# Social Policies and Private Sector Participation in Water Supply

*Social Policy in a Development Context*

General Editors: **Thandika Mkandawire and Huck-Ju Kwon**, both at UNRISD

Social Policy in a Development Context is a new series which places social policy at the centre of research while maintaining the United Nations Research Institute for Social Development (UNRISD)'s unified approach to social development. The series provides a new and exciting contribution to the literature in economic development and social policy. In economic development, social policy has been recognized as an integral part of development, but the literature often falls short of elaborating social policy for a unified approach to economic and social development. In social policy, analysis has concentrated mainly on European and North American countries, and studies on developing countries often lack comparative rigour. The bridge between economic development and social policy will not only contribute to the academic research but also inform the policy debate at the international and national levels.

*Titles include*:
'Jìmí O. Adésínà (*editor*)
SOCIAL POLICY IN SUB-SAHARAN AFRICAN CONTEXT
In Search of Inclusive Development

Giovanni Andrea Cornia (*editor*)
PRO-POOR MACROECONOMICS
Potential and Limitations

Olli Kangas and Joakim Palme (*editors*)
SOCIAL POLICY AND ECONOMIC DEVELOPMENT IN THE NORDIC COUNTRIES

Massoud Karshenas and Valentine M. Moghadam (*editors*)
SOCIAL POLICY IN THE MIDDLE EAST
Political, Economics and Gender Dynamics

Huck-Ju Kwon (*editor*)
THE DEVELOPMENTAL WELFARE STATE AND POLICY REFORMS IN EAST ASIA

Maureen Mackintosh and Meri Koivusalo (*editors*)
COMMERCIALIZATION OF HEALTH CARE
Global and Local Dynamics and Policy Responses

Thandika Mkandawire (*editor*)
SOCIAL POLICY IN A DEVELOPMENT CONTEXT

Naren Prasad (*editor*)
SOCIAL POLICIES AND PRIVATE SECTOR PARTICIPATION IN WATER SUPPLY

Shahra Razavi and Shireen Hassim (*editors*)
GENDER AND SOCIAL POLICY IN A GLOBAL CONTEXT
Uncovering the Gendered Structure of 'the Social'

Manuel Riesco (*editor*)
LATIN AMERICA
A New Developmental Welfare State Model in the Making?

---

**Social Policy in a Development Context**
**Series Standing Order ISBN 1–4039–4295-1 (hardback) 1–4039–4296–X (paperback)**
(*outside North America only*)

You can receive future titles in this series as they are published by placing a standing order. Please contact your bookseller or, in case of difficulty, write to us at the address below with your name and address, the title of the series and the ISBN quoted above.

Customer Services Department, Macmillan Distribution Ltd, Houndmills, Basingstoke, Hampshire RG21 6XS, England

---

# Social Policies and Private Sector Participation in Water Supply

## Beyond Regulation

*Edited by*
*Naren Prasad*

palgrave
macmillan

UNRISD
United Nations
Research Institute
for Social Development

First published 2008 by
PALGRAVE MACMILLAN
Houndmills, Basingstoke, Hampshire RG21 6XS and
175 Fifth Avenue, New York, N.Y. 10010
Companies and representatives throughout the world

PALGRAVE MACMILLAN is the global academic imprint of the Palgrave Macmillan division of St. Martin's Press, LLC and of Palgrave Macmillan Ltd. Macmillan® is a registered trademark in the United States, United Kingdom and other countries. Palgrave is a registered trademark in the European Union and other countries.

ISBN-13: 978–0–230–52082–0 hardback
ISBN-10: 0–230–52082–0 hardback

This book is printed on paper suitable for recycling and made from fully managed and sustained forest sources. Logging, pulping and manufacturing processes are expected to conform to the environmental regulations of the country of origin.

A catalogue record for this book is available from the British Library.

Library of Congress Cataloging-in-Publication Data

Social policies and private sector participation in water supply :
beyond regulation / edited by Naren Prasad.
p. cm. — (Social policy in a development context)
Includes bibliographical references and index.
ISBN 0–230–52082–0 (alk. paper)
1. Water utilities. 2. Social policy. I. Prasad, Naren.
HD4456.S67 2008
363.6'1—dc22

2007052974

10 9 8 7 6 5 4 3 2 1
17 16 15 14 13 12 11 10 09 08

Printed and bound in Great Britain by
CPI Antony Rowe, Chippenham and Eastbourne

# Contents

# List of Tables

# List of Figures

# List of Acronyms and Abbreviations

| | |
|---|---|
| AMF | Association of French Mayors |
| BMA | British Medical Association |
| BNH | The National Housing Bank |
| BOT | Build-operate-transfer |
| BPU | Budget Payment Units |
| CESB | State water and sanitation companies |
| CGE | Compagnie générale des eaux |
| CONPES | National Committee on Social and Economic Policy |
| CPI | Consumer price index |
| CRA | Regulatory Commission for Water and Sanitation |
| CREG | Regulatory Commission for Electricity and Gas |
| CRT | Regulatory Commission for Telecommunications |
| DID | Difference in difference |
| DNP | National Planning Department |
| EC | European Commission |
| EMCALI | Municipal Company of Cali |
| EPIC | Public Enterprise of Industrial and Commercial Nature |
| EU | European Union |
| FAT | Fundo de Amparo ao Trabalhador |
| FDI | Foreign Direct Investment |
| FGTS | Time of Employment Guarantor Fund |
| FNCCR | Federation of local communities delegating public services |
| FNDAE | Fond national pour le développement des adductions d'eau (National Fund for Rural Water Supply) |
| FRS | Family Resources Survey |
| HES | Household expenditure survey |
| IBT | Increasing block tariff |
| IDA | International Development Association |
| IFEN | Institut français de l'environnement |
| IMF | International Monetary Fund |
| INSEE | National Institute for Statistics and Economic Studies |
| MDGs | Millennium Development Goals |
| MMAVDT | Ministry of Environment, Housing and Territory Development |

| | |
|---|---|
| MS | Minimum salary |
| NGO | Non-governmental organization |
| NRW | Non-revenue waters |
| NWRC | National Water Resource Council |
| ODA | Official Development Assistance |
| OECD | Organization for Economic Cooperation and Development |
| OFWAT | Office of Water Services |
| ONEA | National Office of Water and Sewerage Purification |
| ONPF | National Office for Wells and Boreholes |
| PFI | Private Finance Initiative |
| Planasa | National Sanitation Plan |
| PLC | Public Limited Company |
| PME | Programa de Modernización Empresarial (Management Modernization Programme) |
| PMSS | Programme for Modernization of the Sanitation Sector |
| PPP | Private–Public Partnership |
| PSP | Private sector participation |
| PUAS | Perbadanan Urus Air Selangor |
| PWA | Public Water Authority |
| PWD | State Public Works Department |
| RMI | Law on Minimum Income |
| RPB | River Purification Board |
| RWA | Regional Water Authority |
| SCEES | Service Central des Enquêtes et Etudes Statistiques |
| SFS | Sanitation Financial System |
| SNIS | National Sanitation Information System |
| SNSB | National System of Basic Sanitation |
| SOE | State-owned enterprise |
| SPAN | Suruhanjaya Perkhidmatan Air Negara (National Water Service Commission Bill) |
| SPDE | Professional syndicate of water and sewage operators |
| SPDE | Syndicat professionnel des distributeurs d'eau |
| SPIC | Service public à caractère industriel ou commercial (industrial or commercial public services) |
| SSPD | Superintendence for public services |
| SWS | Scottish Water Solutions Ltd |
| TR | Transitional sewerage relief grant |
| UNDP | United Nations Development Program |
| USP | Universal service provision |
| VAT | Value added tax |
| WAMCo | Water Asset Management Company |

| | |
|---|---|
| WaSC | Water and sewerage company |
| WB | World Bank |
| WHO | World Health Organization |
| WIC | Water Industry Commission |
| WSB | State Water Supply Board |
| WSD | State Water Supply Department |
| WSI | Water Services Industry Bill |

# Notes on Contributors

**Zsolt Boda** is senior research fellow at the Institute of Political Science, Hungarian Academy of Sciences, and associate professor at the Business Ethics Center, Corvinus University of Budapest. He graduated from the Budapest University of Economic Sciences (BUES) in 1993 and has an MA in economics. He also received his PhD in political science from BUES in 2000. He has co-edited three books in Hungarian: one on corporate ethics, another on political theory, and a third one on the privatization of public services. His book on global environmental policy was published in 2004. He has published several papers in academic journals, and books on international ethics, trade and environmental issues, environmental policy and the politics of global environmentalism. His publications in English include the following: 'Globalization and International Ethics', in Laszlo Zsolnai (ed.), *Ethics in the Economy: Handbook of Business Ethics* (2002), pp. 233–58, 'Global Environmental Commons and the Need for Ethics', *Society and Economy*, 2003, 213–24; 'No limits? Privatization in Central and Eastern Europe', in Ernst U. von Weizsäcker, Oran R. Young, Matthias Finger (eds) *Limits to Privatization: How to Avoid too Much of a Good Thing* (2005).

**Valerie Dickie** taught at the University of Stirling before being appointed Research Associate and Teaching Fellow in the Department of Economics, Heriot-Watt University, Edinburgh. She has researched and published widely in the fields of water affordability, local government taxation and Scottish economic policy. Recent consultancy work includes projects for the Scottish Water Customers Consultation Panels and the Scottish Executive. She is an invited external member of the University of Stirling's Ethics Committee.

**Andrés Gómez-Lobo** holds a Master's degree in Environmental and Resource Economics and a PhD in Economics from University College London. He currently holds a research and teaching position in the Department of Economics of the University of Chile. Dr Gómez-Lobo has published many papers on issues of natural monopoly regulation and social policies in utility services.

**David Hall** is director of the Public Services International Research Unit in the Business School, University of Greenwich, London. He researches and teaches the politics and economics of public services and privatization. He has special expertise in the sectors of water and energy (and has also worked on waste management and health care), and on the subjects of EU policies on public services, the general history and development of public services, international development policies, and corruption. Before becoming director of PSIRU, David Hall worked for over 25 years in research into public services, public expenditure, privatization, and industrial relations for colleges, trade union research units and other research institutions. For the last 15 years he has worked on these issues internationally. He has a MA from the University of Warwick and a BA and BPhil. from Oxford University. His publications include articles in academic journals, numerous reports published by PSIRU, and two books, and he is guest editor of a special issue of Utilities Policy in 2007. He has been an invited speaker at seminars and conferences at universities and research institutes in Aalborg, Athens, Berlin, Bonn (ZEF), Bradford, Brussels, Bologna, California (UC Berkeley), Cambridge University, London University (UCL), Loughborough (WEDC), Madrid (UCM), Munich (CESifo), New York (Cornell), Newcastle, Oxford University, Paris 8, Sheffield, Tampere, and Uppsala.

**Issaka Kouanda** is a Doctor in Economics of the University Pantheon-Assas (Paris II). A specialist in the study of development, he has led and conducted many researches in rural areas in Mali and Burkina Faso. He is a lecturer at the University Paris XII, researcher and member of the executive committee of Institut CEDIMES, a network of research established in more than forty countries in the world.

**Cassey Lee** is currently Associate Professor of Industrial Economics at the Nottingham University Business School, University of Nottingham Malaysia Campus. Dr Lee specializes in the field of industrial organization (IO). His current research and teaching interests include economics of regulation, competition policy, technological innovation and law and economics. Dr Lee has published papers on industries such as financial services, motion pictures, telecommunications and the water sectors. His academic papers have appeared in peer-reviewed journals such as the *Journal of Economic Dynamics and Control, Quarterly Review of Economics and Finance, Kyklos, ASEAN Economic Bulletin, Metroeconomica,* and *Annals of Public and Cooperative Economics.* Dr Lee received his Bachelor of Economics from University of Malaya, his Master of Philosophy from University of Cambridge and his PhD from the University of California, Irvine.

**Emanuele Lobina** is Senior Research Fellow, PSIRU (Public Services International Research Unit), Business School, University of Greenwich. Emanuele joined PSIRU in 1998, and has contributed to most of PSIRU's work on water services. His work is on the institutional issues revolving around the reform of water supply and sanitation in developed, transitional and developing countries. His interests relate to all types of reform from Private Sector Participation (PSP) to in-house restructuring and Public–Public Partnerships (PPPs), and include governance, capacity building, delivery to the poor, pricing and investment. Emanuele has published refereed articles in journals such as *Utilities Policy*, *Progress in Development Studies*, *Geoforum*, *Natural Resources Forum*, *International Journal of Water Resources Development* and *Development in Practice*. He has contributed book chapters and has made presentations at the Mexico World Water Forum (2006), Stockholm Water Symposia (1999, 2002, 2005) and meetings organized by UNCTAD, UN-Habitat and UN DESA (2006). He has taken part in the EU-funded research project SWITCH and the Govagua network.

**Marcela Meléndez** has a PhD in Economics from Yale University. She is currently Associate Consultant at Economica Consultores Ltd, a Colombian firm that specializes in the regulation of infrastructure services, and external Associate Researcher at Fedesarrollo, the primary policy-oriented think-tank researching the economics of Colombia. Previous to that she was Research Economist at the Inter-American Development Bank and Deputy Director of Fedesarrollo. Her expertise is in the field of applied microeconomics, with a particular emphasis on industrial organization. She has undertaken research on productivity, provision of infrastructure services, intellectual property rights, regulation and antitrust.

**Mouhamad Moudassir** is an independent researcher. He is trained as a statistician and has worked as an advisor in economic affairs at the Ministry of Economy and Planning and Office of Statistics in Chad. He has also been research assistant at the Laboratory of Applied Economy of Geneva University in Switzerland.

**Naren Prasad** is a Research Coordinator at the United Nations Research Institute for Social Development (UNRISD) where he coordinates research projects under two broad programme areas: *Social Policy and Development* and *Market, Business and Regulation*. He holds a doctorate in Economics from the University of Paris and has worked with various United Nations agencies as an economist. He has published on development issues, specifically related to the development challenges of small states.

**Arnaud Reynaud** is researcher at the National Institute for Research in Agriculture (INRA). He is a member of Toulouse School of Economics (TSE) and works in the Laboratory of Natural Resources Economics (LERNA) at the University of Toulouse, France. His research interests include natural resource and environmental economics (integrated water management, aquifer management models, environmental regulation and structure of costs, water demand analysis) and the regulation of public utilities (optimal pricing of water utilities, efficiency and economic regulation, vertical integration and competition). In 2006, Arnaud Reynaud (jointly with Richard Howitt, Siwa Msangi and Keith Knapp) received the 'Quality of Research Discovery Award' from the American Agricultural Economics Association for his work 'Estimating Interporal Preferences for Natural Resource Allocation' published in the *American Journal of Agricultural Economics*.

**André Rossi de Oliveira** is Associate Professor of Economics at the University of Brasília, Brazil. He has served as Director of Graduate Studies in Economics and is currently Vice-Director of the Center for Studies in Regulation of Markets (CERME/UnB). Other positions he has taken up include Visiting Professorships at Tulane University and at the University of Illinois at Urbana-Champaign. Oliveira's main fields of interest are industrial organization, especially the regulation of water and sewerage, telecommunications and electricity, game theory and applied microeconomics. In addition to making contributions to the academic literature, Oliveira has been active in policy making. He has participated in many projects sponsored by Brazilian regulatory agencies and other government bodies, including the training of professionals in the sanitation sector, the revision of electricity distribution tariffs and competition in the mobile telephone market.

**John Sawkins** has held university teaching positions at the universities of Edinburgh and Aberdeen, and is currently Reader in Economics in the Department of Economics, Heriot-Watt University, Edinburgh. He has published widely in the area of water economics, focusing on regulatory issues, and has undertaken consultancy work for the Scottish Water and Sewerage Customers Council, the Scottish Executive and the Scottish Water Customers Consultation Panels. He has given evidence to Scottish Parliamentary Committees on domestic legislation and was a member of the Water Industry Commissioner for Scotland's Academic

Panel and Domestic Forum from April to November 2001. He is currently a member of Waterwatch Scotland, the consumers' representative body for the water industry in Scotland.

**Gábor Scheiring** holds a BA in economics (Budapest Business School), and an MA in sociology and social anthropology (Central Europen University) and an MA in economic sociology (Corvinus University of Budapest). He is a research consultant at Protect the Future (Védegylet), a Hungarian eco-political NGO and think-tank. Scheiring has been a nationally and internationally active member of green and global justice movements since 2002. His academic interests are the restructuring and privatization of public services, and the theory and practice of social movements and civil society. He has published several papers on green politics and the politics of the free trade regime, and has co-edited a book on the privatization of public services. His English-language publications include: (with Zsolt Boda) 'Privatization of Water in the Context of Transition', in Daniel Chavez (ed.), *Public Services Yearbook* (2006); and 'Barbarians at the Open Gate: Public Sociology and the Late Modern Turn', *American Sociologist*, forthcoming.

# Foreword

This book is part of the UNRISD series, *Social Policy in a Development Context*, which seeks to understand the multiple concerns of social policy with production, protection, (re)distribution and reproduction. In doing so, it unifies three different sets of literature on development, democracy and welfare regimes. A range of regional and thematic studies have been carried out since 2000 under the UNRISD research programme on Social Policy and Development. This volume presents the findings of the research project on *Social Policy, Regulation and Private Sector Participation in Water Supply*.

Currently, over 1.1 billion people worldwide do not have access to drinking water. This problem is most acute in developing countries where the health burden is predominantly borne by children. The World Health Organization estimates that in 2005, 1.6 million children under the age of 5 (an average of 4,500 every day) died from unsafe water and inadequate hygiene. In addition, the importance of the connection between water and poverty has now been recognized by the international community. Target 10 of the Millennium Development Goals – *'Halve by 2015 the proportion of people without sustainable access to safe drinking water and basic sanitation'* – is evidence of this growing concern. As a consequence, countries are required to increase access to safe water supply.

Within the general context of liberalization and deregulation that has taken place in recent decades, private sector participation was often proposed for the water sector. However, a previous UNRISD project on *Commercialization, Privatization and Universal Access to Water* concluded that private sector participation itself did not expand network coverage. Moreover, institutional constraints and inefficient regulatory mechanisms were the rule rather than the exception in developing countries, hampering universal access. The research project on social policy, regulation and private sector involvement in water supply takes this inquiry further to investigate the central role of social policies in such circumstances. It is shown that reform of the water sector should be accompanied by appropriate social policies in order to provide affordable access to safe water.

As is the case with all UNRISD projects, the research on which this volume is based would not have been possible without the core funding provided by the governments of Finland, Mexico, Norway, Sweden, Switzerland and the United Kingdom. Let me once again take this opportunity to express our gratitude.

THANDIKA MKANDAWIRE
DIRECTOR, UNRISD

# 1
# Overview: Social Policies and Private Sector Participation in Water Supply

*Naren Prasad*[1]

## Introduction

It is now widely recognized that infrastructure development (transportation, telecommunication, energy, water) are prerequisites for social and economic development. Although private initiatives were historically instrumental in the development of some of this infrastructure, it has traditionally been the responsibility of the state. Expanding and maintaining this infrastructure presents a major challenge for many countries. This chapter presents some of the issues surrounding private sector participation (PSP) in the water supply sector and presents the results of a research project on 'Social Policy, Regulation and Private Sector Involvement in the Water Supply'.

At the time of writing, over one billion people worldwide lacked access to drinking water, especially in developing countries. The World Health Organization estimates that in 2005, 1.6 million children under the age of five (an average of over 4,000 every day) died from unsafe water and inadequate hygiene. In addition, the importance of the connection between water and poverty has been recognized by the international community. Target 10 of the United Nations Millennium Development Goals – 'Halve by 2015 the proportion of people without sustainable access to safe drinking water and basic sanitation' – is evidence of this growing concern. As a consequence, countries are required to increase access to safe water supply.

Infrastructure maintenance is one of the biggest challenges facing the water supply sector in both developed and developing countries. In the latter, an additional challenge is to extend the network and thus increase the coverage of the population. Both network maintenance and network extension require colossal investments. The most common solution proposed consists of market-based reforms, which include operating the system on a full cost-recovery principle, commercialization, or PSP of varying degrees. Given that water is a basic necessity, the affordability of the service becomes a major issue. However, the water industry is a natural monopoly and as such it is not free from the problems associated with lack of competition regardless of who owns or operates the system. Such problems may include charging higher prices, or lowering production costs by decreasing the quality of service. In these circumstances, government intervention, either through public management or through appropriate regulation, is often proposed.

There are several important challenges facing the water sector in both developing and developed countries (Hall 2001). The first challenge consists in maintaining the existing infrastructure, which includes reducing leakages, replacing and expanding networks. In order to achieve this, there is a need for financial autonomy, including sustainable and equitable tariffs, and efficient revenue collection. In addition, the utility company should be properly managed which consists in building managerial capacities and improving efficiency and productivity. Since water is a basic necessity, sociopolitical issues such as having affordable price, transparency and accountability must be considered. And, finally, issues of environment and health, such as public health needs, conservation, and environmental management, must be appropriately dealt with.

One way to tackle these challenges is through the PSP. The debate surrounding PSP in the water industry is one of the most controversial and emotive in the current development discourse. On one side are the proponents who argue that since governments have failed to deliver quality water to everyone, the private sector can solve this problem by the application of market principles. In other words, the private sector can improve efficiency, extend the coverage of service, bring in more investment, and relieve governments from budget deficits. On the other side of the spectrum are those who consider that water is a common good and should not be in the hands of the private sector. They argue that since water is a unique resource and because it is essential to life, it should not be treated like another commodity and market principles should not be applied to it. In other words, the private sector cannot apply just criteria for this merit good. In this context, access to water for everyone becomes a human right and it is the state's obligation to provide this vital resource to everyone. Finally, there is another group which stands in between these two extreme positions. This group thinks that solutions can be found by considering water as an economic good and a human right at the same time. It is within this context that the current debate is taking place.

Although the private sector has a long history of involvement in water supply in industrial countries, PSP is a relatively new phenomenon in developing countries. Privatization has been back on the agenda since the late 1980s. During the early 1990s, many developing and transition countries involved the private sector in their water supply. Different varieties of PSP have been was experimented with, ranging from build–operate–transfer (BOT) models, management, service or lease contracts, concessions (the most common), to joint ownership (but rarely a complete privatization, as in the case of England and Wales or some cities in Chile). After nearly two decades of such experimentation, it is time to investigate the impact of these policy reforms.

This chapter aims to contextualize the debate of PSP and then present the research findings. It starts by outlining the research objectives and the framework. It then presents a historical perspective of PSP in the water supply sector. In the third section, it tries to argue that water is a different kind of good which merits different the adoption of policy options. In the fourth section it presents the arguments for PSP, some statistics and why there was an increase in PSP in the 1990s and the early years of the twenty-first century. In the fifth section it discusses why social policies and public provision were historically important in increasing access to an affordable water supply. The final section presents the research findings and shows why policy makers should not forget about social policies when reforming their water sector.

## Theoretical framework

Market-based reforms, including privatization, have encountered considerable challenges and failures – especially in developing countries. This has led policy makers to argue that in natural monopolies, such as the water industry, where competition is difficult, the state should establish independent regulatory institutions. Within the general restructuring and privatization framework, the establishment of regulation was generally prescribed by donors in order to attract more aid and to provide the private sector with incentives for investment in infrastructure sectors. It was argued that regulatory institutions should be coherent, accountable, transparent, and predictable independent bodies (Kessides 2004). They should have the capacity to protect consumers, investors and the environment.

However, scholars such as Buchanan (1972), Newbery (1999) and Laffont (2000) have argued that the regulatory process is often captured by interest groups while others, such as Stiglitz (1998), have argued that regulation is captured by the politicians. Recent research has shown that building independent regulatory institutions in developing and transition economies presents a major challenge and that the results have been rather disappointing (see, for example, Kirkpatrick and Parker 2004, Jalilian *et al.* 2007; Minogue and Carino 2006; Amann 2006; Cook and Mosedale 2007). This was the result of poor accountability, deficient transparency and the lack of consistency in developing countries (Parker 1999). A World Bank (2006) publication also recognizes that after the creation of over 200 regulatory entities worldwide within the past 15 years, there is now ample evidence to show that regulatory systems have failed to achieve the expected sector outcomes. Very often regulation becomes an end in itself rather than a means of achieving social, economic and environmental objectives for the well-being of the population. Similarly, previous UNRISD research has shown that the regulation of water services through independent bodies has encountered difficulties in many developing countries (Ugaz 2006). This is a result of a poor tradition of independent policy-making bodies, weak institutions and uneven bargaining power among the stakeholders. Lack of effective and transparent regulation hampers the accountability of any service provider.

This takes us back to square one: *plus ça change, plus c'est la même chose*. This research was intended to study how and why social policies can ensure affordable access to water while independent regulatory instruments are still being developed. The following questions were addressed: How do social policies address issues of affordability and access? What is the role of tariffs (social tariffs, increasing block tariffs, metering)? How are policies designed to help the poor (minimum service levels, subsidies)? Are the poor able to benefit from the social policies in place? And, more generally, how can private sector be made to serve poor customers?

In other words, this research investigates the impact of PSP in water supply through a social policy framework. Social policy is any policy put in place by the government or its bodies to improve of the welfare of the population, especially its less privileged members. According to UNRISD (2006: 1), 'Social policy is a state intervention that directly affects social welfare, social institutions and social relations. It involves overarching concerns with redistribution, production, reproduction and protection and works in tandem with economic policy in pursuit of national social and economic goals'. Such policies are also based on the notion of *equity*, which addresses concerns of justice, equality and rights. In this circumstance, equity here implies a distributional principle, which is applied in the allocation of services and benefits in order to achieve what is considered as just and fair division.

Social policies related to water supply are quite common in both developing and developed countries, with the most widespread forms being *income support* and *tariff adjustment*. The former are linked to welfare systems, and include housing benefits, charities, tariff rebates, flexible payment methods, connection subsidies, and vouchers. The latter comprize increasing block tariffs, cross-subsidies, and special tariffs for low-income households.

There is much ambiguity when defining regulation since it depends on whether it is being discussed by an economist, a lawyer, a political scientist or a social scientist.[2] In the case of PSP in the water sector, *regulation* often refers to a diverse set of instruments by which *governments* through an *independent* agency protect consumers, investors and environment. It includes laws, orders and rules issued by all levels of government and by non-governmental bodies to whom governments have delegated regulatory powers. In this view regulation not only means creating institutions, but also defining the 'rules of the game' (Minogue 2005; Kirkpatrick and Parker 2004). In other words, 'regulation refers to the promulgation of an authoritative set of rules, accompanied by some mechanism, typically a public agency, for monitoring and promoting compliance with these rules' (Baldwin *et al.* 1998: 3). In this sense regulation refers to all the efforts of state in order to promote the welfare of its citizens, including economic, fiscal or redistributive policies. It is widely recognized that having an independent agency in place is difficult, especially in developing and transition economies. For example, regulation is likely to be ineffective where corruption is rampant, lack of independence of legal system or even in countries with economic or political crisis.

Therefore we argue that regulation should be complemented by social policies, explicitly pursued by the state. Even though there might be complementarities between social and regulatory policies, what makes them distinct is that the former are executed and pursued by the state, whereas the latter are supposed to be implemented by an independent body.

## Lessons from history

PSP in urban water supply has had a long history (Prasad 2007). Private initiatives were instrumental in establishing modern water supply systems, which led to privately owned or operated systems. This began in the mid-1800s as a result of rapid urban growth in most of the European countries and in North America. England was the precursor of modern water supply systems, which later spread to Germany, elsewhere in Europe and to the United States. However, during the late nineteenth century, as a result of their unsatisfactory performance (inefficiency, high costs and, in some cases, corruption) or due to public health concerns in numerous European countries, many of these services were transferred to public or municipal ownership. Today, in the European countries, the provision of urban water supply is quite diverse, ranging from no private sector participation (the Netherlands), PSP but with no profit motive (Austria, Denmark and Sweden), to an amalgam of PSP arrangements (Belgium, Finland, France, Germany, Greece, Italy and Spain), and to full privatization with strong regulation (England and Wales) (Mohajeri *et al.* 2003).

Water supply (and sanitation), especially in poorer countries, is one of the major challenges facing the development community. Yet debates about increasing coverage are not new. These debates had taken place in developed countries two centuries ago. In major European cities at the beginning of the nineteenth century, water supply was insufficient, of low quality, and often very expensive. By the early twentieth century water had been made available in adequate quantities and its quality had improved drastically. By the mid-twentieth century, access to water was quasi-universal. Looking at how different (now developed) cities dealt with managing their water supply over time can be instructive for understanding today's water supply challenges in developing countries.

Historically, the industrialized countries were concerned with increasing expansion of the water and sanitation systems and the improvements were directly linked to water sector legislation (Juuti and Katko 2005: 220). The drivers of such expansions and improvements were the need for fire fighting, the lack and/or poor quality of water, environmental concerns, public health, industrial use, or various combinations thereof. It is argued that the business motive was the main factors in considering the first private proposal in the mid-1800s (Juuti and Katko 2005).

The historical experiences of England, the United States of America and France could prove instructive. Fragmented, piecemeal and localized systems were abandoned in favour of highly centralized and integrated water supply systems. This occurred in 1802 in Paris, in 1808 in London and in 1856 in Berlin (Gandy 2006). At that time, as in developing countries today, most of these cities originally relied on wells, private water vendors and rivers for their water supply.

Most cities were reluctant to invest in public works such as water supply and therefore called on the private sector. One lesson that could be drawn from this experience is that public authorities started to pay more attention to water supply once the association between diseases (such as cholera, typhoid and diarrhoea) and water (sanitation) was established in the mid-nineteenth century, through progress in research in bacteriology. Not only were the poor affected by water-borne diseases, but increasingly the middle and upper classes were also concerned. In New York, for example, real investment and expansion in the network started through the issuance of municipal bonds. Statistics show that by 1905 the largest category of municipal debt was related to waterworks (Cutler and Miller 2005). The problems were more acute in cities like London where water sources were progressively more polluted due to the growing population and industrialization. The role of the private sector is declining, reflected in London's water supply statistics (Juuti and Katko 2005). In 1861 the share of private provision in the water supply in larger towns was 60 per cent, which decreased overtime reaching 20 per cent in 1881 and only 10 per cent in 1901. Cholera epidemic in France and damages caused by fire in London and Hamburg were instrumental in initiating the development of water infrastructure.

One of the most influential reports on public health published at that time was that of Edwin Chadwick (Chadwick 1842). He argued and demonstrated that insanitary housing conditions caused diseases and poverty in London. He established the correlation between poor sanitation, defective drainage, inadequate water supply and overcrowded housing with disease, high mortality rates and low life expectancy. For example, he claimed that proper sanitation and clean water could increase middle-class life expectancy by 13 years. He also analysed the economic cost of public health and studied why access to water and sanitation should be universal. He argued that it was a waste of valuable time when the poor went to fetch water and waited long hours in the queues, whereas a universal water and sanitation services would increase their levels of productivity. An enlightened public health movement followed the publication of Chadwick's report, starting with the Public Health Act of 1848. In the 1850s, public health was considered as a noble cause and building water supply network became a prestigious symbol of wealth of a city (Breyer 2006).

Despite these breakthroughs in developed countries, today waterborne diseases still prevail in developing countries. The World Health Organization (WHO) estimates that every year around two million people (with 90 per cent of them being children under five) die from diarrhoeal diseases, the sixth most dangerous disease on a global scale.[3] This means that around 4,000 children die each day from water-borne diseases.

What emerges from this historical perspective is that both public and private actors played important roles in developing water supplies. The public authorities started investing in such systems once the link between disease and water had been established. However, the final responsibility lies with the state, through appropriate social policies, to ensure that there is universal coverage and that the poor are not excluded from the service.

## Uniqueness of water

Water is a unique commodity. It is not only a physical good, but also a cultural and social resource with great economic and political significance. The water industry does not easily fit into the standard economic theory of competitive markets (Ballance and Taylor 2005). There are significant *externalities* (social costs and benefits) attached to it and the industry, as is often the case with utility services, is regarded as a *natural monopoly*. These characteristics jointly determine the economics of water.

### Natural monopoly

The drinking water market is not a competitive one because of the existence of economies of scale. Due to very high fixed costs and extremely low, usually constant marginal costs, the average costs of production decline as the level of production increases. To enter such an industry an enormous initial investment is required (laying down transmission networks, such as water pipelines), but the marginal cost of connecting an additional customer to the network is very low (unless the new customer is very far from the existing network). The (sunk) initial costs are usually so high that they constitute an effective barrier to entry and, ultimately, only one firm can survive in such a market. In the absence of competition the sole company may abuse its market power and this can justify government intervention. One traditional solution to this kind of market failure is public ownership. This is often the case when public or national interests are at stake, as, for example, is the case for national defence. However, governments can also choose to regulate private firms by, for example, controlling their prices (see above on regulation). Although economic theory suggests that private ownership should perform better than the public, there is no compelling empirical evidence substantiating this argument. Numerous studies show that operational and economic efficiency comes from competition and rather than from the ownership structure (Vickers and Yarrow 1988).

Although competition is generally desirable, competition within a natural monopoly in particular is very costly and unsustainable. There is an account by Fletcher (1845) of how competition in water supply among different private companies in England (county of Surrey and in St John's Southwark) caused inconvenience to the consumers and difficulties for the companies. The competition was so intense that the companies put two or three mains and pipes in the same street. The public was adversely affected by the poor quality of service and frequent disruption because of continuous works on the street. Moreover, the companies had no incentive to supply water to less dense areas. Finally they collectively decided to increase rates and, in some cases, to divide the areas of operation. This turned out to be detrimental to the consumers and it was later decided that the principle of competition was not applicable to water supply (Wingate 1883).

Though competition *within* such a market is costly, it is possible to establish competition *for* the market. This has been, for example, the dominant organizational method for water services in France, although in this case the resulting degree of competition is limited by contracts often being set for long periods (15–20 years).[4] Equally, competition can be used in one *part* of the market, through outsourcing. Some water companies outsource a considerable proportion of their operations. The extreme case is Welsh Water, Dŵr Cymru, which outsources virtually its entire business, running just a skeleton staff to manage these contracts.

To sum up, the theory says that, if left alone, the water sector (or rather the consumers) will likely be fraught with all the problems associated with natural monopolies. This may justify government intervention in the operation or management and regulation of the industry.

### Private commodity versus merit good

As mentioned earlier, the water industry is not easily accommodated within standard economic theory. This makes it an atypical 'economic good'. Contrary to a private good, a public good is *non-rival* and *non-excludable* (Anand 2007a). Non-rival means that consumption of the good by one individual does not reduce the amount of the good available for consumption by others. Non-excludability means that it is not possible to exclude individuals from the good's consumption and therefore make them pay for it. For these reasons such goods are unattractive to private firms. This can result in market failures, where uncoordinated markets are unable to provide these goods in desired quantities. In such situations, governments may come into play to ensure a sufficient supply (through incentives, investments, and subsidies).

The supply of water is finite and location-specific. In contrast to a public good, there is a marginal cost attached to each unit consumed in the sense that additional costs are associated with production, purification and delivery of water to an individual's home.

Alternatively, there is currently a growing tendency to treat water as an *economic good*. In other words, people should be charged for the water they consume and prices should be based on the cost of production and delivery. This is referred to as 'full cost recovery'. This view has been greatly influenced by key international players such as the Bretton Woods institutions, donor governments, and multinational corporations.[5] The major push for applying market principles to the water sector comes from donor agencies like the World Bank. For example, the World Bank's Policy Paper on Water Resources Management (World Bank 1993) clearly calls for improving water efficiency through the use of prices (markets) and privatization. The World Bank's 2000 Operational Policy, which replaced the 1993 strategy, again emphasized the price mechanism but this time it softened the rhetoric on privatization and instead focused on how public and private entities could forge partnerships.[6]

Because of positive externalities and the merit good argument, water is a very unusual good, which makes a clear-cut classification very hard. Its finite and locally specific supply makes it a rival good and thus implies that market forces should manage supply and demand. However, one should keep in mind that water is an essential resource (increasingly considered to be a human right) (Anand 2007b; UNDP 2006), and in spite of the type of ownership, affordable and universal access to it should be provided. As we will see later, this goal is not easy to achieve, in both developing and sometimes even developed countries, and there is not much consensus about the right solution(s).

## Privatization as a solution

### Arguments in favour of privatization from a historical perspective

Some of the arguments in favour of state ownership rest on the assumption of a market failure. However, state ownership has its own shortcomings and privatization is seen a remedy to these (Megginson and Netter 2001: 329). Megginson (2005) argues that the policy of privatization has been one of the most visible signs of greater reliance on markets to allocate resources. He defines privatization as the sale of state-owned enterprises (SOE) or its assets to private agents. According to him, privatization, for more than 100 countries, has become an increasingly legitimate and accepted tool of statecraft.

In general, there are *three* theoretical reasons for state ownership. One is to ensure that business enterprises balance social and economic objectives rather than focus exclusively on profit maximization. Intervention can also be seen as a response to market failure and the problem of natural monopolies (which rule out competition and hence its supposed benefits). And, thirdly, it can be desirable in situations of informational asymmetries between the principal (public) and the agent (producer).

Historically, state ownership of businesses has arisen as a result of (Megginson 2005): natural expansion of 'royal power' in feudal or tribal societies (antiquity and middle ages) attempts to commercialize complex and new technologies (the industrial revolution of the late nineteenth and early twentieth century), nationalization of failing private businesses aimed at either preserving employment or continuing the production of essential goods and services (during economic crises like the Great Depression), ideology of state ownership (like communism or certain forms of radical socialism), extreme political factionalism (state ownership of key industries as a political tool of reward and punishment).

It is argued that Hayek's *The Road to Serfdom* (1944) had a direct impact on policy makers in the United Kingdom in justifying privatization in the 1970s (Megginson and Netter 2001; Megginson 2005). Hayek's work provided the intellectual basis for Keith Joseph and later Margaret Thatcher and the British Conservative Party (David Howell) who started campaigning for the rolling back of the borders of the British welfare state. What followed in the 1980s and 1990s was a worldwide movement towards privatization as a result of increasing fiscal problems and later due to the collapse of socialism. SOEs were seen as 'inefficient' because government used them to pursue non-economic objectives. Specifically, it was believed that this inefficiency was due to: weak incentives (especially in terms of revenue maximization), the lack of monitoring because of collective action problems, and soft budget constraints since politicians will never apply strict private sector rules in terms of budgetary requirements.

The motives for privatization were different in developed and developing countries. In the latter, state ownership was seen as important in order to promote economic growth, especially in physical facilities.

In addition, after the colonial legacy, most countries resented foreign ownership. Nationalization was justified as a way to overcome decades of colonial exploitation. China, India, Brazil and Russia provided many developing countries with the intellectual leadership in the state ownership.

By the late 1970s, state ownership was common in both developed and developing countries. However, the poor performance of state-owned enterprises triggered the march towards privatization. In the early 1980s, Margaret Thatcher justified the privatization of state-owned firms as a way to: raise revenue for the state, promote economic efficiency, reduce government interference in the economy, promote wider share ownership, introduce competition, and subject state-owned enterprises to market discipline.[7]

Although Margaret Thatcher was not the first to launch a privatization scheme, the Conservative programme had a strategic importance (it was one of the most important ones).[8] After the initial apparent success in Britain, other countries followed suit. In France, for example, this happened after the coming to power of a Conservative government in 1986. Two years later, the arrival of the Socialists stopped the further sale of SOEs, but did not attempt to re-nationalize the privatized companies. Austria, Belgium, Canada, Chile, Denmark, the Netherlands, Italy, Jamaica, Japan, Malaysia, Singapore, Spain, Sweden and the United States all began privatization programmes. For developing countries, the ascendancy of conservative politics was to be felt largely through the international financial institutions. The 1990s witnessed widespread privatization in Latin America. However, it is not yet widespread in sub-Saharan Africa and some observers argue that it is 'something of a stealth economic policy' in this region (Megginson 2005: 19). The last bastion of privatization has been the former Soviet-bloc countries and Eastern Europe after the collapse of communism in 1989–91.

## The push for water privatization

Among the triggers of privatization of the water sector have been increasing debt burdens, fiscal and macroeconomic burdens, public health crises and ideological shifts. It is argued that reform in the water sector had higher social gains (increased coverage, better service quality) but low political benefits (price increase, loss of employment) (Kessides 2004). PSP in the water sector has been *'late and light'* compared to the privatization of other sectors such as electricity, telecommunications, and transport (Davis 2005: 147). There has been much controversy in the water sector due to water a being seen as a basic human need, fears

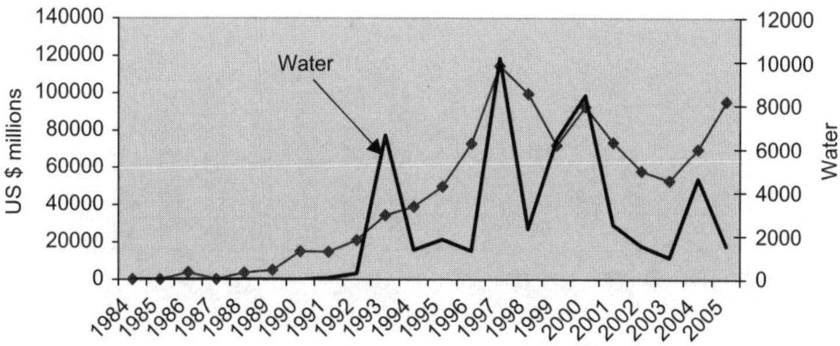


*Figure 1.1* Private sector investment in infrastructure sector, 1984–2005
*Source*: World Bank's private project investment database http://ppi.worldbank.org/.

about price rises, public health concerns, environmental implications, and beliefs that water should not be transferred to a profit-making entity. As we have demonstrated above, these debates took place in the United States and England more than a century ago, when there was a shift from private to municipal ownership.

Privatization has been introduced in different regions of the world for different reasons. In Asia it was launched to reduce budgetary deficits, increase economic growth, develop capital markets and improve services (Ait-Ouyahia 2006). In Latin America, it was initiated because of excessive political interference in public utilities and corrupt government. In the case of Africa, it was aimed principally at reducing the financial burden of the state and increasing access to water among the poor. In Central and Eastern Europe privatization was essentially introduced on ideological grounds (shift from communism to market economy).

Private sector investment in infrastructure increased dramatically in the early 1990s, reaching its peak in 1997 (see Figure 1.1). Subsequently, the Asian financial crisis and successive crises in other countries, together with growing concerns about PSP in infrastructure projects and reservations amongst investors about going into developing countries because of weak regulatory instruments and market failures, led to a waning of private investment in general. With regard to investments in water supply and sanitation in particular, private flows have been very erratic, reaching a peak in 1997 and falling to US$1 billion in 2003. There was a slight increase in 2004, followed by a decline in 2005 to the mid-1990s level of over US$1 billion. During the 1990–2005 period, 55 countries (representing 383 projects)[9] had introduced some form or other of PSP in the water sector (see Figure 1.2). In 2005 alone, there were 41 new

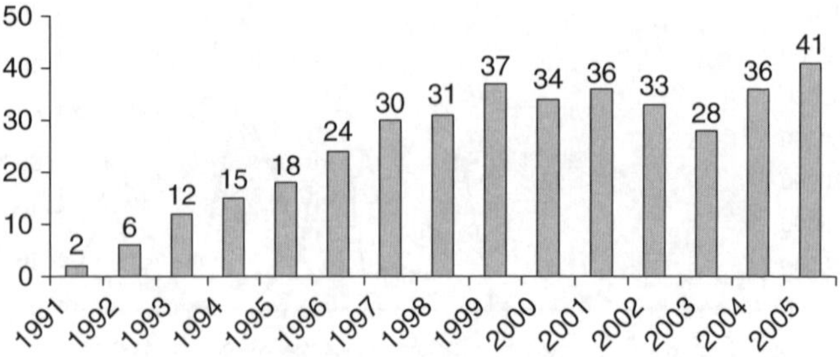


*Figure 1.2* Number of private investments in the water sector, 1990–2005
*Source*: World Bank's private project investment database: http://ppi.worldbank.org/.

investments going to 10 countries in the water sector (China alone had 25 projects).

In order to develop water infrastructure, funds could come either from tax revenues, user charges (and cross-subsidies), private sector investment, aid (bilateral or multilateral), or a combination of some or all of these sources. As regards private investment, Figure 1.3 shows that Malaysia, China, Brazil and Chile received the highest amount of private investment in the water supply sector in the period 2000–05. These four countries also receive a high level of aid. The total household connection rate is also relatively high compared to other countries.

We find that private sector investment generally goes to countries that have higher levels of connection rates. Only seven low-income countries managed to attract private investment in their water sector during 2000–05 (Mozambique, Senegal, Papua New Guinea, Vietnam, India, Niger and Tanzania). South Africa is the only other sub-Saharan African country that received private investment over the course of the same period. In addition, aid and private flows go to the same group of countries. In other words, aid seems to attract private investment and private investment flows to countries that reform their water sector.

One of the main reasons why so many developing countries decided to involve the private sector in water and other infrastructure is the influence and persuasiveness of international donors. One of the main players in international development is the World Bank. In addition to being the largest donor, it has the capacity to produce research that supports its policies.[10] As a result, the World Bank is able to shape the policy agenda of other regional development banks, development agencies, donor countries, and academic community and thus can penetrate the decision-making machinery of a borrowing country.

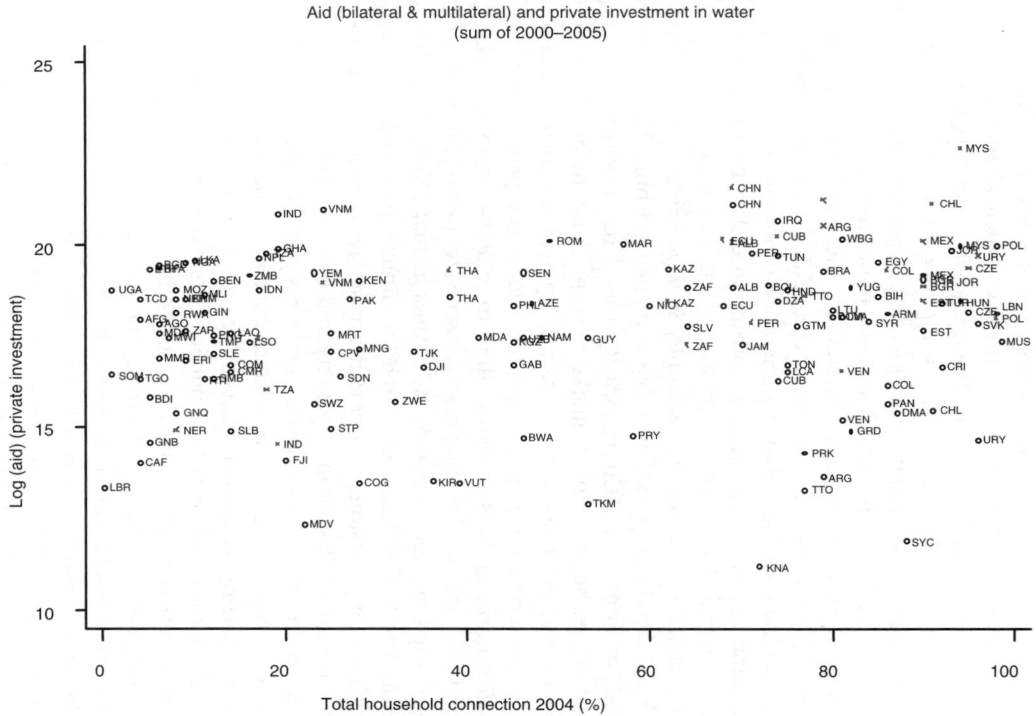


*Figure 1.3* Aid and private investment, 2000–2005
*Source*: OECD Database on Aid (http://www.oecd.org/dataoecd/50/17/5037721.htm), World Bank's private project investment database http://ppi.worldbank.org/, and WHO/UNICEF 2006.

The World Bank started discussion on privatization through the policy of decentralization (privatization is a type of decentralization) (World Bank 1983). In the 1990s a plethora of reports on privatization was published. One of the main messages of the *World Development Report 1994* was that the private sector should be involved in management, financing and ownership of infrastructure to ensure the commercial orientation of the sector (World Bank 1994: 2). In 1995, the World Bank published a high-profile study of SOE reform in developing countries (World Bank 1995). It expressed puzzlement at the slow pace of privatization and was disappointed that 'the bureaucrats' were still in business.

After several years of increased interest by the multinational companies, in 2002 some of the major water companies started to withdraw from developing countries following a series of economic and financial crises, natural disasters, incidences of corruption, risky operating environments, miscalculation by the multinationals, or non-compliance with contractual obligations. For example, Suez pulled back from Latin America and developing economies, but remained in China; Veolia concentrated on Europe and China; SAUR focused its activities only in Europe; RWE withdrew from all markets except Germany and Central Europe (Owen 2006). The result of these developments was that the number of people served by these major international companies declined from 349 million in 2004 to 296 million in 2006. At the same time, the World Bank was starting to doubt its own water privatization advice and was doing some soul-searching (*Wall Street Journal* 2003). In its 2003 evaluation, the World Bank recognized the difficulties associated with the private sector provision of water to the poor: 'getting the private sector to focus on the alleviation of poverty and to design tariffs in a way that does not discriminate against the poor has proved hard to achieve in practice'.[11] It acknowledged its excessive focus on the private sector without recognizing particularities of each country.[12] Moreover reforms, like increasing the efficiency of the public sector through privatization, are more successful if the donor agencies better understood the local context and politics of the reforms (Bangura and Larbi 2006).

It also acknowledged that the private sector might be unable to bring in the additional investment required to increase coverage. In its progress report it further recognized that since the private sector would not be able to increase investment in infrastructure, public funding would continue to be important (World Bank 2005a). Compared to the late 1980s and 1990s, the World Bank's infrastructure strategy has shifted from a reliance on private sector to a mere encouragement of public–private partnerships. Similar conclusions are also drawn by Utting (2006) who argues that the World Bank is fine-tuning its orthodox policy of reliance on market and is paying more attention to social and environmental costs. In addition, civil society organizations have been stepping up pressure against government moves to apply market forces to public services (Ghimire 2005). After two decades of private sector involvement in the water and sanitation sector one can observe increasing popular protests and a growing dissatisfaction of governments and investors (World Bank 2005b).

However, recent research shows that, as a result of such policies, it is only the name that has changed – the main thrust of PSP remains the same. Prasad (2006) argues that reliance on the market to solve water problems through PSP is still alive but repackaged in different terminologies.

## Role of social policies and investment

As regulation is often difficult in developing countries, it emerges that both public and private actors have important roles to play. However, the final responsibility lies with the state and social policies are crucial in increasing coverage and ensuring that the poor are not excluded from the service.

### Social policies in water supply

It is argued that the Romans were the first to manage drinking water as a priced commodity and that social policies were used to guarantee universal access (Salzman 2006). For example, a special tax was levied on those who used pipes from the main system into their residences (the amount varied according to the size of the supply pipe nozzle). The tax funds were used to cover the cost of maintenance of the system. By this method, water for the richer citizens was considered to be an economic good whereas it was free of charge for the average citizen. Each depended on the other in the sense that piped water in private residences was priced as an economic good enabling the authorities to fund and maintain public fountains.

Historically, the industrialized countries were concerned with the increasing expansion of the water and sanitation systems and many improvements in these sectors were linked directly to the water sector legislation (Juuti and Katko 2005: 220). Social policies have been historically instrumental in bringing access to the vast majority of the population in developed countries. This has been the case of France, and England and Wales. In the early 1800s, the London-bridge Waterworks company was practising some sort of cross-subsidy for supplying water (an extra charge was levied on brewers, stable-keepers and tradesmen) (Hunter 1898: 476). The public authorities were concerned that the poor would not be able to afford such services from the private sector and that some poor areas would not be supplied (Fletcher 1845: 174–5). It was argued that the poor could be supplied only through a 'public body'. The private sector was reluctant to supply water to the poor, except through the medium of the landlord or through a separate reservoir with intermittent supply. The rich had their own supplies whereas the poor bought water from private vendors at high prices (two shillings per week – equivalent to their rent) or got it from rivers and wells (Sellers 1997).

Traditionally, the French state provided subsidies to the 'syndicat d'eau' to construct water systems, especially in rural areas. These subsidies were accorded with the framework of the Law on Public Health of 1902. They ranged between 50 and 80 per cent of total investment (Pezon and Petitet 2004) and the rate of subsidy was a function of the total cost of the construction and operation and the number of population. For example, in 1939, access to piped water was almost universal in urban areas, but it was only 25 per cent in rural areas (Pezon 1999). Consequently, a special fund was created in 1954 aimed at increasing access to water in the rural areas (Fonds National pour le Développement des Adductions d'Eau). Public fountains were cross-subsidized by individuals who wanted to have water connected in their residences and also by the industries. It should be remembered that around 50 per cent of the total water networks in France were constructed in the period 1965–80 (Pezon 1999).

Most of the developed economies have introduced some sort of social policies in order to deal with the problem of affordability. The most widespread forms of such social policies are income support (housing benefits, funds, charities, tariff rebate, flexible payments, vouchers) and tariff adjustment (increasing block tariffs (IBT), cross-subsidies, special tariffs for low-income households) (OECD 2003). The most popular form of social policy practised in developed and developing countries is IBT. In Latin American countries, the first block represents 25 cubic metres per month (WHO advises that is should be between 8 and 16 cubic metres) (ADERAS 2006). This implies that most of the residential consumers benefit from such tariffs. In addition, many countries practise social tariffs and subsidy schemes for poorer households. For example, Chile spends US$40 million per year on subsidies which benefit 600,000 people (20 per cent of the population), Colombia spends US$250 million a year for 30 million people (90 per cent of the population, which is considered quasi-universal), 40 per cent of which is funded from internal surcharges, Argentina spends around US$10 million per year for 100,000 people (less than 1 per cent of the population), and Paraguay spends just US$0.1 million for around 5,000 people (Foster and Yepes 2006). In general, social tariffs in Latin America offer a discount of around 67 per cent compared to a normal tariff. However, these authors caution that certain subsidies benefit the rich and the middle class disproportionately.

In many countries, disconnection is not allowed since it is very likely that those who are unable to pay regular water bills are poor. Such policies exist, for example, in the United Kingdom. In certain countries that have involved the private sector in providing water services, social policies such as tariff structures and increasing coverage rates especially to the poorer households are incorporated in the contractual obligations. This has been the case in most developed countries where the private service provider is committed to implement social policy objectives. Since developing countries desperately seek to attract foreign investment in the water sector, private companies in these countries often manage to secure exemption from such obligations.

## Public investment

As mentioned above, although historically the initial construction of the water supply network was often initiated by the private sector, water supply improvements did not take place until the state took full responsibility (increasing public investment and assuming control from the private operators). The main concern of the public authorities was to make access universal, to reduce the incidence of water-borne diseases, and to provide water for fire fighting. Public investment increased as governments recognized the importance of economic, social and political benefits of providing clean, safe and reliable water.

Historically, the funding of the large water supply infrastructure came in the form of 'municipal bonds', as in New York City, and private capital, as, for example, in Britain. In the early twentieth century, waterworks represented the largest component of municipal debt in American cities (Cutler and Miller 2005). However, even in the most prosperous western cities, household connections were uneven, mainly favouring middle-class households. From the middle of the nineteenth century, private monopolies were replaced by public monopolies because the private companies were unwilling to extend coverage to poor neighbourhoods, improve quality, or reduce excessive charges. Today, in the industrialized countries, public investment is important in building and maintaining infrastructure. For example, America has set up a revolving fund for municipalities to borrow from, 33 per cent of capital investment costs in Germany are financed by the central government, even in England and Wales, with its fully privatized firms, 9 per cent of capital investment comes from government subsidies, and in France private companies are subsided through a general taxation on consumers (Hall and Lobina 2006: 22).

In developing countries, funds generally come from government tax revenues, user charges, cross-subsidies, private sector investment, contributions from non-governmental organizations (NGOs) and charity organizations, official development assistance (ODA), or a combination of some or all of these sources. The choice depends on who pays (cross-subsidy, national, or international sources) and how it is financed (either through tax or user charges), and when (now or in the future) (World Development Movement 2006). State aid generally comes from taxation (similarly to ODA). Funds from development banks (national, regional or international) come from taxation and from those who save. Those who save can finance investment cost (through loans, bonds or private equity investment). Loans from savers will be recouped from the users or the government.

There are several estimates undertaken in order to gauge the amount of investment required in order to achieve universal coverage in developing countries. A report published by OECD (Ashley and Cashman 2006) shows that 0.35–1.2 per cent of GDP is required to finance, maintain and service the water supply networks in high-income countries, 0.54–2.60 per cent of GDP in middle-income countries, and 0.70–6.30 per cent of GDP in low-income countries. A more conservative figure is shown in a World Bank (WB) study, which estimates the investment needs for 2005–10 for developing countries to be around 0.5 per cent of GDP (Fay and Yepes 2003). The United Nations Development Programme (UNDP) believes that 1.6 per cent of GDP is required to achieve the target ten of the Millennium Development Goals (MDGs) (UNDP 2006).

As mentioned earlier, there are considerable challenges to securing private funds for the financing of water infrastructure in developing countries. The municipalities who usually operate the water services do not have the capacity to acquire loans to finance their infrastructure. They do not have satisfactory credit-ratings and therefore borrowing is very expensive (either from bank loans or by debt issuance). Some of the municipalities are small which renders them unattractive for private capital. However, there are some innovative approaches (such as pooling) which help decrease administrative costs and provide a more attractively sized bond.

The economic benefits of increasing access, as demonstrated by Edwin Chadwick in the mid-1800s, were recently estimated by WHO for the case of developing countries (Hutton *et al.* 2006). According to this estimate, every dollar invested in making water and sanitation coverage universal will bring in, on average, a return of US$10.3 dollars to developing countries. More precisely, a total of US$16.6 billion investment is required, and it will bring US$171 billion of economic benefits (time savings, productivity gains, healthcare cost savings). This will translate into 673 million fewer diarrhoea cases, resulting in around 600,000 fewer deaths, and saving US$1.7 billion in healthcare costs (over US$200 million in non-medical cost such as food, transport), US$3.5 billion in economic value of work days avoided, and US$7.3 billion as a result of lives saved.

### Tariff and distribution

Different social tariff models for water supply tend to have different distributional impacts. Social policy schemes are, in general, welfare enhancing: several developing countries have succeeded in reducing poverty through universal provision of social services like health care, education and water supply. However, most countries have both universal and targeted social policies since it is argued that even within universal policies, there is a possibility that the poorest may be excluded from accessing some services. Therefore, targeting would be necessary to make 'universalism effective' (Mkandawire 2005: 17).

## Case studies

As academic literature alone does not give a clear answer about the superiority of either private or public provision, it might be insightful to consider some empirical evidence. Having contextualized the water services issues globally, we will now look into our country studies to get a clearer picture.

We conducted seven case studies (in Brazil, Burkina Faso, Colombia, Great Britain, France, Hungary and Malaysia) in which we analysed how the private sector impacts on issues of access and affordability for the poor. We also looked at how social policies were designed and how effective they were at targeting those in need. Household data from selected countries and cities were used to analyse the issues related to access and affordability. These studies examined the debates surrounding PSP within the specific political, cultural and economic settings of each country. The selection of country studies was confirmed after a review of the literature and was based on several criteria. These included regional balance, geographical settings, level of economic development, level of poverty, degree of PSP, degree of regulatory instruments in place, degree of problems in the water supply sector (level of access, availability/scarcity of water) degree of 'success', 'failure' or 'difficulty' in the service provision, and availability of reliable data.

### France

France has historically involved the private sector in the distribution of water. The private sector now supplies 80 per cent of the French population. This very high rate can be compared to the worldwide average of around 10 per cent. The most widely used form of PSP is a concession contract, awarded usually for 10 to 30 years. The author of the French study, Arnaud Reynaud, reminds us that increasing coverage to quasi-universal levels took one or two generations with a high level of subsidies from urban to rural areas. In terms of affordability, Reynaud shows that in 2001 there were still 4.3 per cent of households in France (representing 1.16 million households) who used over 3 per cent of income on water bills.[13] It is estimated that three million people are late in paying their water bills and around 700,000 households request to reschedule their bills.

Despite these affordability problems, there is currently no explicit pricing scheme, rebate or discount tariff for the poorest households in France. Instead, the mechanism put in place by the public authorities corresponds to an *ex-post* financial aid designed to help qualified low-income households pay their water bills.[14] The main reason for this approach is that, according to the French definition of a public service, all customers with similar characteristics must face the same price (different pricing systems are therefore 'illegal'[15]). The prominent size of the private sector (and the lobby against such social tariffs) might also constitute a plausible explanation for the *ex-post* choice.

During the past two decades, water prices increased twice as fast as the consumer price index. In addition, water tariffs are 33 per cent higher in areas where the private sector operates than they are in those regions supplied by the public companies. Although the marginal cost and marginal price are not very different, the private companies tend to have a high fixed charge in order to secure their revenues. Reynaud concludes by saying that the private sector has negatively impacted the poor and that the *ex-post* financial assistance has not succeeded in solving affordability problems for the poor.

**Great Britain**

Studying the water sector in Great Britain is instructive and fascinating for two reasons. *First*, from the early nineteenth century Great Britain was a pioneer in the private sector provision of water services. Later its ownership reverted to the public provision. We learn that from the middle of the nineteenth century government policy makers have given priority to providing every household, regardless of geographical location, social class or income, with access to treated piped water. By the early twentieth century, this had been achieved for the vast majority of urban residents (and the mid-twentieth century for most of the rural areas). This was accomplished through an extensive, and costly system of cross-subsidies.

And, *secondly*, it is interesting to investigate the British model of unprecedented full-scale privatization since 1989. The authors of the England and Wales and Scotland study, John Sawkins and Valerie Dickie, argue that one of the reasons for privatization was the belief that the private sector could deliver services in a more efficient and effective way than the public sector, provided there was appropriate economic regulation. Hence an independent economic regulator – the Office of Water Services (Ofwat)[16] – was established. Sawkins and Dickie demonstrate that with this transformation, there was a shift in government policy and more emphasis was given to economic equity such as cost-recovery, dismantling of certain social policies (for example, cross-subsidies). They also argue that changes in policy did not impinge detrimentally on the underlying principle of universal access. However, with the arrival of the Labour government in 1997, there was a move towards reprioritizing social over economic equity, as demonstrated by the prohibition of domestic disconnection for non-payment, and a ban on the use of limiting devices (for example, trickle valves). The authors provide a detailed analysis of such policies and how the government tried to influence OFWAT to take up some social obligations.

What were the effects on affordability in the aftermath of privatization? Data reveal, for example, that in 1988, the poorest were using 3.5 per cent of their gross household income for water bills compared to 0.4 per cent for the richest. This figure increased for the poorest in 1991 and remained unchanged for the richest; that is, the poorest bore most of the burden. In 1997 the poorest were still using 4 per cent of gross household income on water and sewerage charges whereas the richest spent only 0.5 per cent. The 2002–03 figures show that this burden for the poorest has started to decrease, whereas it increases for the middle class. In addition, problems related to water debt have also been increasing recently. After comparing England and Wales with Scotland, Sawkins and Dickie conclude that there is no marked difference between a private and a public delivery of service and that the poor do not seem to be more or less affected by either model. However, with a public management in Scotland, there is more emphasis given to social equity concerns. Indeed, effective regulation (an independent economic regulatory body)[17] and appropriate social policies seem to cushion the adverse effects of privatization.

### Colombia

As a result of poor management and the lack of sufficient capital, the World Bank proposed the privatization of the water services in many Latin American countries. PSP in Colombia's water sector is representative of developments observed in other Latin American countries. These experiences were often controversial and characterized by considerable failures. The two well-known cases are Cartagena (privatized services) and Bogota (refusing privatization). The authors of the Colombian study, Andrés Gómez-Lobo and Marcela Meléndez, show that significant participation through management or concession contracts is relatively recent in this country, as it started only in 1994.

Data on access show that only around 68 per cent of the poorest do have access to piped water compared to around 96 per cent of the richest. However, the lack of access is almost exclusively a problem for the rural poor, for which the connection rate is still less than 50 per cent. As expected, the poorest are paying more in terms of their share of expenditure on water bills: 0.05 per cent compared to 0.01 per cent for the richest (this figure remains unchanged between 1997 and 2003).

Gómez-Lobo and Meléndez demonstrate that PSP tends to have a neutral to positive effect on access, especially to the poor and neutral impact of affordability. They argue that the generous subsidy scheme cushions the potential negative impact of PSP. The subsidy scheme is financed by the higher income and business sector groups, by the national and local governments, and by a special 'solidarity and income distribution fund' which was designed as a cross-subsidy scheme for the poorer regions. The subsidy is based on the socioeconomic stratification of dwellings. The authors show that over 80 per cent of households are classified in the first three groups eligible for subsidies. As such, it is more akin to a universal subsidy scheme than a focused social programme. The main policy conclusion to emerge from this study is that in the presence of appropriate social policies, PSP does not necessarily imply that the welfare of poorer households is negatively affected.

**Brazil**

PSP in Brazil is still in its infancy, since only 2 per cent of water companies are in private hands. However, in terms of the percentage of population supplied by the private sector, Brazil comes second (25 per cent) in Latin America after Chile (Owen 2006). In his contribution, André Rossi de Oliveira presents an in-depth analysis of the sector's development since the 1960s and shows how the government managed to increase coverage from 60 per cent in 1970 to 86 per cent in 1990. He argues that this was achieved by heavy public investments, especially through two institutions: the National Housing Bank (BNH) and the national Sanitation Plan (Planasa). This led to the emergence of regional (state) companies, which still hold concessions from municipalities. Following the dismantling of these institutions in the late 1980s (due to an economic crisis), the country has been struggling to develop a coherent water policy. There is confusion as to who (municipalities or the federal/state government) has the right to grant concessions. After much discussion, a new bill was passed in 2007, which allows the municipalities and states to access federal financing and establishes a council including civil society institutions to influence tariff setting and termination of service. However, it falls short of defining the authority in according concession.

De Oliveira presents some social polices that were put in place to increase access to water for the poor in the 1990s, and argues that all these policies gave greater priority to access than to issues concerning affordability. He shows that only 52 per cent of the poorest households had access to water supply in 1995, compared to nearly 100 per cent of the richest. By 2003, this figure had increased to 68 per cent of the poorest households. This increase is due mainly to the heavy public investments mentioned above and by forcing private operators to invest. However, 45 million Brazilians still have no access to water supply. The author provides some evidence that private companies are present mainly in areas with higher coverage rates, that the productivity is higher in private companies, private companies invest less, and the private companies tend to have higher tariffs. In terms of affordability, the study shows that water and sewage bills are much more burdensome for low-income families than high-income families. The poorest use around 1.4 per cent of their expenses on water bills compared to only 0.3 per cent for the richest. The affordability problem is generally dealt with the tariff structure and all companies (public or private) practice social tariffs such as increasing block tariff and use other *ex-post* measures designed to help the poor households.

## Malaysia

Malaysia started PSP in the water sector in the early 1990s, mainly through BOT. In recent years, this has been changing in favour or concession-type contracts granted for longer periods. The private sector currently supplies water to 64 per cent of the population of the country. This figure is among the highest in the Asia Pacific region (Owen 2006). One particularity of the country's water sector is that apart from the big multinational companies, local firms have also been very active in the market, having ambitions to expand beyond its national territory (for example to China, Thailand and Indonesia).

Cassey Lee argues that the development of the water sector in Malaysia has been fairly uneven, with the more developed states achieving almost universal coverage, while the less developed states continue to have great difficulties in increasing access, particularly in rural areas. He also shows that the more developed states tend to attract PSP while those that are poor have public provision of water supply. Lee's study shows that only 56 per cent of the poorest had access to water in 1994 compared to 94 per cent for the richest. These figures changed to 74 per cent and 96 per cent, respectively, in 1999. Water affordability for the households with lower income worsened during the same period. On the other hand, the affordability for the richer households has improved. In 1999 the poorest used 1.5 per cent of their expenditure on water compared to 0.7 per cent for the richest. Social policies such as lifeline consumption rate, cross-subsidy (from industrial to domestic consumers), increasing block tariff are implemented to address the concerns for the poor households. The author shows that there is a general trend in reducing water subsidies.

Lee finds that privatization does not seem to have improved access to water. As illustrated by the case of Kelantan, water privatization in Malaysia has not always been successful. In other words, PSP has not brought in additional investments to increase coverage, nor have they increased efficiency. He shows that most of the companies are highly deficient since they are unable to recover their operating costs. The main reason for this weak financial performance is the loss of revenues from non-revenue waters, primarily through leakages (but this is lower where the private sector is operating the system). However, because of strict policies and political sensitivity regarding tariff increases, there does not seem to be an association between PSP and higher tariffs. But privatized states do tend to revise tariff (upwards).

### Hungary

Hungary is representative of what is taking place in other transition economies, where a large-scale privatization started after the regime change in the early 1990s. Within the privatization wave (and with little public debate), the water sector was reformed, with the ownership being transferred first to the municipalities and then to the private sector. Zsolt Boda *et al.* remind us that an overall privatization of the assets was prohibited by law. However, partial privatization did take place, and this was combined with long-term management rights given to private companies. Today about 40 per cent of the water is distributed by private companies/joint ventures and about 20 per cent of the water companies were privatized.

Although piped water is available to almost all residential areas, connection is still not universal. By disaggregating data, Boda *et al.* show that 20 per cent of the poorest households still have no access to piped water (this figure has remained relatively unchanged since 1992). The authors argue that if people are not connected, it is because of financial, rather than physical constraints and therefore the issue of access can be redefined as a question of affordability. In general, there does not seem to be an affordability problem (with most of the households paying less than 3 per cent of their income on water bills), but the proportion of expenditure on water bills paid by the poorest has increased from 1.1 per cent to 1.5 per cent over the period 1992–2003.

The authors argue that water is affordable thanks to the specific social policies put in place in the country. These policies include keeping the tariffs low (which does not reflect investment and depreciation costs), providing state subsidies and assistance (maintenance or debt relief) by the local governments, and the existence of regional cross-subsidies. The prices are kept deliberately low for political reasons because in the socialist era water services were free of charge. As a result of this scheme, investments cannot be imposed on the companies but instead fall under the responsibility of the municipality (backed by the state subsidies and EU funding). Another consequence is that the water tariffs are between 5 and 90 per cent lower than the actual cost of production and this benefits both the rich and the poor (universal social policy).[18]

In terms of the differences between public and private provision, Boda *et al.* find that the rate of price increase is slightly higher in the private companies, but that PSP did not lead to price increase. This is due to the strict political control of prices (as discussed above), or due to the practices of the water companies that seek compensation from fixed management fees, increasing efficiency, or by choosing regions with low costs of production (cherry picking). Overall, the authors find that although the private water companies (especially multinational corporations) have been successful in increasing efficiency (productivity) without increasing investment, this did not result in a lowering of tariffs.

**Burkina Faso**

Burkina Faso is one of the poorest countries in the world, and is confronted by major development challenges. Studying this country could illustrate the challenges of increasing access to water, in conditions where less than half of the people have access to safe drinking water. The other half either buy water from private vendors at exorbitant prices or consume unsafe water from rivers and other sources. In other words, there are three groups of private actors in the water services: private firms, fountain managers, and private vendors who sell water to individual domiciles. The authors, Issaka Kouanda and Mouhamad Moudassir, start their discussion of Burkina Faso by emphasizing that it is a landlocked country, which suffers from extreme climatic conditions. Reform of the Burkinabe water sector started in the mid-1990s with loans from the World Bank. In common with their approach to other developing countries, and cautious about the country's ability to respect its financial obligations, the lenders set the privatization of the public water company as a condition. In 2001, a compromise was reached in the form of a service contract with a multinational water company (Veolia). The objective of this partnership was to operate the company on a commercial basis, improve access and increase the efficiency of the water services.

The study shows that the share of population with access to safe drinking water has been increasing constantly – from 43 per cent in 1994 to 52 per cent in 1998 and to 61 per cent in 2003, benefiting all income groups. In addition, the time spent on fetching water has also decreased as a result of putting to use more water fountains. Kouanda and Moudassir present a detailed account of how the private management tries to prioritize economic efficiency to the detriment of social objectives. These take the form of increasing tariffs, dismantling social policies, privileging larger consumers, and decreasing the level of lifeline consumption. As a result, the share of expenditure used for water increased for the poorest quintile, but decreased for the richest income groups. The fact that the number of poor people using more than 3 per cent of expenditure on water has increased also illustrates this point. Moreover, the authors caution that the poorest are often not connected to the network and therefore have to purchase water from private vendors.

The authors conclude that although coverage seems to have increased for all groups and efficiency has improved, the commercialization objective pursued by the private sector has been detrimental in terms of affordability, especially to the poorest sectors of the population.

## Policy implications: social policies are instrumental

All of these country studies show the shortcomings of PSP in terms of access and affordability. Increased coverage comes from increased investment or increases in efficiency (increasing productivity, organizational restructuring and rationalization, reducing leakages, and more efficient collection of tariffs). The private sector does not necessarily invest more. However, they tend to be more efficient (in Burkina Faso, Hungary and Malaysia), but this efficiency does not seem to translate into a lowering of tariffs. On the contrary, the evidence shows that the private sector has higher tariffs (Burkina Faso, France, Colombia). Our studies show that affordability is a major issue in most countries. In all of the countries, it is demonstrated that the poor are affected disproportionately. Governments try to neutralize this by designing various social policies such as cross-subsidies, public subsidies, increasing block tariffs, lifeline consumption, *ex-post* assistance and by keeping tariffs deliberately low.

The choice of social policies varies from country to country. In the two developed countries (France and Great Britain), heavy public investment was used to ensure that everyone had access to piped water. In these countries, even with high regulatory capacity, social policies in the water sector have been crucial. For example, in France, it consists predominantly of *ex-post* assistance to those who cannot afford to pay water bills, operating a fund for rural water supply, and the prohibition of disconnection. British social policies include income support based on property values, subsidies, a ban on disconnections, various forms of social security support and social assistance in paying water bills. In addition, there exists an effective and independent economic regulatory body.

In the case of Colombia, our findings suggest that it is the subsidy that helps the poor to have access to affordable water. In addition, private investment commitments prescribed to the private sector have been useful in increasing coverage. Similarly, in Brazil, the desire to make water supply universal led to heavy investment in the 1970s and effective social policies (cross-subsidies) helped to increase the coverage to the poor. However, the current impasse on who has the right to grant concessions (the state or municipality) to the private sector is jeopardizing further progress. The government in Hungary provides subsidies to those regions that have high costs of production. In addition, industrial users cross-subsidize domestic consumption and income transfers by central or local authorities shoulder some of the burden of households' water expenditures. The tariffs are kept low ('hidden social policy'), and no disconnection is allowed due to the non-payment of bills. The private sector has increased efficiency in the system, but the investment is financed by the state. In Malaysia, the social policies that are in place comprise state financing of water supply in rural areas, cross-subsidy (industrial users to domestic), and lifeline block tariffs. In addition, the private sector is contractually obliged to increase coverage in the urban and rural areas. In Burkina Faso, although the efficiency of the network has substantially improved with commercialization through PSP, it is now putting pressure on dismantling social policies.

And, finally, our studies also show that once the private sector comes in, it tries to dismantle such social policies.

## Conclusions

The results of our research are consistent with other research findings.[19] Increasing coverage requires many things and investments is one of the key inputs. As we have seen, the private sector can, and often does, assume a critical role in the provision and operation of the water supply. However, loans have to be recovered from the users or from the government. One of the water specialists puts this bluntly: '*whatever* the purists say, water services need to be able to cover their operating costs and to finance debt' (Owen 2006: 28). In the countries that cannot service loan repayments, the private sector does not provide a new source of financing. The financing of water facilities is unappealing to private investors for reasons such as the 'lumpiness' of necessary investments, long payback periods (of 20 years or more), and the political difficulties inherent in charging and collecting cost-recovering tariffs. Ironically, it is the developing countries that need the most assistance in terms of investment requirement and yet the private sector finds these countries '*aggressively challenged*'. As discussed above, water projects are risky compared to other forms of capital-intensive projects. In such circumstances, there is no need to be overoptimistic that the private sector will solve the water supply problem. It is rightly pointed out by one of the leading experts on privatization that operating water business which is profitable to the service providers and affordable to consumers, especially the poor, is extremely difficult because of the huge capital investment requirements (Megginson 2005: 399–400).

As discussed above, it is ultimately the public authorities that can make the difference in terms of providing the adequate social policy framework and mobilizing investments. Expenditure in water supply, rather than creating regulatory bodies, would be more effective in increasing coverage. Increased coverage will benefit the poor *the most* since they are not connected to piped water sources and they have to pay more in order to obtain water from alternative sources. Improved coverage will also save their time (spent on fetching water) and could drastically improve their health (since they will have access to better quality of water).

Our results, the growing failures of large-scale privatization and increasing public pressure against privatization, show that there is a need to rethink PSP strategy in terms of water supply. PSP in the water sector was oversold during the 1990s without realizing the challenges of such policy reforms. In this context, Mahbub ul Haq argued that the development pendulum is swinging from a reliance on the public sector to an overenthusiasm for the private provision and he fears that this pendulum may swing too far (Haq 1995: 140). In other words, one should be more cautious about private sector involvement in the water sector.

In conclusion, theory and evidence show the ambiguities of PSP in the water sector. The political economy of water is such that any benevolent reform can lead to an impasse if the reforms are not well thought through. Our country studies, together with a historical perspective, show that any reform intending to increase coverage (either through commercialization, PSP, additional investment or increasing efficiency) should be accompanied by appropriate social policies. These policies should be able to address the issue of access and affordability, especially to the poor.

## Notes

1. Research Coordinator, United Nations Research Institute for Social Development (UNRISD), prasad@unrisd.org. Anna Sagan provided excellent research assistance for this project.
2. Lawyers would incorporate a broader meaning of rules and institutions, while political scientists will also include the policy process.

3. http://www.who.int/water_sanitation_health/publications/facts2004/en/index.html, accessed on 22 January 2007.
4. Following the introduction of laws governing the PSP in water and the bidding procedures, the duration of delegation contracts has significantly dropped, however, and most contracts are now signed for 12 years or less.
5. Although the United Nations does not have the power in terms of financial resources, it has managed, however, to shape policies through UN conferences and declarations. One such international conference took place in 1992 in Dublin and focused on water and the environment (Dublin 1992). It was organized to prepare a statement for the Rio Earth Summit in the same year. The Dublin statement proposed four guiding principles including the Principle 4: *Water has an economic value and it should be recognized as an economic good.* This principle has been used to justify the commercialization of water supply. Coincidently, the emergence of water multinationals and the Dublin/Rio principles are linked where the multinationals becoming the vehicle for these principles.
6. http://www.worldbank.org, accessed on 22 January 2007.
7. It should be noted that the Federal Republic of Germany (government of Konrad Adenauer) launched the first large-scale ideologically motivated 'denationalization' programme in 1961. It sold Volkswagen and the chemical firm VEBA.
8. She adopted the term 'privatization' which was originally coined by Peter Drucker (1968).
9. Based on the World Bank's private participation in infrastructure (http://ppi.worldbank.org), the following countries have involved the private sector in their water supply: Albania, Algeria, Argentina, Armenia, Azerbaijan, Barbados, Belize, Bolivia, Brazil, Bulgaria, Central African Republic, Chile, China, Colombia, Croatia, Cuba, Czech Republic, Ecuador, Egypt, Arab Republic, Estonia, Ghana, Guyana, Honduras, Hungary, India, Indonesia, Jordan, Kazakhstan, Lebanon, Malaysia, Mexico, Mozambique, Namibia, Niger, Panama, Papua New Guinea, Peru, the Philippines, Poland, Romania, Russian Federation, Senegal, Serbia and Montenegro, Slovak Republic, South Africa, Tanzania, Thailand, Trinidad and Tobago, Turkey, Uganda, Uruguay, Uzbekistan, Venezuela, Vietnam, West Bank and Gaza.
10. See Evaluation of the World Bank Research (1998–2005) at http://econ.worldbank.org, accessed on 22 January 2007.
11. *Implementing the World Bank Group Infrastructure Action Plan*, 13 September 2003: 25.
12. See *Implementing the World Bank Group Infrastructure Action Plan*, 13 September 2003: 5.
13. Although still subject to debate, there is an international norm that expenditure on water should not exceed 3–5 per cent to total expenditure (or, in the absence of expenditure data, 3 per cent of houseld income).
14. For example, there exists a specific fund created to help low-income households who cannot pay their bills (by writing off water debts).
15. The last Water Law No. 2006–1772, promulgated on 30 December 2006, has however recognized a right for all users to benefit from water at an economically acceptable cost. This is a first step towards the implementation of social water pricing.

16. Ofwat is a non-ministerial government department, and therefore not subject to direction from ministers. It is accountable to Parliament, provides evidence for Parliamentary Select Committees and provides an annual report to the Secretary of State and the First Minister of Wales.
17. The economic regulator is to regulate through the use of a price cap mechanism with periodic reviews every five years. In setting price caps Ofwat's primary duty was to ensure that the companies were able to finance their functions, in particular by securing a reasonable rate of return on their capital.
18. However, there is a concern that the national-level social policy scheme in the form of reduced price and cross-subsidy is contrary to the EU Guidelines on Water Framework Directive. These guidelines emphasize that the cost of water should be covered by the operator. This will likely lead to a price increase in Hungary and the targeted assistance at the local level will probably be enhanced.
19. For a literature review on PSP and their results, see Prasad (2006).

## References


ADERAS (2006) *Las Tarifas de Agua Potable y Alcantarillado en America Latina* (ADERAS, Asociación de Entes Reguladores de Agua Potable y Saneamiento de las Américas). Web document at http://www.aderasa.org/en/documentos3.htm?x=654. Accessed on 29 October 2007.

Ait-Ouyahia, M. (2006) *Public–Private Partnerships for Funding Municipal Drinking Water Infrastructure: What Are the Challenges?* Discussion Paper (Government of Canada, Policy Research Initiative).

Amann, E. (2006) *Regulating Development: Evidence from Africa and Latin America* (Cheltenham: Edward Elgar).

Anand, P.B. (2007a) 'Right to Water and Access to Water: an Assessment', *Journal of International Development* 19, 511–26.

Anand, P.B. (2007b) *Scarcity, Entitlements, and the Economics of Water in Developing Countries* (Cheltenham: Edward Elgar).

Ashley, R. and A. Cashman (2006) 'The Impacts of Change on the Long-term Future Demand for Water Sector Infrastructure', in OECD (ed.), *Infrastructure to 2030: Telecom, Land Transport, Water and Electricity* (Paris: OECD).

Baldwin, R., C. Scott and C. Hood (1998) *A Reader on Regulation* (New York: Oxford University Press).

Ballance, T. and A. Taylor (2005) *Competition and Economic Regulation in Water: The Future of the European Water Industry* (London: IWA Publishing).

Bangura, Y. and G. Larbi (eds) (2006) *Public Sector Reform in Developing Countries: Capacity Challenges to Improve Services* (Geneva: UNRISD and Basingstoke: Palgrave Macmillan).

Breyer, H. (2006) *Mortality, Morbidity and Improvements in Water and Sanitation: Some Lessons from English History*. Occasional Paper 2006/35, Human Development Report 2006 (New York: Human Development Report Office, UNDP).

Buchanan, J.M. (1972) *Theory of Public Choice* (Ann Arbor, MI: University of Michigan Press).

Chadwick, E. (1842) *Report ... from the Poor Law Commissioners on an Inquiry into the Sanitary Conditions of the Labouring Population of Great Britain* (London). http://www.victorianweb.org/history/chadwick2.html.

Cook, P. and S. Mosedale (2007) *Regulation, Markets and Poverty* (Cheltenham: Edward Elgar).

Cutler, D. and G. Miller (2005) *Water, Water, Everywhere: Municipal Finance and Water Supply in American Cities* (Cambridge, MA: National Bureau of Economic Research).

Davis, J. (2005) 'Private Sector Participation in the Water and Sanitation Sector', *Annual Review of Environment and Resources*, 30, 145–83.

Drucker, P. (1968) *The Age of Discontinuity: Guidelines to Our Changing Society. With a New Introduction by the Author* (New Brunswick, NJ: Transaction Books).

Fay, M. and T. Yepes (2003) *Investing in Infrastructure: What is Needed from 2000 to 2010*? World Bank Policy Research Working Paper No. 3102 (Washington, DC: World Bank).

Fletcher, J. (1845) 'Historical and Statistical Account of the Present System of Supplying the Metropolis with Water', *Journal of the Statistical Society of London*, 8(2), 148–81.

Foster, V. and T. Yepes (2006) *Is Cost Recovery a Feasible Objective for Water and Electricity? The Latin American Experience*. World Bank Policy Research Working Paper No. 3943 (Washington, DC: World Bank).

Gandy, M. (2006) *Water, Sanitation and the Modern City: Colonial and Post-Colonial Experiences in Lagos and Mumbai*. Occasional Paper 2006/6, Human Development Report 2006 (New York: Human Development Report Office, UNDP). http://hdr.undp.org/hdr2006/pdfs/background-docs/Background_papers/Gandy%20Matthew.pdf.

Ghimire, K.B. (2005) *Civil Society and the Market Question: Dynamics of Rural Development and Popular Mobilization* (Geneva: UNRISD and Basingstoke: Palgrave Macmillan).

Hall, D. (2001) *Water in Public Hands* (London: Public Services International Research Unit/PSIRU). www.psiru.org, accessed on 12 April 2007.

Hall, D. and E. Lobina (2006) *Water as a Public Service* (London: Public Services International Research Unit/PSIRU). www.psiru.org.

Haq, M. (1995) *Reflections on Human Development* (New York: Oxford University Press).

Hunter, W. (1898) 'London Water Supply', *Journal of the Society of Arts* 47(2422), 475–94.

Hutton, G., L. Haller and J. Bartram (2006) *Economic and Health Effects of Increasing Coverage of Low Cost Water and Sanitation Interventions*. Occasional Paper 2006/33, Human Development Report 2006 (New York: Human Development Report Office, UNDP).

Jalilian, H., C. Kirkpatrick and D. Parker (2007) 'The Impact of Regulation on Economic Growth in Developing Countries: a Cross-country Analysis', *World Development* 35(1), 87–103.

Juuti, P. and T. Katko (eds) (2005) *Water, Time and European Cities: History Matters for the Futures*. WaterTime Project (Brussels: European Commission). http://www.watertime.net/Docs/WP3/WTEC.pdf, accessed in January 2007.

Kessides, I.N. (2004) *Reforming Infrastructure: Privatization, Regulation and Competition*. World Bank Policy Research Report (Washington, DC: Development Economics Vice Presidency, World Bank).

Kirkpatrick, C. and D. Parker (2004) 'Regulatory Impact Assessment and Regulatory Governance in Developing Countries', *Public Administration and Development* 24(4), 333–44.

Laffont, J.J. (2000) *Incentives and Political Economy* (New York: Oxford University Press).

Megginson, W.L. (2005) *The Financial Economics of Privatization* (New York: Oxford University Press).

Megginson, W. L. and J. Netter (2001) 'From State to Market: a Survey of Empirical Studies on Privatization', *Journal of Economic Literature* 39(2), 321–89.

Minogue, M. (2005) 'Apples and Oranges: Problems in the Analysis of Comparative Regulatory Governance', *Quarterly Review of Economics and Finance* 45(2–3), 195.

Minogue, M. and L. Carino (2006) *Regulatory Governance in Developing Countries* (Cheltenham: Edward Elgar).

Mkandawire, T. (2005) *Targeting and Universalism in Poverty Reduction*. Programme on Social Policy and Development, Paper No. 23 (Geneva: UNRISD).

Mohajeri, S., B. Knothe, D.-N. Lamothe and J.-A. Faby (2003) *Aqualibrium: European Water Management between Regulation and Competition* (Brussels, European Commission).

Newbery, D.M.G. (1999) *Privatization, Restructuring, and Regulation of Network Utilities* (Cambridge, MA: MIT Press).

Organisation for Economic Co-operation and Development OECD (2003) *Social Issues in the Provision and Pricing of Water Services* (Paris: OECD).

Owen, D.L. (2006) *Pinsent Masons Water Yearbook, 2006–2007* (London: Masons Solicitors).

Parker, D. (1999) 'Regulation of Privatised Public Utilities in the UK: Performance and Governance', *International Journal of Public Sector Management* 12(3), 213–35.

Pezon, C. (1999) *La gestion du service d'eau potable en France de 1850 à 1995*. Thèse es sciences de gestion (Paris: Conservatoire national des arts et métiers).

Pezon, C. and S. Petitet (2004) *L'intercommunalité en France de 1890 à 1999, la distribution d'eau potable en question, Arras, communication à la Journée d'études 'Les territoires de l'eau'* (Arras: Université d'Arras).

Prasad, N. (2006) 'Privatisation Results: Private Sector Participation in Water Services after 15 Years', *Development Policy Review* 24(6), 669–92.

Prasad, N. (2007) 'Water Privatization: A Historical Perspective', *Law, Environment and Development Journal* 3(2), 217–37.

Salzman, J. (2006) 'Thirst: a Short History of Drinking Water', *Yale Journal of Law and the Humanities* 17, 94–121.

Sellers, D. (1997) *Hidden Beneath Our Feet: The Story of Sewerage in Leeds* (Leeds: Leeds City Council).

Stiglitz, J. (1998) 'The Private Uses of Public Interests: Incentives and Institutions', *The Journal of Economic Perspectives* 12(2), 3–22.

Ugaz, C. (2006). *Commercialization, Privatization and Universal Access to Water*. Mimeo (Geneva: UNRISD).

United Nations Development Programme (UNDP) (2006) *Human Development Report 2006: Beyond Scarcity: Power, Poverty and the Global Water Crisis* (New York: Human Development Report Office, UNDP and Palgrave Macmillan).

United Nations Research Institute for Social Development (UNRISD), (2006), *Transformative Social Policy: Lessons from UNRISD Research.* Research and Policy Brief No. 5 (Geneva: UNRISD).

Utting, P. (ed.) (2006) *Reclaiming Development Agendas: Knowledge, Power and International Policy Making* (Geneva: UNRISD and Basingstoke: Palgrave Macmillan).

Vickers, J. and G. Yarrow (1988) *Privatization: An Economic Analysis* (Cambridge, MA: MIT Press).

*Wall Street Journal* (2003) 'The World Bank as Privatization Agnostic', 21 July.

Wingate, C.F. (1883) 'The Water-Supply of Cities', *North American Review* 136, 364–74.

World Bank (2006) *Handbook for Evaluating Infrastructure Regulatory Systems* (Washington, DC: World Bank).

World Bank (2005a) *Infrastructure Development: The Roles of the Public and Private Sectors. World Bank Group's Approach to Supporting Investments in Infrastructure* (Washington, DC: World Bank).

World Bank (2005b) *Infrastructure and the World Bank: A Progress Report* (Washington, DC: Development Committee, World Bank).

World Bank (1995) *Bureaucrats in Business: The Economics and Politics of Government Ownership* (New York: Oxford University Press).

World Bank (1994) *World Development Report 1994: Infrastructure for Development* (New York: Oxford University Press).

World Bank (1993) *Water Resources Management.* A World Bank Policy Paper (Washington, DC: World Bank).

World Bank (1983) *World Development Report 1983* (New York: Oxford University Press).

World Development Movement (2006) *Piped Dreams: The Failure of the Private Sector to Invest in Water Services in Developing Countries* (London: World Development Movement).

World Health Organization (WHO) and United Nations Children's Fund (UNICEF), (2006), *Meeting the MGD Drinking Water and Sanitation Target* (Geneva: WHO and New York: UNICEF). www.who.int/water_sanitation_health/monitoring/jmp 2006/en/index. html, accessed on 12 April 2007.

# 2
# France

*Arnaud Reynaud*

## Introduction

Given the substantial size of the French private water industry and the specific concession-type arrangement for private sector participation (PSP), it is natural to investigate how the private sector impacts on equity, access and affordability issues. Issues surrounding access to and the affordability of water have been discussed in France since the beginning of the 1990s. For example, access to water was incorporated into the 1992 law on a minimum insertion income, stating that 'all families must have access to energy and water'. Another example is the creation in 2000 of a fund (financed by private and public operators) to help poor households pay their bills. Although these social measures show that both private and public operators are concerned about water affordability, there is still a lack of research to investigate the affordability of the water service for low-income and other vulnerable household groups in France. This chapter explores the various social policies and regulations implemented by private water companies and by public authorities in helping the poor households.

France has been a pioneer of PSP in the water sector. The first well-documented case of private participation in France dates back to 1776 when the city of Paris decided to allocate to '*Sieurs Perrier*' a 15-year exclusive concession of the water supply system (Duroy 1996).[1] In this period, water affordability to poor households was already an important issue since the concession contract stipulated that 'The Sieurs Perrier must build water fountains in order to guarantee appropriate price for poor households'. Currently, the water industry in France is organized on a municipal level. Local communities can either directly manage water services or they may choose to delegate it to a private company through various contractual agreements, including management contracts, affermage (lease contract) and concessions (here the private operator is responsible for financing all new investments over the period of delegation). Whatever the type of arrangement, water services must have the characteristics of a *public service*: equal access for all consumers, continuity of the service and adaptability to technical innovations. The participation of the private sector has steadily increased in France during the twentieth century to reach around 80 per cent of the market share (Guérin-Schneider and Lorrain 2004; Pezon 2000).

The rest of this chapter is organized as follows. The following two sections present the main characteristics of the French water industry and discuss the main issues related to private participation and water affordability. Then, we switch our focus to social policies and regulations dealing with water affordability in France. In particular, we describe and analyse critically the recent, current and proposed support mechanisms to assist low-income households in paying water and sewerage charges. We also discuss alternative approaches to the measurement of water affordability in France. Using the Family Income and Expenditure surveys published by the National Institute for Statistics and Economic Studies and the existing literature, we provide a formal definition of water affordability in France. In the final section we identify the determinants of water affordability. We focus in particular on private participation in the water sector as a potential determinant of affordability. We conclude by deriving some policy implications from our findings.

## Characteristics of the French water industry

### Organization of water services in France

#### *A local organization*

French local communities have been responsible for water supply, treatment and sanitation since 1790. But local communities only started to organize water delivery from the middle of the nineteenth century. At the end of the nineteenth century, the Conseil d'état (the highest administrative jurisdiction in France) recognized that the water service was a prerogative of French municipalities.[2] In 2003, there were approximately 29,300 water services in France for 36,679 local communities (Bureau d'informations et de prévisions économiques et Syndicat professionnel des distributeurs d'eau 2005), of which 14,900 deal with water supply and 14,400 with sewage.

### *The legal status of water services*

Water services in France are considered to be public services.[3] Being a public service means that water services must have a certain number of characteristics, including equal access for all consumers, continuity of supply in quantity and quality and adaptability to the technical innovation (Mescheriakoff 1985).

But the French water services belong to a specific category of public service called *industrial or commercial public services* (*Service public à caractère industriel ou commercial,* in French, SPIC). Belonging to the industrial or commercial public service category means that the local public authority can delegate the management of the water service to a private firm. Local public authorities may decide to cooperate with an external operator. If the municipality retains this option, it will have a wide variety of contractual arrangements at its disposal. These contractual arrangements differ according to the degree of the firm's involvement in the service and the proportion of the risk that the external operator bears.

The delegation of water services is currently governed by the *'Sapin Law'*, passed on 23 January 1993. In case of private management, the relationship between the local municipality and the firm can take different forms: management contracts, affermage (lease contract) where the municipality remains the owner of assets, and concession where the private operator is responsible for financing all new investments over the period of delegation. Typically, all these contracts specify the nature of expected services and the water pricing schemes (including price adjustment formula). Affermage is the most common form of contract, usually awarded for a period of seven to 12 years. The private firm is responsible for the operation and maintenance of the water utility; it collects tariff revenues from users and pays a special additional charge to the local community, which is included in the water rate determined by the contract. It has *no* obligation to invest in the infrastructure. Whatever the type of management chosen by the local community (public versus delegated), water services must have the characteristics of a public service.

### *Institutional organization of the water sector*

One important characteristic of the institutional organization of the water sector in France is the complexity of public authority intervention. There are several levels at which public authorities may have an impact on water utility management (from European Union/EU level to the local community level).

*1 The European Union level.* Most environmental regulation currently takes place at the European level. The two most important EU provisions dealing with water regulation are the Water Framework Directive and the Urban Wastewater Treatment Directive.

The Water Framework Directive[4] establishes a European framework for the protection of all water bodies in the European Union – rivers, lakes, coastal waters, groundwater and inland surface water. Its objective is to achieve 'good quality' of water resources by 2015. This objective is to be reached through integrated management based on river basins, as water systems do not stop at administrative borders. The Water Framework Directive operates with clear deadlines for various steps that are required to move toward sustainable, integrated water management in Europe. The national legislation necessary to implement the Directive became effective in December 2003.

The Urban Wastewater Treatment Directive[5] addresses nutrient-based, bacterial and viral pollution caused by urban wastewater. Urban wastewater that discharges excessive levels of nutrients, in particular phosphorous and nitrogen, into rivers and seas promotes excessive growth of algae and other forms of aquatic plants. This process, known as 'eutrophication', leads in turn to a lowering of oxygen levels, threatening the survival of fish, which depend on oxygen. It can also make the water unsafe for drinking. By introducing potentially harmful bacteria and viruses, the discharges also pose human health risks in waters that are used for bathing or shellfish farming.

*2 The state level.* As a result of the decentralization laws (March 1982 and January 1983), the role of the central state has been limited to water law enforcement (withdrawal and wastewater discharge), and to guaranteeing public health and safety. Water services are controlled by the territorial administration of the state: control of the legality of public procurements and, generally speaking, of all activities of local communities (Prefecture) and compliance with technical standards (Local Directorate of Agriculture and Forestry, Directorate of Public Works, Directorate of Health and Social Affairs).

The state also guarantees solidarity between users at two levels:

- At the level of each of the six large river basins, a Water Agency (a public establishment under state supervision) levies water charges on withdrawals and wastewater discharges. These water charges are used to subsidize investments to improve water resources and to treat effluents or to improve the operation of treatment plants.

- At the national level, the National Fund for Rural Water Supply (Fond national pour le développement des adductions d'eau, FNDAE) levies a tax that amounts to 10.5 per cent on all cubic metres of water supplied in France, and allocates each Department (administrative district) subsidies for small rural communities to enable them to invest in potable water supply system. This fund has however ceased to exist since January 2005.

*3 Water agencies and drainage basins.* The water agencies oversee the application of the 'polluter pays' principle and implement the policies for the basins drawn up by the committees, in order to protect water resources and control pollution. Six water agencies (one per major basin) were set up in 1964. They are independent public institutions under the dual supervision of the Ministry of the Environment and Sustainable Development and the Ministry of the Budget. They distribute financial aid to industry, local authorities and farmers who undertake to protect water resources and quality.

In order to support these operations they collect fees from water users, calculated on the 'polluter pays' principle. In the course of the seventh investment programme (1999–2001), the agencies invested EUR16 billion and collected EUR7.8 billion in fees. The difference between these organizations and those established in other countries is that they play no role either in carrying out projects or in regulating or supervising water. The agencies are supplementary to the existing structures and their role is to accelerate or stimulate necessary projects by offering technical and financial incentives. The arrangement based on the major drainage basins means that water policy could be adapted to the specific features of each region. This is one of the unique aspects of the French system.

*4 Regions.* Water is the largest item of environment expenditures at the regional level, accounting for an average of 33.4 per cent. The regions, however, have a very limited regulatory jurisdiction over water (they only grant funds for investments that are of regional benefit, for example for major infrastructure projects) and they do not have specific environmental financial resources.

*5 Departments.* Water is also the biggest item in terms of environment expenditure at the department level, accounting for 61.4 per cent. Departments assist local communities at the technical and financial level. They manage the bulk of the above-mentioned FNDAE budget. This budget was on average equal to EUR122 million per year from 1996 to 1999. After the water agencies, the French *Départments* are the second largest source of water sector financing.

*6 Local communities and intercommunal arrangements.* The production and distribution of drinking water and sewage are the responsibility of the communes. The latter are also responsible for the quality and the cost of each of these services and their proper operation.

## Economic, social and environmental performance of the French water industry

### *Population connected to the water network*

Berland and Juery (2002) and Guérin-Schneider and Nakhla (2004) report data on the evolution of connection rates in France of the rural population (see Table 2.1). These figures show that the rural population has, on average, less coverage than the whole population.

*Table 2.1* Evolution of the rural population connected to the water supply network

| *Year* | *1954* | *1960* | *1966* | *1971* | *1976* | *1981* | *1990* | *1995* |
|---|---|---|---|---|---|---|---|---|
| Rural population (million) | 21.6 | 21.8 | 26.1 | 26.7 | 28.4 | 29.6 | 36.9 | n.a. |
| Connected rural population (million) | 8.1 | 10.4 | 16.6 | 20.1 | 25.0 | 27.8 | 36.3 | n.a. |
| Connection rate (%) | 37.6 | 47.4 | 63.6 | 75.3 | 88.0 | 93.7 | 98.2 | 98.2 |

*Source*: Berland and Juery (2002); Guerrin-Schneider and Nakhla (2004); Pézon (2000).

At the beginning of the 1950s, less than 40 per cent of the rural population was connected to the water supply network (it was just 25 per cent in 1939 – Pezon 1999). From 1954 to 1995, the connection rate increased by more than 2.5 times to reach almost a full coverage of rural population at the end of the 1990s. This rapid increase in the connection rate was mainly as a result of the creation of the FNDAE in 1954 (mentioned above).

The fact that the FNDAE focuses primarily on development of water networks in small communities can be easily understood from a consideration of Table 2.2. Hence, it is important to stress that at the beginning of the 1950s the connection rate to the public water network depended largely on the size of local municipalities. Although more than 90 per cent of inhabitants living in large local communities (number of inhabitants greater than 10,000) were already connected to the public water

*Table 2.2* Total population connected to the public water network, 31 December 1960

| *Size of water supply network* | *Population connected (million)* | *Connection rate (%)* |
|---|---|---|
| Less than 2,000 inhabitants | 10.4 | 50.5 |
| 2,000 to 5,000 inhabitants | 5.1 | 71.2 |
| 5,000 to 10,000 inhabitants | 3.8 | 84.8 |
| 10,000 to 20,000 inhabitants | 4.1 | 90.4 |
| 20,000 to 50,000 inhabitants | 5.3 | 93.4 |
| 50,000 to 100,000 inhabitants | 2.8 | 93.2 |
| Greater than 100,000 inhabitants | 4.6 | 90.8 |

*Source*: Berland and Juery (2002).

*Table 2.3* Evolution of the French population connected to the water supply network by income class for 1984, 1992 and 2002

| *Income decile class* | *1984* | | | | *1992* | | | | *2002* | | | |
|---|---|---|---|---|---|---|---|---|---|---|---|---|
| | *1* | *5* | *10* | *All* | *1* | *5* | *10* | *All* | *1* | *5* | *10* | *All* |
| Households only supplied with cold water (%) | 33.0 | 5.1 | 0.4 | 7.7 | 11.9 | 2.1 | 0.2 | 2.8 | 3.9 | 0.8 | 0 | 1.1 |
| Households not connected to the water network (%) | 2.2 | 0.3 | 0 | 0.4 | 1.0 | 0.1 | 0 | 0.5 | 0.3 | 0.1 | 0 | 0.1 |

*Sources*: INSEE housing surveys 1984, 1992 and 2002 and author's own calculation.

network in 1960, the percentage significantly drops in the case of small local communities (fewer than 10,000 inhabitants). For the smallest municipalities, only one in two inhabitants were connected in 1960. The fact that the connection rate was highly dependent upon the size of local communities was clearly incompatible with the notion of public service.

Another measure to show the evolution of the connection rates would be to use household surveys conducted by the National Institute for Statistics and Economic Studies (INSEE). Table 2.3 reports that connection rates for households belonging to the lowest (1), median (5), the highest income decile (10) and the national average (all).

In 20 years, the proportion of French households supplied only with cold water has dropped from 7.7 per cent in 1984 to 1.1 per cent in 2002. For the poorest households, the change is very significant (from 33 per cent to 3.9 per cent). We observe a similar trend for the share of households not connected to the water network. The proportion of French households not connected has dropped from 0.4 per cent in 1984 to 0.1 per cent in 2002. For the poorest households, the change is also very significant (from 2.2 per cent to 0.3 per cent).

Based on the data presented in Tables 2.1 and 2.3, it is clear that access is not a major issue in France today, except perhaps in very specific areas (very small local rural communities) where building a water network is either impossible or too costly to undertake. But one should keep in mind that:

- the process of getting universal coverage has taken one or two generations;
- achieving a full coverage required a high level of investment (subsidies from urban to rural areas);
- the process of universalizing coverage may have benefited from long periods of economic growth.

One of the major challenges now is to maintain and replace the water infrastructure. According to Berland and Juery (2002), 29 per cent of the network pipes are 30 years or more in age and 10 per cent of the network are more than 60 years old. The investment required to renew the network is estimated to be between EUR1.5 and 2 billion per year from now to 2015.

*Evolution of household sanitary equipment and quality of water*

Looking at the sanitation and sanitary facilities in households may also provide additional information on the water sector in France. According to the figures in Table 2.4, in 2002, less than 1 per cent of the French population did not have an inside bathroom. This figure was around 4 per cent in 1990, illustrating that there has been significant progress in recent years. The proportion of population without any toilets has also dropped significantly, from 2.3 per cent in 1990 to 0.7 per cent in 2002. It could be argued that access to basic sanitary equipment is no longer a major issue, except for the poorest households. 7.5 per cent of the poorest still did not have any bathrooms in their houses in 2002 (Table 2.5). This situation has dramatically improved since 1984 where

*Table 2.4* Evolution of household sanitary equipment

| | *1990*[1] | *1996*[2] | *1999*[1] | *2002*[2] |
|---|---|---|---|---|
| *Households* | | | | |
| No bath, shower or WC inside (%) | 814,755 (3.8) | 388,000 (1.7) | 298,468 (1.3) | 199,339 (0.8) |
| No bath, shower but WC inside (%) | 596,246 (2.7) | 302,000 (1.1) | 257,069 (2.2) | 197,387 (0.9) |
| No WC but bath or shower (%) | 575,486 (6.6) | 244,000 (2.7) | 532,899 (1.9) | 214,818 (1.2) |
| *Persons* | | | | |
| No bath, shower or WC inside (%) | 1,428,824 (2.5) | 621,000 (1.0) | 458,230 (0.8) | 303,063 (0.5) |
| No bath, shower but WC inside (%) | 997,232 (1.8) | 469,000 (0.8) | 390,808 (0.6) | 253,043 (0.4) |
| No WC but bath or shower (%) | 1,321,197 (2.3) | 504,000 (0.8) | 1,192,485 (2.0) | 428,954 (0.7) |

*Note*: Figures in parentheses are based on the total number of households or the total number of persons.
*Sources*: 1. French census and author's own computation.
2. INSEE housing surveys and author's own computation.

*Table 2.5* Evolution of household sanitary equipment by income class for 1984, 1992 and 2002

| *Income decile class* | *1984* | | | | *1992* | | | | *2002* | | | |
|---|---|---|---|---|---|---|---|---|---|---|---|---|
| | *1* | *5* | *10* | *All* | *1* | *5* | *10* | *All* | *1* | *5* | *10* | *All* |
| Households without bathroom (%) | 40.2 | 10.9 | 1.4 | 13.6 | 20.9 | 3.9 | 0.4 | 5.6 | 7.5 | 1.1 | 0.3 | 2.1 |
| Households without WC (%) | 5.6 | 0.8 | 0.1 | 1.3 | 3.1 | 0.5 | 0.1 | 0.7 | 1.3 | 0.2 | 0.1 | 0.3 |

*Sources*: INSEE housing surveys 1984, 1992 and 2002 and author's own calculation.

40 per cent the poorest households did not possess any bathroom in their home.

*Quality of water delivered*

One of the tasks of the French Ministry of Health and Solidarity is to ensure that the water delivered to customers complies with the EU drinking water standards. Every year, around 300,000 sample

*Table 2.6* Quality of water delivered according to the size of distribution units in 2002 (per cent)

| | | *Volume produced (in m³ per day)* | | | | | | |
|---|---|---|---|---|---|---|---|---|
| | | *<100* | *100–1,999* | *2,000–9,999* | *10,000–49,999* | *50,000–99,999* | *>100,000* | *Total* |
| Nitrates | Non-compliant distribution units | 2.70 | 4.36 | 2.80 | 1.61 | 0.00 | 0.00 | 3.41 |
| | Non-compliant tests | 3.04 | 3.81 | 1.30 | 0.31 | 0.00 | 0.00 | 2.66 |
| Pesticides | Non-compliant distribution units | 13.45 | 16.28 | 16.52 | 22.53 | 22.73 | 7.69 | 15.73 |
| | Non-compliant tests | 2.04 | 1.27 | 0.48 | 0.32 | 0.09 | 0.04 | 1.04 |
| Microbiology | Non-compliant distribution units | 28.39 | 13.52 | 10.73 | 9.55 | 4.40 | 0.00 | 21.51 |
| | Non-compliant tests | 2.77 | 10.02 | 2.33 | 1.00 | 0.59 | 0.38 | 2.77 |

*Source*: Ministère de la Santé et des Solidarités (2005).

are taken and 4.5 million laboratory tests are conducted (including tests on nitrates, pesticides and microbiological parameters). Table 2.6 presents the percentage of water production units and test results, which do not comply with the EU drinking water standards in 2002 (SISE-EAU database).

In 2002, 3.41 per cent of the distribution units presented a maximal nitrate concentration greater than 50 mg/l. On average, 2.66 per cent of the tests reveal a contamination by nitrates. The non-compliance rate decreases with the size of the distribution unit. Data show that on average 2.77 per cent of the tests reveal a contamination by pathogenic micro-organisms. The average rate of non-compliance with microbiological parameters is higher than 20 per cent for the water distribution units. This shows that the water quality delivered to consumers in France may be a concern.[6]

## Modalities of private sector involvement

Local public authorities in France are responsible for the maintenance and operation of water services. Full privatization is not an option in view of the French law (which derives from the Roman law), stating that the public domain in France (including the infrastructure such as pipes built on the public domain) is *'inalienable'*. This implies that no one can own it except a public authority. The local public authorities define the general principles governing the service (for example, it has to monitor the prices, control the firms that enter the market, oversee bidding and competition, ensure that there is no interruption in the service provision, and so on).

Nevertheless, even though the responsibility rests upon the public authority, the management of the service can be either public (direct management) or private. Therefore, local public authorities may decide to involve a private operator. Hence, in spite of the public domain of being *'inalienable'*, private participation is a major component of the water sector in France.

## Political and economic rationale for private involvement in the water sector

As mentioned earlier, France has been a pioneer in terms of private–public partnership (PPP). As early as the twelfth century, French legal texts mention *'affermage'* and *'concession'* – terms which are still in use today (Ménard and Saussier 2003). According to the French legal system, the delegation of a public service takes the form of a contract through which a local municipality gives a private firm the right to build and/or to operate a public service.

As we will show, an increased level of PSP took place in the period from the 1950s to the 1970s. During this period, there was a large investment need in water networks and in treatment facilities. This need of investment may have led local authorities to involve the private sector.

## The size of the private sector

As mentioned earlier, PSP in the water sector in France has a long history (Paris allocated an exclusive concession to a private company in 1776; less than a century later, in 1853, Napoleon III created the Compagnie générale des eaux).[7] At the beginning, the two main objectives were *'to irrigate the countryside and to supply water to towns and cities'*. However, only after the 1940s did a significant change take place in terms of public–private market shares, as shown in Table 2.7.

For the water service, the market share (in terms of customers) of the private sector stood at 17 per cent in 1938, before rising to 44 per cent in 1964 and reaching 80 per cent in 2001. The main characteristic of the private sector is its oligopolistic form with three major companies: Générale

*Table 2.7* Recent evolution of the private participation in the water supply sector (per cent)

| *Year* | *1938* | *1964* | *1975* | *1979* | *2001* |
|---|---|---|---|---|---|
| Public | 83 | 56 | 50 | 47 | 20 |
| Private | 17 | 44 | 50 | 57 | 80 |
| CGE | | | 42.3 | 35.6 | 51.1 |
| SLE | | | 26.9 | 24.6 | 24.3 |
| SAUR | | | 5.8 | 10.4 | 13.1 |
| Other | | | 19.2 | 16.4 | 9.9 |
| SODEBA | | | 5.8 | 6.8 | — |
| SDEI | | | — | 6.5 | — |
| Independent | | | — | — | 1.9 |
| Total French population (millions) | 42 | | 52 | 53 | 60 |

*Source*: Guérin-Schneider and Lorrain (2004).

des eaux (Véolia Environnement), Lyonnaise des eaux (ONDEO-SUEZ group) and SAUR (Bouygues group). They represent almost the entirety (98 per cent) of the private water market (other private companies operate at a local level but their importance remains low).

## Contractual relationship between local communities and private operators

Local communities may either directly manage their water supply services or entrust their management to a private company.

### *Direct management*

The community, or an intercommunity syndicate of which the community becomes a member, takes full responsibility for investments and the operation of water supply services, customer relations, invoicing and billing (generally through a municipal collector). The staff of the water authority is composed of municipal agents with a civil servant status. Today, except in some medium and large towns that have established their own technical municipal services, this kind of water authority is found principally in small rural communities.

### *Delegated management*

In this case, communities delegate the management of all or part of their water supply services to a private water operator for a certain period of time through contracts; 'affermage' (leasing) and concession are the two types of contracts that are usually used. In Paris, for example, the current water service is delegated through a concession contract. One part of the city is delegated to the Suez group ('Paris rive gauche') and the rest of the network to Véolia Environment ('Paris rive droite'). Prior to 1985, the water service was publicly managed. The City Council decided first to use 'affermage' contracts, before switching to a concession regime.

In the 'affermage' contract, the local authority is responsible for investments and only entrusts the operation of installations to a private operator. Some of the income collected through tariffs becomes the operator's service fee and the rest goes to the local authorities to meet the technical depreciation cost and financial amortization of the infrastructure. In a concession contract, the private company builds infrastructure, operates this at its own expense and recovers its cost by collecting tariffs for water use. As specified in the contract, the operator hands back the network to the public authority at the end of the contract. The concession contract implies a higher degree of risk for the operator since it is responsible for all investments. But the level of risk depends of course on the type of price regulation implemented.

In some cases, there could be a mixed-type management where the local authorities may decide to operate water production and intakes and choose to delegate the distribution and billing component to a private operator.

## Important issues related to private involvement in the French water sector

### *Regulation of the private sector*

Economic regulation of the French water services is carried out directly by local authorities. They must ensure that users' interests are protected with respect to prices and that the quality of the service is assured. They must also make sure that there is no undue discrimination between users.

This decentralized system creates a number of challenges. In particular, as a result of the lack of information or information asymmetry, local authorities are not always in a position to exercise an efficient control over water service operators. As a consequence, and contrary to other industrialized countries such as England and Wales, there is no price-cap or rate-of-return regulation imposed on water utilities in France. Such regulation is carried out through a contract between the private operator and the local authority, or through a municipality board (regarding the way in which the water utility is managed) in the case of solely public operation. In other words, regulation is based on the contract.

This form of delegation contract sets the price and describes the obligations of the private operator (in terms of both service and economic information that must be given each year to the local authority). Water prices for the first year are calculated from financial forecasts. For the following years, the modification of tariffs is based on input price index changes. The main sanction in the case of non-compliance with delegation rules may be the non-renewal of the delegation contract after expiration. There are examples in France where the non-renewal of the delegation contract has resulted from the non-respect of delegation rules such as a disagreement on water price.[8]

In contrast to the England and Wales model, no centralized public authority is responsible for the regulation of the water industry in France. The economic regulation of the operator results from the national legislative framework which governs both the form of private sector participation, and also the procedure of the delegation bidding process. The Sapin Law (1993) and the Barnier and Mazeaud Laws (1995) are the main legislative texts defining these relationships between local communities and private firms. Environmental regulation takes place both at the national level, through the Ministry of Environment, and at the European level, through the European Commission.

### *Private sector participation and water price*

In France, water-pricing schemes have been affected by the decisions of public authorities. For example, the January 1992 Water Law has attempted to reduce water wastage and to promote equity between users. It has prohibited the use of flat tariffs, entirely ruling out both non-volumetric pricing schemes and tariffs combining a fixed charge covering a given volume of consumption with volumetric charging on the remainder. This law has been instrumental in moving towards one- or two-part tariff systems without minimum consumption charges.

The process of price setting may be different depending on whether or not the local community has delegated the service to a private operator. If the local community manages the water service directly, it can set the price of water by itself. In this case, the rate is designed in order to generate revenue that allows the utility to cover its costs (both operating and capital). Since French legislation requires the water utility budget to be balanced, the 'revenue-recovery principle' is usually the primary objective in the design of water prices.

If the local community decides to delegate water services to a private operator, the tariff structure is determined by projecting financial accounts given by the operator over the period of delegation. Periodic revisions of water tariffs are defined using a price index adjusting formula. The relationship between the local municipality and the firm is formalized by means of a contract that specifies a price structure, a formula of price revision and clauses allowing for exceptional conditions or *force majeure*. This contract is the result of a negotiation: the local community and the firm have mainly to agree on a price structure that achieves a balanced budget (or cost recovery) for the firm while remaining consistent with the social or economic policy objectives of the local community. Since the bargaining power is in most cases favourable to private operators, the price structure is likely to reflect monopolistic behaviour rather than social welfare maximization. Whatever the choice of water service delegation, the question of price efficiency is hotly debated.

*Private sector participation and competition*

The 'Sapin Law' limits the duration of the delegation contracts and sets out a procedure for tendering and procedures for renegotiation in the case of renewal. The main objective of this law is to ensure transparency when choosing the private operator. To this end, the law defines a specific procedure that is to be followed by the execution of the delegation agreements. This procedure includes a negotiation stage where the local communities wishing to delegate their water services (or to renew the delegation) must negotiate with one or more contractors in order to obtain specifications and detailed information about the content of their bids.

In order to evaluate the impact of the Sapin Law on the water sector, the public authorities have conducted a set of surveys targeted towards water services where the delegation agreement was renewed between 1998 and 2001. The results of the survey are reported in Table 2.8. Since 1998, there have been around 500 contracts negotiated each year and it was around 2000 in 2005 because of a huge number of contracts which came into expiration.

There has been an increase in the number of agreements leading to a change in operator. However, in 80 to 90 per cent of the cases, the existing operator has their contract renewed for another term. The number of offers received by local communities is still very low – 2.2 in 2001. In 28 per cent of the cases, the local community receives only one offer, which means that there is no *ex-ante* competition for the market. In

*Table 2.8* Impact of delegation agreement renewal on the water sector

| | *1998* | *1999* | *2000* | *2001* |
|---|---|---|---|---|
| Number of delegation agreements | 582 | 684 | 509 | 477 |
| Number of delegation agreements in the sample | 333 | 195 | 211 | 208 |
| Length of contracts before/after delegation agreement | 17/11 | 16.8/11 | 15.2/10.8 | 15.7/10.9 |
| Private operators renewed (%) | 92 | 82 | 88 | 89 |
| Average number of offers received | N/A | 2.4 | 2.1 | 2.2 |
| Price change (%) | −9 | −10 | −12 | −8 |
| Price change in % (local communities with less than 10,000 inhabitants) | 4 | −4 | −3 | −3 |
| Price change in % (local communities with more than 10,000 inhabitants) | −16.5 | −14 | −17 | −12 |

*Source*: Guérin-Schneider and Lorrain (2004).

other words, in France the level of competition among private companies through the delegation contract biding process is still low. In terms of water and sewage rates, the renewal of the delegation agreement leads to an average fall in price of between 8 and 12 per cent. The largest price decreases are observed for populations of more than 20,000 inhabitants. This decrease in tariff may be linked to the threat of introducing competition.

### *Quantitative assessment of a private firm's performance*

One possible way to compare the performance of private and public water services is to compare the water price of these services. One must be very careful, however, since a direct price comparison is meaningful only if there is consistency in the data generating process. As demonstrated by Carpentier *et al.* (2006), this is not the case in France. The probability of delegating the water service to a private firm increases with the complexity of the service (low quality of raw water, complex water treatment process, high level of interconnection with other water network, and so on).

In Figure 2.1 we have plotted the consumer price index (CPI), the consumer price index for housing expenses (CPI housing), and the consumer price index for water expenses (CPI water) for the past ten years which are published by the National Institute for Statistics and Economic Studies (INSEE). What do we learn from this figure?

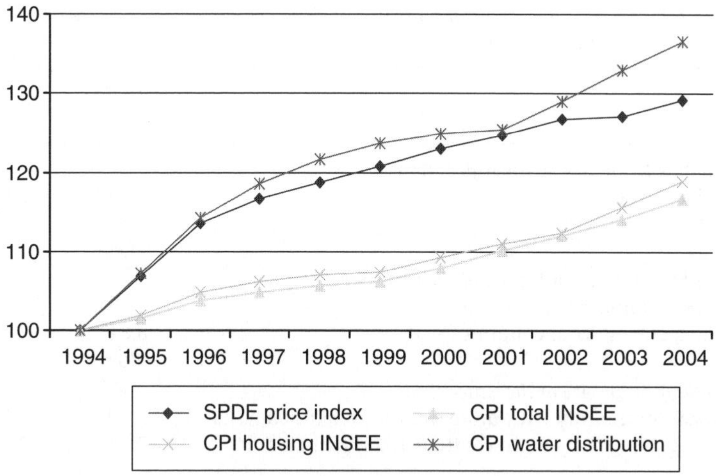


*Figure 2.1* Evolution of CPI and water-related price index

First, the burden of water charges for households has increased more rapidly than total household expenses. Over the course of the last ten years, the Syndicat professionnel des distributeurs d'eau (SPDE) price index[9] and the CPI water index have increased more than twice as rapidly as the general CPI index. Secondly, the SPDE and the CPI water indexes follow similar dynamic paths, except over the last two years.

Next, it is interesting to compare the water price for private and public water services. Carpentier *et al.* (2006) provided an econometric analysis of water prices in France with a special focus on the comparison between those prices charged by public and private services.

As shown in Table 2.9, in France in 1998 the average domestic water price was FF7.85 on average. *On average, the price for the water service was 33 per cent higher in the case of private management than it was in the case of public management.* However, any direct policy implication drawn from this result should be treated with caution since it would suffer from a self-selection bias problem. Indeed, Carpentier *et al.* (2006) saw that local communities tend to delegate water services in case of difficult operational conditions.[10] Taking into account these complex operational conditions (complex water network, large seasonal population, large need for capital investment), the water price would still be 15 per cent higher in the case of private management for small local communities (fewer than 10,000 inhabitants) and only 5 per cent for

*Table 2.9* Average domestic water price (in FF per cubic metre) in France in 1998 for the water supply service (FF1 represents EUR0.152)

| | *Average price* | *St. dev.* |
|---|---|---|
| *According to the type of the water service* | | |
| Private water service | 8.73 | 2.80 |
| Public water service | 6.57 | 2.21 |
| | +33% | |
| *According to the organization of the water service* | | |
| Inter-communal agreement | 8.59 | 2.64 |
| Independent local community | 6.81 | 2.64 |
| | +26% | |
| *According to the size of the water service* | | |
| Local community with more than 10,000 inhabitants | 7.69 | 2.13 |
| Local community with less than 10,000 inhabitants | 7.88 | 2.90 |
| | −2% | |
| *All local communities* | 7.85 | 2.78 |

*Source*: Adapted from Carpentier *et al.* (2006).

large communities (population greater than 10,000 inhabitants). Moreover, the price difference between private and public water utilities is not significantly different from zero for large local communities.

Another interesting result from the study by Carpentier *et al.* (2006) is that a model can explain whether or not a local authority would choose to delegate the services. This choice reflects efficiency considerations since the water tariff is expected to increase slightly if it chooses to delegate their water service to a private operator. Therefore, the impact of PSP on the water price depends upon local conditions.

Next, we focus on the organization and the size of water services. On average, in 1998, the domestic price was higher in instances of intercommunal management of the water service than in the case of an independent local service (+26 per cent on average) (Table 2.10). This reflects the higher technical complexity of water services operating under an intercommunal agreement since they usually operate in rural areas with very low population densities (high cost per capita due to the network pipe maintenance). Finally, the size of water services does not seem to have a strong impact on the price since the water price for water utilities serving less than 10,000 inhabitants is not significantly different from the price for services serving more than 10,000.

*Table 2.10* Average domestic water price (in EUR per cubic metre) in France in 2001 for the water supply service

| | *Public* | *Private* | *Total* |
|---|---|---|---|
| Independent local community | 1.03 | 1.26 | 1.19 |
| Intercommunal agreement | 1.19 | 1.58 | 1.47 |
| Total | 1.12 | 1.46 | 1.36 |

*Source*: Coutelier and Basso (2004), based on the IFEN-SCEES water survey.

In addition, according to a study by the Institut français de l'environnement and by the Service central des enquêtes et études statistiques (IFEN-SCEES), the average price paid for one cubic metre of water can vary across French Départments by as much as 100 per cent. Between 1998 and 2001, the price of water rose by around 5 per cent for drinking water. We have to bear in mind that in France, supplying drinking water accounts for 47 per cent of the price of water in the bill, wastewater collection and treatment for 37 per cent, and taxes represent the rest. As we demonstrated, this price is higher if the water service is managed at an intermunicipal level and if the water management is delegated to the private sector. Whatever the type of water service organization considered (independent versus intercommunal agreement) or the type of water service considered (water supply or sewage), the price is significantly higher in the case of private management.

## The issue of water affordability in France

### Water affordability in France – some empirical facts

In 2005, according to the French Observatoire des inégalités, between 3.6 and 7.1 million people were facing poverty in France.[11] More than three million lived in insanitary housing. In addition, 2.9 million people were unemployed (10 per cent of unemployment) and around 3 million used to depend upon social assistance.

According to Smets (2004), 300,000 households have accumulated important debts (relating to their rent) and at least 3 million people are late in paying water, electricity, gas or phone bills. Around 300,000 poor households receive a specific social aid in order to pay their electricity bills and 700,000 households have asked to reschedule their water bills. These figures show that the affordability of water is an important issue in France, at least for poor households.

Charitable and non-profit organizations offer an interesting picture for assessing water affordability in France since those institutions deal with the poorest people. In 2003, 1.6 million people (2.5 per cent of the French population) went to a centre managed by the Secours catholique[12] in France. According to the Secours catholique (2004), half of these people live below the poverty threshold (12.8 per cent do not have any income and 41.7 per cent relied exclusively on social aid) and 58 per cent of those in poverty, present at least one type of unpaid charges (electricity, gas, water or banking services). The average debt per household in 2003 represented EUR1,646, which corresponds to two months of average income. Of the poor households, around 10 per cent of them have not paid their water bills.

Another way to empirically assess the issue of water affordability in France is to analyse the disconnection policies of private firms in charge of water services. According to Fauquez-Avon (2005), the number of customers served in France by the Compagnie générale des eaux (CGE) was 6.3 million in 2002. In that year the CGE granted 250,000 payment facilities to customers facing financial difficulties (representing 20 per thousand of the water bills or 40 per thousand of the customers). 80,000 disconnections have been realized by the CGE (13 per thousand of the customers) that year. According to the Ministry of Social Affairs, the rate of disconnection due to *serious financial difficulties* is around 15 per cent in France. Hence, the number of disconnections by the CGE due to serious financial difficulties is estimated to be 12,000 (2 per thousand of the customers). Among them 1,200 (0.2 per thousand of the total number of customers) disconnections last more than 24 hours.

Finally, in order to assess the importance of water affordability for poor households in France, one could analyse the social actions undertaken directly by municipalities through Social Action Centres. On average, in 2000, 64 per cent of the French municipalities offered water debt payment programmes oriented towards low-income households facing financial difficulties (Dutheil 2004). Moreover, the share of municipalities implementing household debt payment programmes is significantly higher for water than for any other basic goods (phone, gas or electricity). This may reflect that, at the local level, water bills for low-income households are a significant problem.

## Private and public regulation of water affordability

### *A system of* ex-post *social help*

In France, there is currently no specific water price rebate or discount tariff for the poorest households (in other words, there is no formal social water pricing). Historically, the mechanism put in place by public authorities and private firms in order to guarantee an affordable access to water may be viewed as an *ex-post* financial aid to help poor households facing difficulties in paying their water bill. In cases of financial difficulties, qualified low-income households can have access to a specific fund in order to write off their water debts.

There are two main reasons explaining the choice of an *ex-post* help system in France. First, according to the definition of a public service, all customers having similar characteristics must pay the same price. As the level of income is not considered to be a particular characteristic of a household, this implies that no specific tariff can be implemented for the poorest households.[13] Of course, increasing block rate pricing may be used to help consumers of small amounts of water (poor households) but this is not an explicit social pricing system. Secondly, it is clear that the size of the private water sector may constitute a possible explanation for the *ex-post* choice.

In France, the Water Law project presented in March 2005 had first confirmed that social pricing was not an objective per se of the state and that maintaining water affordability to low-income households did not necessarily lead to a system of social water pricing. However, the Water Law No 2006-1772, promulgated on 30 December 2006, has recognized a clear right for all users to benefit from water at an economically acceptable cost. This may be viewed as a first step towards the implementation of social water pricing in France.

### *A historic view of state social and regulatory mechanisms*

Although there is at present no specific tariff oriented towards poor consumers, the state has defined a set of regulatory instruments aiming at guaranteeing the affordability of water for French households. We briefly describe and discuss the most important of them.

As mentioned earlier, one such policy was the creation of the National Fund for Rural Water Supply (FNDAE) in 1954.[14] The FNDAE levies a tax on every cubic metre of water supplied in France, and allocates each *Départment* (administrative district) subsidies for small rural communities to enable them to invest in potable water supply and flood and wastewater collection and treatment. These subsidies compensate for low population densities and the small size of human settlements. The main objective of this fund was to finance water supply equipment in rural areas. The FNDAE has been quite successful: at the beginning of the 1950s, less than 40 per cent of the rural population was connected to the water supply network; by the 1990s, it had reached quasi-universal coverage.

It was not until the early 1990s that some form of social policy was introduced to address the issue of water affordability. For example, the main objective of the 29 July 1992 Law on the Minimum Income (RMI) was to guarantee each person (older than 25 years of age) a minimum income level. But some articles of this law were dedicated to basic human needs, including water. In particular, article 43 states that '*Mechanisms aiming at dealing with serious financial difficulties and social exclusion include financial aids for household unpaid water and energy bills*'. However, since no specific fund dedicated to unpaid water bills was created at that time, this law has not helped the poorest households.

Four years later, in 1996, the Water Solidarity Charter was promulgated. The key fact about this charter is that it is neither a law nor a legislative text. The Water Solidarity Charter is a voluntary contractual agreement between the state, the Association of French Mayors (AMF), the Federation of Local Communities Delegating Public Services (FNCCR) and the Professional Syndicate of Water and Sewage Operators (SPDE). The charter is based on two general principles. First, the access to water must not be disconnected in the case of unpaid bills due to serious financial difficulties. Secondly, in cases of payment default the water and sewage bills can be paid, totally or partially, by local communities, private water operators or charitable associations. Although this charter has been a step towards guaranteed access to water for all low-income households, its impact in terms of access to water services has been limited as the result of a complex system involving several institutions with divergent interests. There is no clear definition of obligations and responsibilities between institutions and there is a lack of sanctions in case of the non-application of the Charter (Billard *et al.* 2001). As a consequence, in the late 1990s, 130,000 disconnections a year were still taking place. Of this, 20,000 concerned low-income households.

A National Water Solidarity Convention took place in 2000 to clarify the 1996 Water Charter. This Convention has been signed by the state, the AMF, the FNCCR and the SPDE. The Convention specifies explicitly that households must not be disconnected in case of unpaid bills due to serious financial difficulties (up to three months while the case is put to a specialized commission), that disconnection of households with babies or elderly people will be prohibited and that households in serious financial difficulties must be identified by state social agencies at the local level. As a result, a financial fund was created (mainly from state resources, EUR4.6 million and from the SPDE resources, EUR3 million in

2000[15]). For the first time, public and private institutions involved in the water sector have clearly outlined their respective financial contribution to a social water fund.

A recent law on housing (2005) reinforces the protection of poor households in case of the non-payment of water bills. No disconnection will be allowed for low-income households facing financial difficulties for paying water charges.

*Private utilities' water pricing practices*

Pricing policies for public services are often used to satisfy several requirements and to pursue several objectives. In the specific context of urban water supply, some criteria have been emphasized, including efficiency, equity, and/or public acceptability and transparency. Many empirical studies have analysed efficiency issues, but only a few have dealt with distributional aspects of water pricing (see, for example, García-Valiñas 2005). It has been argued that the cost-recovery pricing approach goes against the equity principle since low-consumption and low-income households are characterized by a more price-inelastic water demand. As a consequence, a redistributive pricing mechanism has been promoted.

For example, increasing block rates may favour small consumers (that is, poor households). By contrast, large consumers (rich households) will benefit from decreasing block rates. Similarly, a small fixed charge will reflect a more socially oriented tariff policy. Hence, the choice of pricing schemes implemented by water utilities (increasing or decreasing block rates, flat rates, constant unit rate, and so on) has a significant impact on distribution.

It has been found that the marginal cost and marginal price of water is not substantially different (Garcia and Reynaud 2004). The private sector secures its profit through fixed charges. The average fixed charge (EUR25.85 per user) is more than half of the average capital expenditure (EUR16.12 per user). As a result of these high fixed charges, poor households are affected disproportionately.

## Measuring water affordability in France

To the best of our knowledge, there is currently no formal accepted definition of water affordability in France (or even elsewhere).[16] The international norm has been that a household should use between 3 and 5 per cent of its expenditure/revenue on water bills. However, several authors have consequently used 3 per cent in the context of developed countries (Sawkins and Dickie 2002; Fitch and Price 2002). Following these authors, we define water affordability as the share of income spent on water charges. Moreover, we define a *'water-poor'* household as a household spending 3 per cent or more of its income on paying water charges. One should, however, be cautious with using the term *water-poor* in case of high-income classes. For a rich household, being *water-poor* results from a high water bill. It is likely that such a high water bill is the consequence of a high level of water consumption associated with equipment such as air conditioning, swimming pools, gardens, and so on. Hence, being *water-poor* in the case of a high-income class is likely to be the result of a voluntary decision on the part of the household. By contrast, being *water-poor* in the case of a low-income class is likely to mean that a significant part of the total income must be devoted to the water bill for insuring basic human needs.

*Measuring water expenses and household income*

Water affordability has been defined by reference to the share of income spent on water charges (*water income share*). Assessing the affordability of water for a household involves the straightforward comparison of their water bill with their income.[17] Obviously, the definition of income is critical and we need to clarify our approach. But it is also necessary to have a clear definition of water charges.

As presented in Figure 2.2, water charges in France may be divided into three parts: namely the water supply charges, the sewage treatment charges and the taxes and fees. The first and main component of water price corresponds to the supply process which involves the extraction of water, and its treatment and distribution to customers. In 2003 the share of the supply represented 46 per cent of total price paid by a consumer (Bipe 2005). The second component of the price corresponding to the

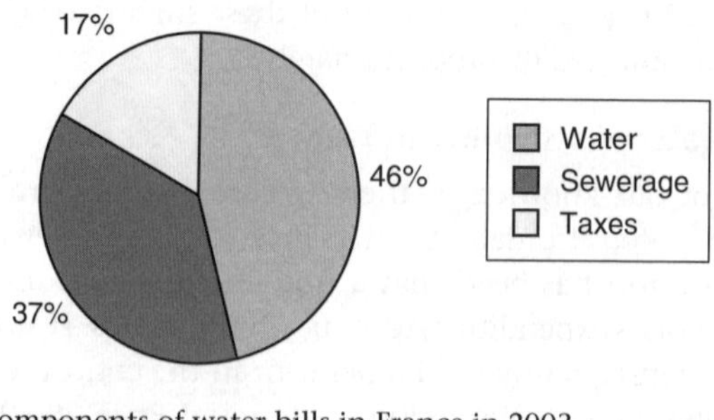


*Figure 2.2* Components of water bills in France in 2003
*Source*: Bipe (2005).

sewage service used to represent, on average, 37 per cent of the total water price in 2003. It is important to notice that not all consumers necessarily pay sewage charges. This is, for instance, not the case in small rural local communities, where no collective sewage service exists. The last component, which corresponds to taxes and fees, includes the river basin agency fees, the National Fund for the Development of Water Supply System fee (eliminated in January 2005) and the Value Added Tax (VAT) at 5.5 per cent. These taxes now represent more than 17 per cent of the price. This component has registered the sharpest increase over the last decade (+256 per cent for the basin agency fees and +115 per cent for other taxes from 1991 to 1998).

Since our focus here is exclusively on the water service, we will exclude from the water charges those that relate to the sewage service. Hence, the water charges we consider are those corresponding exclusively to the water supply service (the extraction of water and its treatment and distribution to customers) plus the taxes and fees that must be paid by each household (63 per cent of the water bill). In order to avoid any problem of seasonality, we consider the annual water charges paid by each household. The source of data for water expenses at the household level is from the *family income and expenditure surveys* conducted regularly by INSEE.

### *An empirical assessment of water affordability in France*

The water income shares have been calculated using the INSEE *family income and expenditure surveys* (1979, 1984, 1989, 1995 and 2005) by dividing the annual water bill paid by each household by the total income. In Table 2.11, we report the water income shares by income deciles (income classes).

In 2001, the average income spent on paying water charges was 1.20 per cent. This implies that the average French household is not water-poor (based on our definition of 3 per cent of total income being devoted to paying water charges). From 1979 to 2001, the share of income devoted by French households to paying water bills has increased significantly, from 0.79 per cent to 1.20 per cent. For example, in 1979, water expenses were less than 1 per cent of the total income for deciles 3–10. In 2001, the share of the total income devoted to water bills is smaller than 1 per cent only for deciles 8–10. One may suspect that a significant part of this change is due to the water price increase observed during that period (during the past two decades, water prices have increased twice as fast as the consumer price index) (see Figure 2.1).

*Table 2.11* Water income shares from 1979 to 2001 by income classes (per cent)

| | *1979* | *1984* | *1989* | *1995* | *2001* |
|---|---|---|---|---|---|
| Total sample | 0.79 | 1.11 | 1.05 | 1.19 | 1.20 |
| Income class 1 | 2.256 | 4.692 | 3.915 | 3.100 | 2.311 |
| Income class 2 | 1.079 | 1.234 | 1.252 | 1.725 | 1.663 |
| Income class 3 | 0.736 | 0.949 | 0.994 | 1.339 | 1.588 |
| Income class 4 | 0.699 | 0.845 | 0.941 | 1.267 | 1.292 |
| Income class 5 | 0.647 | 0.728 | 0.774 | 1.117 | 1.166 |
| Income class 6 | 0.598 | 0.634 | 0.769 | 1.087 | 1.041 |
| Income class 7 | 0.546 | 0.613 | 0.618 | 0.889 | 1.002 |
| Income class 8 | 0.474 | 0.558 | 0.609 | 0.873 | 0.873 |
| Income class 9 | 0.412 | 0.494 | 0.524 | 0.735 | 0.742 |
| Income class 10 | 0.335 | 0.391 | 0.407 | 0.574 | 0.607 |
| 1% poorest households | 9.70 | 22.61 | 22.65 | 17.64 | 4.80 |
| 5% poorest households | 3.25 | 8.48 | 6.47 | 4.25 | 2.69 |
| 5% richest households | 0.29 | 0.34 | 0.35 | 0.47 | 0.51 |
| 1% richest households | 0.19 | 0.25 | 0.27 | 0.36 | 0.37 |

*Note*: This table gives the water income shares by income classes (deciles). Data sources: INSEE family budget and income surveys, and author's own calculation.

However, if we disaggregate data according to income groups, we find that the percentage of income spent on paying water charges varies significantly according to income level. For the highest income decile, the water expenditures represented only 0.335 per cent of the total income in 1979, compared to 2.256 per cent for the lowest income class. For the one per cent of poorest households the water charges represent 4.80 per cent of their total income in 2001 compared to 0.37 per cent for the one per cent of the richest.

The issue of affordability is important for water, electricity, gas or even telephone services. Yet it is difficult to say precisely whether or not a particular expenditure is affordable in absolute terms because that involves value judgements about priorities. From the 2001 INSEE *family income and expenditure surveys,* we have calculated the share of household income spent on four basic commodities (water, electricity, gas, telephone) by income decile (Table 2.12). For all income deciles, the percentage of income devoted to water charges ranks third, below electricity and gas but above the share of income spent on telephone charges. The poorest households spend on average 14 per cent of their total income on water, electricity, gas and telephone. For households belonging to the

*Table 2.12* Basic good income shares by income decile in 2001 (per cent)

| *Income decile* | *Water* | *Electricity* | *Gas* | *Phone* |
|---|---|---|---|---|
| 1 | 2.32 | 6.45 | 4.31 | 1.04 |
| 2 | 1.67 | 4.04 | 2.40 | 0.61 |
| 3 | 1.59 | 3.77 | 2.01 | 0.60 |
| 4 | 1.29 | 3.14 | 2.73 | 0.55 |
| 5 | 1.17 | 2.75 | 2.01 | 0.45 |
| 6 | 1.04 | 2.52 | 1.90 | 0.40 |
| 7 | 1.00 | 2.32 | 1.58 | 0.33 |
| 8 | 0.88 | 2.03 | 1.40 | 0.31 |
| 9 | 0.74 | 1.86 | 1.35 | 0.29 |
| 10 | 0.61 | 1.42 | 0.96 | 0.20 |

*Note*: This table gives the percentage of income spent on water, electricity, gas and telephone charges by income classes (deciles). Data sources: 2001 INSEE Family budget and income survey and author's own calculation.

higher income class, the share of income devoted to these basic services represents less than 3.3 per cent.

All of these questions lead us to further empirically investigate the issues of affordability of water in the French private and public sectors.

## An empirical investigation of affordability

### Assessing the determinants of water affordability in France

Reynaud (2007) used an econometric model to investigate the impact of PSP on the poor, and here we present some of the main findings. There are several potential determinants that may explain the level of the income spent on water, including household and housing characteristics, the type of water pricing scheme implemented by the water service, the level of participation of the private sector into the management of the service and the state regulation (either social or economic).

It is demonstrated that single-parent families (especially if the head of the household is a woman) or a large family for which social aid represents a large proportion of the household total income could be considered as the most vulnerable groups in terms of water affordability (Reynaud 2007). In addition, private participation in the sector seems to have a detrimental impact on water affordability for low-income households and almost no impact on rich households. In this case, we could argue that the private utilities are more likely to implement pricing structures that favour large consumers (wealthy consumers, with decreasing block rates or tariffs with a large fixed charge).

### Being 'water-poor' in France

As shown in Table 2.13, in 2001 4.31 per cent of households in France (representing around 1.16 million households) spent more than 3 per cent of their income on water charges. The percentage of income these households are obliged to devote to water (4.50 per cent) is on average around four times that of the population as a whole.

Those households that are vulnerable to water poverty share a number of specific characteristics. First, the share of social income to total income is higher in the case of water-poor households. As expected, the average total income of water-poor households is significantly smaller than the average income for the whole French population. The groups most vulnerable to water poverty are the single-adult families. 14.15 per cent of those single-adult families where the head of the household is a woman are water-poor (compared to 4.31 per cent of the whole population). Unemployment of the head of household is also a clear determinant of water poverty since 11.53 per cent of the households where the head is unemployed are water-poor (compared to 4.31 per cent of the whole

*Table 2.13* Descriptive statistics for water-poor and non-water-poor households for 2001

| | *All households* | *Non-water-poor households* | *Water-poor households* |
|---|---|---|---|
| Proportion of households (%) | — | 95.69 | 4.31 |
| Total income (euros per year) | 27,534 | 29,108 | 12,169 |
| Percentage of income spent on water charges (%) | 1.19 | 1.05 | 4.50 |
| Share of social income to total income (%) | 41.08 | 43.03 | 66.88 |
| Private participation (%) | 72.75 | 69.00 | 72.79 |
| Average water price (euros per cubic metres) | 1.32 | 1.31 | 1.33 |
| Share of the fixed water charge to the total bill (%) | 16.40 | 16.50 | 16.09 |
| Periodicity of the water bill (months) | 7.06 | 7.65 | 6.80 |
| Number of persons | 2.42 | 2.58 | 2.17 |
| 1 Adult only (%) | — | 92.32 | 7.68 |
| 1 Adult (man) and children(%) | — | 93.32 | 6.68 |
| 1 Adult (woman) and children (%) | — | 85.85 | 14.15 |
| Head of the household unemployed (%) | — | 88.47 | 11.53 |
| Head of the household 65 years old or more (%) | — | 93.65 | 6.15 |

population). And, finally, the average number of persons per household is smaller in the case of water-poor households.

Using another model (probit), Reynaud (2007) demonstrates that being a single-parent family increases the probability of being water-poor. This is especially true if the head of the household is a woman. Being elderly results in a small, but significant increase of the probability of being water-poor. Finally, the larger the size of the household the greater the chances of being water-poor. Here we assume that there exists a positive relationship between household size and levels of water consumption. In terms of the impact of housing characteristics of water affordability, we find that living in an individual house produces a higher probability of being water-poor. In addition, we find that a high percentage of votes for the Socialist or Communist Party at the previous local election results in a lowering of the probability of being water-poor. This implies that these political parties are more pro-poor and have more social policies.

We also find that the predicted probability of being water-poor decreases significantly with the income class. For example, the probability of being water-poor is 24 times higher for a family belonging to the lowest income class than it is for a family in the highest income class. Some micro-simulations reveal that, if we increase the PSP by 10 per cent, the probability of being water-poor increases for all income groups, and especially for the lower classes.

To summarize, the impact of PSP differs according to the level of income in that PSP significantly increases the probability of being water-poor for households belonging to the lowest income classes.

## Conclusions

Using historical data we were able to show that the process of securing universal coverage in France has taken one or two generations and that substantial investment, in the form of subsidies from urban areas, were required to increase coverage to rural areas. We also argued that the decision to involve the private sector resulted from the need for heavy investment in the water infrastructure which the local authorities did not have.

We also presented some elements which highlight the fact that water charges for households have increased more rapidly than total household expenses, and that water charges have increased twice as fast as the consumer price index. The price is significantly higher when the private sector is providing the service. However, differences in operating conditions may explain a large part of this price difference.

We have seen that one specificity of the French water sector is that there is currently no specific pricing scheme, rebate or discount tariff for the poorest households. The mechanism put in place by public authorities and private firms in order to guarantee affordable access to water corresponds to an *ex-post* financial aid designed to help low-income households who face difficulties in paying their water bills. Our empirical evidence shows that there is still a need for specific social policy to guarantee that water is affordable to poor households.

We also demonstrated that water affordability depends upon a certain number of household characteristics. For example, being a single parent results in an increasing share of income being spent on water charges – more so if the head of the household is a woman. Despite the social regulation mechanisms put in place by public authorities, the most vulnerable households in terms of water affordability are those heavily dependent upon social aid. In addition, a high percentage of votes for the Socialist or the Communist Party at the previous local election results in a lowering of the share of income spent on water charges since these parties tend to be more pro-poor.

The empirical analysis has also revealed that the water affordability of the poor in France was a relevant social policy issue. There is a strong probability that poor people will also be water-poor. In other words, the *ex-post* financial assistance system has not fully succeeded in achieving water affordability objectives for poor households.

Finally, econometric simulations suggest that an increase in PSP results in a significant increase in the water income share spent on water, especially among the poor. Moreover, the type of delegation arrangement also has an impact on the affordability of water. For example, a concession-type contract results in having a higher share of income being spent on water. One possible explanation could be that, since concession contracts are usually long-term contracts, regulation of the delegated firm may become more difficult, especially if the municipality lacks technical skills. This calls for the better monitoring of the private sector by municipalities (in particular with respect to the type of tariff).

## Notes

1. On 7 February 1778, Louis XVI gave the Perrier brothers the exclusive right 'to build and establish all facilities (pumping machines, pipes, and so on) required to bring water from the Seine to all Parisian districts and suburbs'.

2. See the 28 April 1977 decision of the Conseil d'état for the city of Poitiers or the 6 August 1978 decision for the city of Lille.
3. The definition of water services as a public service has a long history in France. According to the Cour de cassation (the highest judiciary authority in France), the public water fountain service was already considered in 1863 as a public service (Duroy 1996: 17).
4. Directive 2000/60/EC of the European Parliament and that of the Council of 23 October 2000 establish a framework for Community action in the field of water policy.
5. Council Directive 91/271/EEC concerns urban wastewater treatment.
6. For example in October 2004 (case C-505/03), the European Union's Court of Justice condemned France for excessive concentrations of nitrates in tap water in Brittany.
7. In 1999, the Compagnie générale des eaux changed its name to Vivendi Environment and became Véolia Environment in 2003.
8. *Le Monde Diplomatique* (March 2005) reports the example of the city of Neufchâteau located in the East of France. In Neufchâteau, the water service used to be delegated to a private firm, la Compagnie de l'eau et de l'ozone, for a long period (more than 15 years of contract delegation). In 1992, the mayor decided to conduct an audit of the water price. The conclusion of this audit was that the average water price should be equal to EUR2.90 per cubic metre compared to EUR3.65 actually paid by Neufchâteau customers. After the 2001 local election, the city council decided to cancel out the delegation contract and to manage the water service directly. As a result, the water price, which used to be EUR3.84 per cubic metre in 2000, went down to EUR2.92 in 2004.
9. The SPDE price index is based on the average price for water services belonging to the professional association.
10. There is a typical self-selection problem. Some observed and unobservable characteristics of local communities that have an impact on the water price also influence the choice of delegating the water service. To correctly relate the price difference between private and public management of the water service, a choice delegation model must be first estimated. This is the approach followed by Carpentier *et al.* (2006) using a treatment effect framework.
11. The number of poor people varies according to the definition of the poverty threshold (either 50 per cent or 60 per cent of the median income). According to the National Institute for Statistics and Economic Studies (INSEE), 3 million households (representing more than 12 per cent of the population) are considered as being poor (their income per consumption unit is lower than 50 per cent of the median income).
12. The Secours Catholique is a non-profit association created in France in 1946 which is committed to assist the poor and to fight poverty, exclusion, intolerance and discrimination.
13. Duroy (1996) reports that the Conseil d'état (the highest French administrative jurisdiction) used to consider that any price discrimination based on customer income was not allowed by the administrative code. In 1982, the Conseil d'état published a decision stating that the rebate implemented in Charente-Maritime for the sewage service for low-income households and elderly people was illegal since any category of customers can benefit from a specific pricing.

14. The FNDAE has ceased to exist from 1 January 2005.
15. For instance, the financial participation of private operators belonging to the SPDE represents EUR0.2 per customer and per year.
16. The OECD, however, has proposed several methods for measuring the affordability of water charges. 'Macro-affordability' indicators are developed by relating national average household water charges to either average household income (disposable or gross) or average household aggregate expenditure. 'Micro-affordability' indicators disaggregate the former by income groups, family types or regions. Available evidence of affordability indicators suggests that, in about half the OECD countries (15 out of 30), affordability of water charges for low-income households is either a significant issue now or might become one in the future, if appropriate policy measures are not put in place.
17. Water affordability could also be defined by comparing the water expenses to the total household expenses. We prefer to use the household income for two reasons. First, the statistical information is more reliable for income than for household expenses. Secondly, the intra-year variability of household expenses is higher than that of income (total expenses are registered for a given period of year, hence they may be subject to problems of seasonality). It follows that a water affordability index based on household expenses would more heavily depend upon the date at which the survey is conducted than an index based on household income.

## References

Berland, J.-M. and C. Juery (2002) *Inventaire et scénario de renouvellement du patrimoine d'infrastructures des services publics d'eau et d'assainissement* (Limoges: Office international de l'eau).

Billard, M., D. Legrain and J.-L. Prime (2001) *Rapport sur l'évaluation de la mise en oeuvre des dispositifs départementaux d'aide aux personnes et familles qui éprouvent des difficultés à acquitter leurs factures d'eau.* Rapport 20010161 de l'Inspection générales des affaires sociales (Paris: Ministère de l'emploi et de la solidarité).

Bureau d'informations et de prévisions économiques and Syndicat professionnel des distributeurs d'eau (2005) *Les services collectifs d'eau et d'assainissement en France: Données économiques, sociales et techniques.* Working paper.

Carpentier, A., C. Nauges, A. Reynaud and A. Thomas (2006) 'Effets de la délégation sur le prix de l'eau potable en France. Une analyse à partir des résultats de la littérature sur les "effets de traitement" ', *Economie et Prévision,* No. 174, 2006–3.

Commission de régulation de l'énergie (2004) 'Avis du 27 juin 2002 sur le projet de décret relatif à la tarification spéciale de l'électricité "produit de première nécessité" '. *Journal Officiel,* No. 86, 10 April, page 6813, texte No. 31.

Dutheil, N. (2004) *L'action sociale des communes de 5,000 à moins de 200,000 habitants. Etudes et Résultats,* No. 307, April (Paris: Direction de la recherche des études de l'évaluation et des statistiques/DREES).

Duroy, Stéphane (1996) *La distribution d'eau potable en France. Contribution à l'étude d'un service public local.* Bibliothèque de droit public, Tome 177 (Paris: Librairie générale de droit et de jurisprudence).

Fauquez-Avon, S. (2005) *L'accès à l'eau pour tous: Un impératif social.* Article presented at the 84th Congress of the ASTEE (Association scientifique et technique pour l'eau et l'environnement), Paris, 30 May–3 June.

Fitch, M. and H. Price (2002) *Water Poverty in England and Wales* (Leicester: Centre for Utility Consumer Law and Chartered Institute of Environmental Health).

García-Valiñas, M. (2005) *Optimal Pricing: A Proposal for Urban Water Distribution* (mimeo) (Oviédo, Spain: University of Oviédo).

Garcia, S. and A. Reynaud (2004) 'Estimating the Benefits of Efficient Water Pricing in France', *Resource and Energy Economics*, 26, 1–25.

Guérin-Schneider, L. and D. Lorrain (2004) 'Les relations puissances publiques – Firmes dans le secteur de l'eau et de l'assainissement', in *Eau, le temps d'un bilan* (Paris: Editions Groupe Moniteur).

Guérin-Schneider, L. and M. Nakhla (2004) 'Les indicateurs de performance: Une évolution clef dans la régulation des services d'eau', in *Eau, le temps d'un bilan* (Paris: Editions Groupe Moniteur).

IFEN (Institut français de l'environnement) (2003) *La gestion de l'eau potable en France en 2001. Etudes et Travaux*, No. 44 (Paris: IFEN).

Ménard, C. and S. Saussier (2003) 'La délégation de service public, un mode organisationnel efficace? Le cas de la distribution d'eau en France', *Economie Publique*, 2003(1), 99–129.

Mescheriakoff, Alain (1985) *Droit des Services Publics* (Paris: Presses Universitaires de France).

Pezon, C. (2000) *Le service d'eau potable en France de 1850 à 1995* (Paris: Presses du CEREM).

Pezon, C. (1999) *La gestion du service d'eau potable en France de 1850 à 1995*. Thèse es sciences de gestion (Paris: Conservatoire National des Arts et Métiers).

Reynaud, A. (2007) *Social Policies and Private Sector Participation in Water Supply: The Case of France*. Programme on Markets, Business and Regulation (Geneva: UNRISD).

Reynaud, A, S. Renzetti and M. Villeneuve (2005) 'Estimating Domestic Water Demand under Complex Pricing: the Canadian Case', *Water Resources Research*, 41, W11409, doi:10.1029/2005WR004195.

Reynaud, A. and A. Thomas (2005) 'Demande domestique en eau et choix de délégation', *Revue Economique*, 56(5), 1145–68.

Sawkins, J.H. and V.A. Dickie (2002) *Affordability of Water and Sewerage Services in Great Britain*. Report by ScotEcon.

Secours Catholique (2004) *Statistiques d'accueil 2004*. Annual report.

Secours Catholique (2003) *Statistiques d'accueil 2003*. Annual report.

Smets, H. (2004) *La solidarité pour l'eau potable: Aspects économiques* (Paris: Rapport pour l'Académie de l'eau).

Swallow, S. and S. Marin (1988) 'Long-run Price Inflexibility and Efficiency Loss for Municipal Water Supply', *Journal of Environmental Economics and Management*, 15, 233–47.

# 3
# Great Britain: England and Wales, and Scotland

*John W. Sawkins and Valerie A. Dickie*

## Introduction

One of the most contentious political issues in the United Kingdom in the second half of the twentieth century was the relationship between individual citizens and the state. In the years immediately following the Second World War a consensus emerged between the main political parties on the role of the state as a provider to citizens of a range of goods and services – particularly those associated with the utility industries – in order to achieve specific distributional ends.[1] By the mid-1970s, however, doubts were being raised by leading politicians[2] about the efficacy of public corporations in meeting redistributive or other social obligations, and the consensus began to break down. The 1979 election, of a Conservative administration committed to changing the relationship between the citizen and the state marked the beginning of a period in which alternatives to the public sector provision of goods and services were explored. A technically challenging and politically ambitious privatization programme followed, in which many nationalized industries, including some but not all of the utilities (previously considered the exclusive preserve of the state), were restructured, divested of particular social obligations, given clearer economic objectives, made subject to new forms of economic regulation, and sold to private sector investors.[3]

The water and sewerage industry in Scotland, England and Wales was not immune to these wider policy developments. Indeed, according to Bakker (2001: 1), the English and Welsh industry's evolution over the last thirty years may be understood in terms of shifting policy priorities, resulting in a changed perception of the relationship between the service supplier and recipient. Thus, instead of suppliers prioritizing social equity in seeking to supply all citizens at subsidized rates, changes in policy ensured that they gradually came to prioritize economic equity in selling to those customers able to pay on a full-cost recovery basis. In other words the 'public service' model[4] of the relationship between producer and consumer began to give way to a 'business organization' model.

Against this background the Great Britain case study analyses the issue of affordability of water services and how social policies and regulation are designed, in Scotland, England and Wales,[5] with particular reference to low-income households.

## Institutional setting

During the early and mid-twentieth century a wide variety of organizations, both public and private, undertook the tasks of supplying water and sewerage services to domestic households across Great Britain. While local municipalities generally came to assume responsibility for the provision of sewerage and sewage disposal services within their own jurisdictions, private sector organizations worked alongside public sector bodies in the abstraction, treatment and distribution of water. A process of consolidation and amalgamation gradually reduced the numbers of separate undertakings in both branches of the industry from over 2000 at the beginning of the century to around a tenth of this number by 1970.[6]

### England and Wales 1974 to date

In England and Wales, the most significant organizational change to the industry in the second half of the twentieth century came about through the passing of the 1973 Water Act, which created ten Regional Water Authorities (RWAs).[7] These bodies, organized under the general principle of 'Integrated River Basin Management', assumed responsibilities relating to the planning and control of all uses of water in each river catchment area: responsibilities which had previously been exercised by a large number of separate water and sewerage organizations.[8] As public bodies, they were ultimately responsible to central government, in particular the Department of the Environment (the Welsh Office for Welsh Water) except on matters of land drainage and fisheries where they reported to the Ministry of Agriculture, Fisheries and Food.

A significant feature of this reorganization was the fact that the 29 private (statutory) water companies existing in 1973 were allowed to continue operating under section 12 of the 1973 Water Act, even though the RWAs assumed responsibility for the supply of water in all areas. Where a private company operated within the area of the RWA, the RWA was required to discharge its water supply and distribution functions through the company. Close cooperation was required as responsibility for water resource development lay with the RWA. However, in many areas the company acted as agent of the Authority. All 29 private water supply companies in existence in 1973 continued to operate under tight regulatory control until 1989. Supplying approximately one-quarter of the population in England and Wales, their combined contribution was significant throughout the period. Thus private and public water suppliers coexisted in England and Wales from 1974 to 1989.

In 1989 the RWAs were privatized[9] and ten public limited companies were created. These were group holding companies sharing similar corporate structures, in which a subsidiary water and sewerage company (WaSC) assumed the main operational responsibilities. The WaSCs delivered services under an 'Instrument of Appointment' granted by the Secretaries of State for the Environment and Wales.

The assets and liabilities of the RWAs were transferred to the subsidiary Appointees on 1 September 1989 with shares in the holding (Group) companies being offered for sale in November 1989. The share offer was oversubscribed, due in part to the success of previous public share offerings in the large utilities, and the perception on the part of potential investors that the companies had been underpriced in order to maximize the chance of a successful floatation.

Each Appointee's Licence to operate, granted either by the Secretary of State for the Environment or the Secretary of State for Wales, was awarded initially for a period of 25 years. Licence terms and conditions, binding the companies in various ways, were enforced by the industry's new economic regulator, Office of Water Services (Ofwat), and covered matters such as charging, codes of practice on consumer matters, debt and leakage, levels of service, asset management plans and the provision of information.

A special or 'golden' share in the WaSCs was retained by the Secretary of State until 31 December 1994. This share gave ultimate ownership rights to the Secretary of State, effectively ruling out the threat of merger or takeover for the initial post-privatization period. For all water companies the Director General of Water Services was required to refer any proposed merger of companies which breached a particular financial threshold to the Competition Commission. For larger mergers, European Commission (EC) Mergers Regulations came into play.

As far as the 29 private water companies were concerned, the Act preserved their status and areas of supply. They were appointed to supply water services (only) within their own areas under licence in the same way as the ten WaSCs. Restrictions on their ability to borrow and pay dividends were loosened, some became PLCs, and many attracted the interest of domestic and foreign companies as potential takeover targets. To date, the majority of the original 39 companies have either merged or been taken over and now operate as subsidiaries of larger companies. Only a minority retain a separate London Stock Exchange listing.

As far as economic regulation was concerned, the main innovation of the 1989 Water Act was the appointment of an independent economic regulator, the Director General of Water Services (Ian Byatt), who headed Ofwat.[10] The economic regulator's duties set out in section 2 of the consolidating 1991 Water Industry Act as updated by section 39 of the 2003 Water Act included; the promotion of consumer interests (through the promotion of competition where appropriate), ensuring that the functions of the companies were properly carried out and that they abided by the terms of their licence to operate. Significantly, the economic regulator was to regulate through the use of a price cap mechanism, with periodic reviews every five years. In setting price caps Ofwat's primary duty was to ensure that the companies were able to finance their functions, in particular, by securing a reasonable rate of return on their capital. From 1 April 2006 the functions of the Director General of Water Services transferred to the new Water Services Regulation Authority.[11]

## Scotland 1975 to date

Scotland's response to the 1974 reorganization of the English and Welsh industries in 1974 came about as part of wider local government reform. Thus, under the terms of the Local Government (Scotland) Act 1973 the nine regional and three islands councils established on 16 May 1975 became responsible for water and sewerage services within their own areas, and responsibility for the prevention of pollution of inland and defined coastal waters on mainland Scotland was transferred to seven River Purification Boards (RPBs).[12]

Overall responsibility for the economic regulation of the industry post-1975 remained with the Scottish Office, a department of central government. It continued to set the macroeconomic framework within which the bodies were to work, but delegated some regulatory powers to regional and islands councils that set charges at a level high enough to cover annual expenditure. The councils were responsible for their actions to the local electorate. Funds for capital investment were allocated by the Scottish Office on an annual basis under section 94 of the Local Government (Scotland) Act 1973.

Following privatization of the ten English and Welsh RWAs in 1989, the Conservative government signalled its intention to restructure the Scottish industry as well. After lengthy public consultation and heated debate, during which a proposal to privatize the industry was decisively rejected, the statute reforming the industry passed into law as the Local Government etc. (Scotland) Act 1994. Under its terms, responsibilities for water and sewerage services were transferred from the nine regional and three islands councils to three new Public Water Authorities (PWAs) on 1 April 1996. The Secretary of State for Scotland became responsible for the appointment of all PWA board members, effectively removing responsibility for these services from local government control for the first time. He also remained ultimately responsible for the setting of prices, and for the release of money for large-scale capital investment through fixed External Financing Limits. The amount of money available through this route, however, was restricted and PWAs were encouraged to bridge any funding gap with money from the Private Finance Initiative (PFI) and increased charges. Thus, although privatization of the industry had not been implemented, the principle of private sector involvement had been established for the first time since 1975.

An important regulatory change came about through the Water Industry Act 1999 which established the post of Water Industry Commissioner for Scotland.[13] The Water Industry Commissioner's primary functions were to promote the interests of the water authorities' customers and to advise the Scottish Executive on the level of water charges over periods of several years. Responsibility for approving charges, however, remained with the Minister. For the first time Scottish water authorities were issued with individual price caps or limits on annual price increases.

Concerns over the impact on customer charges of the large investment programme and a desire to capture further unexploited economies of scale led to the creation of a single public water authority for Scotland. Under the terms of the Water Industry (Scotland) Act 2002 the North, East and West of Scotland PWAs merged on 1 April 2002 to become Scottish Water. Most recently the Water Services etc. (Scotland) Act 2005 replaced the Water Industry Commissioner for Scotland with a Water Industry Commission (WIC) which began operating on 1 July 2005. This new body acts independently of Scottish Ministers to set periodic price caps for Scottish Water. Should Scottish Water contest price determinations of the Commission the appeal is now to the United Kingdom's Competition Commission rather than to Scottish ministers.

Although a public authority, Scottish Water has inherited a set of commercial relationships with private sector firms, and has sought to develop others. Inherited commercial relationships included, significantly, the nine large-scale wastewater projects that were eventually commissioned under PFI agreements and which currently process around half of the waste water in Scotland. More recent public–private partnerships include a joint venture enterprise – Scottish Water Solutions Ltd (SWS) – the purpose of which is to manage and deliver a large part of the industry's capital investment programme.

To summarize, over the course of the last 30 years the pattern of water and sewerage service provision across Great Britain has evolved in ways which have increased private sector participation. Having sketched in this background we turn now to consider the broad changes in government and regulatory policy relating to service provision that precipitated many of the institutional reforms.

## Changing policy priorities

### From social to economic equity and back

A survey of water service pricing practices in OECD countries (OECD 1987) listed criteria used by governments and regulatory bodies in designing charging systems. Ten years later (OECD 1999) the list of criteria remained largely intact.[14] However, the author drew attention to the way in which particular criteria had been given greater priority over others by different governments and regulatory agencies during that time. Some, for example, had introduced policies which had given greater emphasis to criteria emphasizing narrow economic efficiency objectives; others had prioritized broader social equity goals.[15]

### England and Wales

In a penetrating study of the English and Welsh water industry, Bakker (2001) developed this theme of changing government and regulatory priorities within a British context, arguing that institutional developments, in general, could be helpfully understood in terms of changing government and regulatory policies. Changes to tariff structures resulting from new regulatory arrangements, for example, could be seen to reflect a shift towards the prioritization of economic equity over social equity: a movement from the ability to pay principle to the benefit principle.[16] Thus, it is notable that in the early 1980s an English and Welsh interregional charge equalization levy was phased out and Keynesian regional employment policies, which had contributed to high staffing levels within the industry, fell out of favour. RWA boards were restructured, reduced in size and populated with central rather than local government appointees.

Challenging financial targets were set which required RWAs to achieve particular rates of return. Cost–benefit analysis was embedded in company decision making and attempts made to introduce long run marginal cost pricing.[17]

Despite these developments it would be wrong to assert, in terms of charging, that all post-privatization policy changes exclusively prioritized the principle of economic equity over social equity. Rather, in order to achieve the aims of privatization, the government had to articulate more precisely and clearly the social obligations laid upon the companies. This is quite different, of course, from removing social obligations altogether, and in the years following privatization, distinct spatial patterns of consumption and access to water services did not emerge in the water industry to the extent that they did in the post-privatization energy industry. This was due to statutory measures which have continued to include both a *universal service obligation* on suppliers[18] and specific protection for rural customers.[19]

Concern that the movement towards prioritizing economic over social equity in industry policy had gone too far lay behind the newly elected Labour government's decision to hold a 'Water Summit' in May 1997. Water companies and their regulators were brought together, and a ten-point plan devised in which new political priorities were articulated. Immediate measures included the introduction of mandatory leakage targets and an announcement that the government would conduct a broad review of water charging and metering policies.[20] Legislative changes reflecting the new policy emphases came through the Water Industry Act (1999). The Act prohibited domestic disconnection for the non-payment of charges, prohibited the use of limiting devices (for example, trickle valves), and gave ministers the authority to provide statutory guidance to the economic regulator on charging and to make provisions for the protection of vulnerable groups.

### Scotland

In Scotland, the principle of social equity in relation to water industry policies enjoyed a prominence and longevity exceeding that in England and Wales. The reasons behind this are explored in more detail by Sawkins and Dickie (2006). Thus, rather belatedly, following the 1996 restructuring of the industry, policy measures marked out the change in emphasis with new policies including the introduction of designated sewerage charges,[21] the phasing out of water and sewerage charge reliefs for charitable organizations, the imposition of strict performance targets and the consequent sharp decline in employee numbers within the organizations. Against this must be set the single most significant social policy innovation of the period, charge harmonization for the whole country, which was achieved in 2004/05.

Despite a delay in the reorientation of industry policies towards prioritizing economic over social equity in Scotland, the movement gathered momentum. However, as in the case of England and Wales, it is also possible to discern politically inspired movements in the other direction, an example being the phasing out of reliefs to voluntary organizations. Bakker's (2001) conclusion drawn in the context of England and Wales therefore has relevance too to Scotland.

## Implications of changing policy priorities for low-income households

Having outlined recent changes to institutional arrangements and broad policy priorities, we examine in more detail changes in policies aimed at addressing the access and affordability-related concerns of low-income households across Great Britain.

### Access

Since the middle of the nineteenth century government policy makers in Great Britain have attached great importance to providing all households with access to treated water piped directly into individual residences, and corresponding sewerage systems for the conduct of foul flows away from the same residence, regardless of geographical location, social class or income. This was achieved, technically,[22] for the vast majority of urban residents across Great Britain by the middle of the twentieth century. However, in remote rural areas, small-scale private supplies have only gradually been joined to larger public networks.[23] The extent of this work continues to be limited by the costs of extending the network, which remains prohibitive in some areas.

Nevertheless for Scotland, England and Wales, physical access to water and sewerage services for domestic consumers may be regarded, for all practical purposes, as being universal. Changes in policy priorities to emphasize economic over social equity have not impinged seriously upon the underlying principle of universal access which has continued to enjoy a degree of statutory protection.[24] Tables 3.1 and 3.2 record the percentage of the resident population connected to mains water and sewerage in England, Wales and Scotland. They highlight the fact that there is little geographical variation in connection rates.

*Table 3.1* Percentage of resident population connected to mains water and sewerage in England and Wales, 1987/88

| *Year* | *% Resident population connected to mains water* | *% Resident population connected to mains sewerage* |
|---|---|---|
| Anglian | 99 | 92 |
| Dŵr Cymru | 98 | 94 |
| Northumbrian | 99 | 98 |
| North West | 99 | 97 |
| Severn Trent | 100 | 98 |
| Southern | 100 | 95 |
| South West | 95 | 85 |
| Thames | 100 | 98 |
| Wessex | 97 | 94 |
| Yorkshire | 99 | 96 |
| Total: England and Wales | 99 | 96 |

*Note*: Figures relate to water authority areas in 1987/78.
*Sources*: Water Authorities Association (1988a, 1988b).

*Table 3.2* Percentage of resident population connected to mains water and sewerage in Scotland, 2000/01

| *Year* | *% Resident population connected to mains water* | *% Resident population connected to mains sewerage* |
|---|---|---|
| North East | 96 | 93 |
| North West | 94 | 82 |
| South East | 98 | 97 |
| South West | 99 | 98 |
| Islands | 94 | 67 |
| Total: Scotland | 98 | 96 |

*Source*: Scottish Executive (2001b). Figures relate to 2000/01. Areas are those used by Scottish Water. Islands include the Western Isles, Orkney and Shetland.

## Affordability

An enduring feature of government efforts to secure universal access to water and sewerage services for households has been continuous downward pressure on prices, either applied directly or mediated through quasi-independent economic regulatory bodies. Prior to the privatization of the English and Welsh RWAs in 1989 and the reorganization of the Scottish industry in 1996, prices were generally some way below a level that, together with government lending, was necessary to recover the full economic costs of service provision, and despite increases particularly in the mid-1980s in England and Wales and the late 1990s in Scotland, this remained the position up to the end of the respective decades.

Where households were unable to pay for services, financial support was offered through the tax and benefits system. Thus in the 1980s, claimants of Supplementary Benefit received an amount of money which reflected the actual costs of water and sewerage bills. Where households were unwilling rather than unable to pay for services, suppliers in England and Wales had the power of disconnection. This power did not extend to Scotland.

As part of the Conservative government's reform of social security arrangements Supplementary Benefit was abolished in 1988 and replaced by Income Support. Significantly, for water and sewerage consumers, this broke the link between benefit and bills and a system was introduced in which a series of personal allowances – related to particular household circumstances – were granted to cover day-to-day living needs.[25] Water and sewerage service charges were thereafter deemed to be met by the personal allowance element in the overall Income Support payment.[26] This change effectively passed responsibility for meeting water and sewerage charges from the Department of Social Security, which no longer automatically rebated charges in full to the benefits claimants themselves – a further example of the way in which government policy came to prioritize economic over social equity.

From the point of view of low-income water and sewerage customers across Great Britain two features of the post-1988 system are notable. First, Income Support rates did not – and do not – vary regionally despite the fact that local variations in water and sewerage charges in England and Wales began to open up following the abolition of interregional equalization grants.[27] This clearly disadvantaged those in higher-charging regions such as the southwest of England (Kempson and Bennett 1997). Secondly, the index used to up-rate means-tested benefits – the Rossi Index – did not include water charges until 1992, and generally lagged well behind water and sewerage charge increases in the post-1989 period in England and Wales, and the post-1996 period in Scotland. In Table 3.3 we show the annual percentage change in the benefit up-rating index (Rossi/New Rossi) against changes in the Retail Price Index and for the purposes of illustration the average water and sewerage charge for England and Wales.

The erosion in the value of support for water and sewerage charges through the Social Security system was outlined by Fitch (2002), who quoted figures given in a reply from the House of Commons Library to

*Table 3.3* Indices and prices

| *Year* | *Annual % change in Retail Price Index (RPI)* | *Annual % change in Rossi/New Rossi Index* | *Annual % change in average English and Welsh water and sewerage charge* |
|---|---|---|---|
| 1988/89 | 4.2 | 3.2 | – |
| 1989/90 | 5.9 | 4.7 | 11.2 |
| 1990/91 | 7.6 | 5.2 | 12.6 |
| 1991/92 | 10.9 | 8.1 | 16.4 |
| 1992/93 | 4.1 | 7.0 | 8.3 |
| 1993/94 | 3.6 | 3.6 | 9.5 |
| 1994/95 | 1.8 | 3.9* | 7.6 |
| 1995/96 | 2.2 | 1.8 | 6.0 |
| 1996/97 | 3.9 | 3.0 | 3.3 |
| 1997/98 | 2.1 | 2.6 | 5.5 |
| 1998/99 | 3.6 | 2.4 | 5.7 |
| 1999/90 | 3.2 | 2.1 | 1.2 |
| 2000/01 | 1.1 | 1.6 | −11.0 |
| 2001/02 | 3.3 | 1.6 | 2.3 |
| 2002/03 | 1.7 | 1.7 | 1.8 |
| 2003/04 | 1.7 | 1.3 | 3.5 |
| 2004/05 | 2.8 | 1.8 | 5.5 |

*Source*: Department for Work and Pensions (2004b) Table 2, Uprating History, p. 31. Ofwat's (various) Tariff Structure and Charges Reports.
*Note*: Income Support is uprated annually in early April using the Rossi/New Rossi index which is currently defined as RPI (all items) less rent, local taxes and mortgage interest payments. Pre-April 1992 the Rossi index excluded water charges. The RPI and Rossi indices in this table relate to the uprating date (April), however the data on which the uprating figures are based relate to the previous year to September (for example, the uprating of 11 April 1988 used September 1986 to September 1987 data). Note that Ofwat adopts a November RPI figures in its regulatory functions (see Ofwat 2005).
*In April 1994 Income Related Benefits were uprated by 3.9 per cent to take account of the introduction of VAT on fuel. The Rossi factor for this period was 3.5 per cent.

Helen Jackson MP on 17 May 1996. The base Social Security figure of GBP1.65 per week[28] was not an amount included in Income Support for the payment of water and sewerage bills, but the estimated average bill for those in receipt of Supplementary Benefit in 1988. In Table 3.4 we extend the time series of Fitch (2002) by uprating the benefit element within Income Support (notionally ascribed to water and sewerage in 1988) by the Rossi index, setting this alongside the average water and sewerage charge for England and Wales. Benefit as a proportion of the average charge has clearly fallen quite markedly over the period: a point underlined recently by the National Consumer Council.[29] In Table 3.5 the effect of the large regional variation in water and sewerage charges

*Table 3.4* Changes in Income Support Benefit Element and English and Welsh charges, 1988/89 to 2004/05

| *Year* | *Benefit element (weekly) GBP (uprated by Rossi)* | *Average water and sewerage charge (GBP) annual (weekly)* | *Benefit element as % of average charge* |
|---|---|---|---|
| 1988/89 | 1.65 | 107 (2.06) | 80 |
| 1989/90 | 1.73 | 119 (2.29) | 76 |
| 1990/91 | 1.82 | 134 (2.58) | 71 |
| 1991/92 | 1.97 | 156 (3.00) | 66 |
| 1992/93 | 2.11 | 169 (3.25) | 65 |
| 1993/94 | 2.19 | 185 (3.56) | 62 |
| 1994/95 | 2.28 | 199 (3.83) | 60 |
| 1995/96 | 2.32 | 211 (4.06) | 57 |
| 1996/97 | 2.39 | 218 (4.19) | 57 |
| 1997/98 | 2.45 | 230 (4.42) | 55 |
| 1998/99 | 2.51 | 243 (4.67) | 54 |
| 1999/00 | 2.56 | 246 (4.73) | 54 |
| 2000/01 | 2.60 | 219 (4.21) | 62 |
| 2001/02 | 2.64 | 224 (4.31) | 61 |
| 2002/03 | 2.68 | 228 (4.38) | 61 |
| 2003/04 | 2.71 | 236 (4.54) | 60 |
| 2004/05 | 2.76 | 249 (4.79) | 58 |

*Sources*: Annual average water charges, 1988/89: Water Services Association (1989). 1989/90 to 1990/91: CRI (1994). 1991/92 to 1994/95: Ofwat Annual Reports 1990–93. 1995/96 to 2004/05: Ofwat Report on Tariff Structure and Charges 1995/96–2004/05. 1988/89 to 1994/95 average household charges for unmeasured water and sewerage. 1995/96 to date for measured and unmeasured. Weekly charges = annual charges/52. When Supplementary Benefit was replaced by Income Support no specific amount was included for water and sewerage charges in the latter. However in correspondence from the House of Commons Library to Ms Jackson MP (17 May 1996) an amount of GBP1.65 was cited. This is used as the basis for the benefit series (uprated by Rossi/New Rossi). At the time of writing (May 2007) the US$:GBP exchange rate stood at US$1.98 = GBP1.

on effective support levels is teased out for two of the English and Welsh water companies: South West Water, a high-charge area, and Thames Water, a low-charge area. In the case of South West Water the benefit element as a percentage of the average charge has been under 50 per cent since 1992/93.

In order to set these figures quite briefly within the broader context of poverty measures in the United Kingdom we report the results of a recent analysis by Brewer *et al.* (2007) which considers changes in levels of relative poverty – the 'headline' approach used by the UK government – for key subgroups of the population. In Table 3.6 the percentage and number of individuals in households with incomes below 60 per cent of median

*Table 3.5* Changes in element of Income Support Benefit and charges for Thames and southwest, 1988/89 to 2004/05

| *Year* | *Benefit element (weekly) GBP (uprated by Rossi)* | *Average water and sewerage charge GBP annual (weekly) Thames* | *Average water and sewerage charge GBP annual (weekly) South West* | *Benefit element as % of average charge Thames* | *Benefit element as % of average charge South West* |
|---|---|---|---|---|---|
| 1988/89 | 1.65 | 93 (1.79) | 128 (2.46) | 92 | 67 |
| 1989/90 | 1.73 | 100 (1.92) | 146 (2.81) | 90 | 62 |
| 1990/91 | 1.82 | 113 (2.17) | 164 (3.15) | 84 | 58 |
| 1991/92 | 1.97 | 130 (2.50) | 192 (3.69) | 79 | 53 |
| 1992/93 | 2.11 | 138 (2.65) | 228 (4.38) | 80 | 48 |
| 1993/94 | 2.19 | 152 (2.92) | 266 (5.12) | 75 | 43 |
| 1994/95 | 2.28 | 162 (3.12) | 304 (5.85) | 73 | 39 |
| 1995/96 | 2.32 | 172 (3.31) | 317 (6.10) | 70 | 38 |
| 1996/97 | 2.39 | 181 (3.48) | 329 (6.33) | 69 | 38 |
| 1997/98 | 2.45 | 191 (3.67) | 343 (6.60) | 67 | 37 |
| 1998/99 | 2.51 | 201 (3.87) | 354 (6.81) | 65 | 37 |
| 1999/00 | 2.56 | 206 (3.96) | 356 (6.85) | 65 | 37 |
| 2000/01 | 2.60 | 187 (3.60) | 314 (6.04) | 72 | 43 |
| 2001/02 | 2.64 | 194 (3.73) | 313 (6.02) | 71 | 44 |
| 2002/03 | 2.68 | 197 (3.79) | 326 (6.27) | 71 | 43 |
| 2003/04 | 2.71 | 201 (3.87) | 342 (6.58) | 70 | 41 |
| 2004/05 | 2.76 | 209 (4.02) | 361 (6.94) | 69 | 40 |

*Sources*: Annual average water charges – see notes to earlier tables.

income (after the deduction of housing costs) is recorded. Despite a small rise in relative poverty for children and working-age adults with and without children in 2005/06 the general picture is one of falling poverty since 1996/97. This pattern is particularly marked for children and pensioners, whose position has been the object of anti-poverty government policies since 1997.

As far as overall income inequality is concerned, however, it may be noted that a marked rise occurred during the 1980s and early 1990s. Since then the level has stabilized. Thus Brewer *et al.* (2007) report that the Gini coefficient[30] rose from around 0.25 in 1979, peaking at 0.34 in the early 1990s. Since 1997 the measure has moved from 0.33 in 1996/97 to 0.35 in 2005/06. The increase over this period has been statistically significant.

### Affordability in England and Wales

Turning to examine the question of affordability for low-income households in England and Wales we note that the combination of rapidly

*Table 3.6* Relative poverty: Percentage and number of individuals in households with incomes below 60 per cent of median after housing cost income

| | *Children* | *Pensioners* | *Working-age parents* | *Working-age non-parents* | *All* |
|---|---|---|---|---|---|
| | *% (million)* | *% (million)* | *% (million)* | *% (million)* | *% (million)* |
| 1996/97 | 34.1 (4.3) | 29.1 (2.9) | 26.6 (3.3) | 17.2 (3.5) | 25.3 (14.0) |
| 1997/98 | 33.2 (4.2) | 29.1 (2.9) | 25.9 (3.2) | 15.9 (3.3) | 24.4 (13.6) |
| 1998/99 | 33.9 (4.3) | 28.6 (2.9) | 26.3 (3.2) | 15.5 (3.2) | 24.4 (13.6) |
| 1999/00 | 32.7 (4.2) | 27.6 (2.8) | 25.5 (3.1) | 16.1 (3.4) | 24.0 (13.4) |
| 2000/01 | 31.1 (3.9) | 25.9 (2.6) | 24.7 (3.0) | 16.2 (3.4) | 23.1 (13.0) |
| 2001/02 | 30.8 (3.9) | 25.6 (2.6) | 24.5 (3.0) | 15.6 (3.4) | 22.7 (12.8) |
| 2002/03 | 29.8 (3.9) | 24.2 (2.5) | 24.1 (3.0) | 16.5 (3.7) | 22.4 (13.1) |
| 2003/04 | 28.7 (3.7) | 20.6 (2.2) | 23.5 (2.9) | 16.6 (3.7) | 21.5 (12.6) |
| 2004/05 | 28.4 (3.6) | 17.6 (1.9) | 23.0 (2.9) | 16.1 (3.6) | 20.5 (12.1) |
| 2005/06 | 29.8 (3.8) | 17.0 (1.8) | 24.8 (3.1) | 17.5 (4.0) | 21.6 (12.7) |

*Note*: Calculations based on FRS data. Figures for 1996/97 to 2001/02 relate to Great Britain. Figures for 2002/03 to 2005/06 relate to the United Kingdom.
*Source*: Extracted from Brewer *et al.* (2007, table 5, page 29).

rising charges, diminishing social security support (in relative terms), the ending of direct subsidies to firms from government and the unwinding of cross-subsidies within the charging regime resulted in growing political pressure on central government and the economic regulatory agency in the early 1990s, to address the problem of water affordability and reverse the direction of policy. For the economic regulator, Ofwat, a symptom of the underlying problem – the number of domestic disconnections for non-payment – acted as the focus of political and media attention in this debate.

In framing the original privatization legislation the government had given Ofwat a general customer protection role.[31] It did not, however, regard this as encompassing responsibility for the mitigation of financial hardship caused by water and sewerage tariffs. Ofwat was careful, therefore, to ensure that it remained an economic regulatory agency, operating at 'arm's length' from both industry and government. In its policy statements it carefully avoided giving the impression of having any sort of social security role; of being merely another arm of the Department of Social Security. It sought also to defend this principle for the water companies themselves. 'It would be unfair to other water customers if general tariff policy were to reflect social objectives. These should be part of health and social services policy. Any costs from providing support to customers with particular needs should be met by the appropriate agency, and not by water customers generally' (Ofwat 1990: 10).

Nevertheless Ofwat came under early pressure to take a more proactive stance with regard to affordability in the light of information on the number of domestic disconnections for non-payment that was emerging.

## Disconnection policies

In contrast to Scotland, where the disconnection of domestic households for non-payment of charges had not been permitted, the practice was not uncommon in England and Wales among the public RWAs and private statutory water companies. Among the statutory provisions of the 1989 Water Act was a requirement for companies to prepare a code of practice on debt and disconnection,[32] which would be approved by Ofwat. These company codes were to include guidance to households who had difficulty in paying bills, and an outline of procedures to be followed by companies before disconnection.[33] In the year before privatization, the number of domestic disconnections for non-payment was 15,255.[34] This fell sharply post-privatization as companies began to 'feel their way' with regard to the new statutory procedures. By 1991, however, there was a rapid rise in the number of county court summonses and judgements which resulted in a record number of disconnections that year (Table 3.7).

At the same time as the number of disconnections was growing, Ofwat undertook a consultation on the principles of charging for water and sewerage services (Ofwat 1990). In the report outlining the Director General's conclusions (Ofwat 1991) the principle of domestic metering was endorsed subject to certain caveats[35] and approval given to the extension of domestic metering on a voluntary basis. The Ofwat policy stance and the enthusiasm of some companies[36] to extend metered provision – consistent with prioritization of economic over social equity – raised concern among charitable organizations and consumer bodies which highlighted the budgeting problems faced by low-income families connected to a metered supply of water. In a well-publicized study[37] of the potentially health-endangering measures taken by low-income families to conserve water, Save the Children concluded that '70 per cent of the sample, were taking measures to reduce their use of water. Common measures included sharing baths, taking fewer baths or showers, washing clothes less often, flushing the toilet less often and preventing children from playing with water... Save the Children calls on the Government to ensure that water for basic human needs is affordable for

*Table 3.7* Disconnections (England and Wales): household water supply disconnections for non-payment of charges

| *Year* | *Number of disconnections* | *Percentage of households* |
|---|---|---|
| 1989/90 | 8,426 | 0.042 |
| 1990/91 | 7,673 | 0.038 |
| 1991/92 | 21,282 | 0.105 |
| 1992/93 | 18,636 | 0.092 |
| 1993/94 | 12,452 | 0.062 |
| 1994/95 | 10,047 | 0.050 |
| 1995/96 | 5,826 | 0.029 |
| 1996/97 | 3,148 | 0.016 |
| 1997/98 | 1,907 | 0.009 |
| 1998/99 | 1,129 | 0.005 |

*Source*: House of Commons Hansard Written Answers for 30 November 2000 (part 22), Water (Disconnections), Column 795W. Also for 1990/91 to 1998/99 see Ofwat's (2004) Debt and Disconnection Figures 2003–04, http://www.ofwat.gov.uk/aptrix/ofwat/publish.nsf/Content/debt_disc180804. Figures are years to 31 March 1998/99 was the last full year in which domestic disconnection for non-payment of bills was permitted. The disconnection of domestic properties for non-payment of water bills in England and Wales was abolished by the Water Industry Act 1999 with effect from 1 July 1999. Industry data is not available pre-privatization split down by domestic and non-domestic. However total disconnections for 1988/89 for water authorities and statutory water companies for domestic and non-domestic was 15,255 (House of Commons Hansard Debates for 24 June 1992, Water Disconections, column 203). Water Authority only data on total disconnections is available for 1986/87 onwards.

all families. The impact on children in low-income families should be taken into account in deciding on methods of charging for water' (Save the Children 1996: 7).

## Public health

Another issue arousing public concern at about the same time was the reported rise in notified cases of dysentery and hepatitis. In a House of Commons written answer[38] the Secretary of State for Health highlighted a rise in the incidence of dysentery in 1992 in all major conurbations other than London. Commenting on this he noted that trends in dysentery exhibit a periodicity with peaks every seven to eight years in the United Kingdom, although the peak in 1992 was higher than other peaks in the previous two decades. Although the association between disconnections for non-payment of bills and incidents of dysentery was not a clear one, the media began to make this link. For example, 'New evidence from the West Midlands points to a "very significant" link between water disconnection and risk of disease outbreaks. Dr John Middleton, director of public health at Sandwell Health Authority, compared the postcodes of people whose water was cut off with those of notified dysentery and hepatitis cases, and found a "strong correlation"' (*Healthmatters*,[39] Issue 14, Summer 1993: 4).

More thorough research into the issue was carried out by the British Medical Association (BMA 1994). While not finding the simple causal link characteristic of media reports, the BMA did raise public health concerns related to the disconnection policy.[40]

## Consumer debt

Meanwhile with diminished levels of social security support, water-related consumer debt levels rose rapidly. During 1994 nearly two million households defaulted on water bills and by the end of the year over one million, or 5 per cent of all households, were in payment arrears (Herbert and Kempson 1995). Another survey[41] found that 75 per cent of those claiming Income Support had difficulty in paying water bills and that for low-income families the most rapidly rising component of overall debt related to water.

## Review of policy

Under pressure to respond to all of these developments Ofwat reviewed company practice in relation to disconnection and debt, identifying substantial differences between companies in terms of the number of summonses issued, the level of disconnections and the overall approach to customer relations. This review led to the publication of Guidelines on Debt and Disconnection (Ofwat 1992) which emphasized the importance of companies minimizing the use of court action, improving information for customers and providing a range of payment methods to help customers to budget for water and sewerage charges. Thereafter the number of disconnections fell rapidly until by 1996–97 five water companies[42] had what amounted to a 'no-disconnection' policy for domestic premises. Overall disconnection figures fell far below pre-privatization levels.

Undoubtedly this action by Ofwat resulted in some households which would otherwise have faced disconnection for non-payment remaining connected to the supply. Nevertheless Ofwat took care to ringfence its activities, ensuring that together with the water companies it fulfilled its statutory obligations but did not offer any form of additional financial assistance for those unable or unwilling to pay their bills.

Two other initiatives taken by Ofwat in the early 1990s related to the wider affordability debate. The first was an Ofwat-commissioned report by the Institute for Fiscal Studies into the distributional impact of alternative charging schemes (Ofwat 1993). Information from this study underpinned discussions of alternatives to unmeasured tariff regimes, and their effect on low-income households. Second was its support for Budget Payment Units (BPUs) – restrictive flow devices, which were offered to households at risk of disconnection for non-payment to assist them to budget effectively for water services. The devices, operated by means of payment cards, were declared unlawful in February 1998 on the grounds that the possibility of self-disconnection posed a health risk to those using them and the wider public. The decision disappointed Ofwat, which had seen them as a helpful and popular budgeting device for a particular class of customer.

In general, Ofwat's careful refusal to transgress the strict statutory limits of its operations was a stance congenial to Conservative central governments from 1989 onwards. In 1997, however, the new Labour administration quickly showed itself eager to become more involved at a micro level in the economic and environmental regulation of the industry, convening the Water Summit discussed earlier. The limited return to the prioritization of social over economic objectives in water-related policy matters was handled with care by the economic regulator. Ofwat quickly showed itself to be adept at working in the new political environment, managing once again to resist pressure – this time from central government – to add a range of social objectives to its portfolio of responsibilities. In this it succeeded; for the Government chose to address its particular social concerns in England and Wales – including affordability of water and sewerage services – by means of primary legislation.

Following a period of intense lobbying and political discussion over the plight of vulnerable households in relation to disconnection and debt, the Water Industry Act 1999 put in place various protections for particular groups in line with governmental social objectives. Although not designed to address the affordability problem directly the measures did offer some support to particular vulnerable groups. The Act prohibited the disconnection of households for non-payment of charges (section one) thereby bringing England and Wales into line with Scotland. It prohibited the use by companies of limiting devices, for example trickle valves, to enforce payment (section two). It gave powers to the Secretary of State to make Regulations on charging to issue regulations setting out requirements that should be included in companies' charges schemes, and in particular to make provision for the protection of vulnerable groups (section five). Finally it gave domestic consumers the right to opt for a measured charge (section six).

The effects of these measures were wide ranging. The prohibition of domestic disconnection for non-payment of charges led, predictably, to an increase in the numbers of customers in debt and the overall level of outstanding revenue for companies. It is not possible of course to identify the extent to which this reflects a growing reluctance on the part of customers to pay for the service, as against changes in ability to pay. However, Ofwat suggested that the change itself was due, in no small part, to blunted payment incentives. Indeed, following the 1999 Periodic Review it was formally recognized that companies might spend more recovering debt, and that interim price determinations might therefore be required to reflect these new circumstances.[43]

Vulnerable group regulations were made in the Water Industry (Charges) (Vulnerable Groups) Regulations 1999[44] and Water Industry (Prescribed Conditions) Regulations 1999. Both offered tariff-based assistance to particular target groups. However, recent evidence offered by the National Consumer Council to the House of Commons Environment, Food and Rural Affairs Committee stated that the scheme had been a failure with only a 1.4 per cent take-up among eligible customers in 2001/02.[45] It further alleged that the scheme cost more to administer than it paid out to customers.

One company-led innovation to address the problem of affordability, however, enjoyed limited success, and did not fall foul of legislation or economic regulation. This innovation was the establishment of charitable trust and hardship funds. These funds, discussed in detail by Fitch (1998), were established by most water and sewerage operators in the mid-1990s, and offered targeted assistance to customers who had difficulty in paying their bills. They varied greatly in scale and constitution. Some were administered by boards of independent trustees, others run by water companies on informal lines, dealing with cases on an ad hoc basis. Trust funds were derived largely from the companies themselves which, in 2000–01, contributed GBP3.7 million – a fall of nearly 20 per cent from 1998–99 levels.[46] Levels of support and take-up rates vary quite widely across the country and there is no automatic entitlement to assistance. Nevertheless the existence of such bodies at the very least indicates some level of concern for financially disadvantaged customers by the companies themselves.

## Social policies: Scotland

A slightly different pattern of events affected consumers of water and sewerage services in Scotland. Social security provision in the form of Income Support arrangements applied to low-income consumers in Scotland as in England and Wales, however the option to disconnect domestic households for non-payment of charges was not available to Scottish suppliers throughout the period. Other differences are also evident.

First, it is important to note that from 1996 onwards domestic consumers in Scotland (as well as the large majority in England and Wales) continued to be charged for water and sewerage services on the basis of property valuations (that is non-volume related charges[47]), however this was related to the council tax banding of their residence[48] and not its rateable value.[49] In addition, local authorities remained responsible for billing and collection which was undertaken in parallel with the ingathering of general council tax revenues. A corollary of this was that single-person households were eligible for a 25 per cent reduction in council tax liability if they were sole eligible occupants of the property. This reduction extended to water and sewerage charges and was in effect a benefit over and above that available through the Income Support system. We note the significance of this point later.

Secondly, the large price rises experienced by consumers in England and Wales in the late 1980s and early 1990s were delayed in Scotland until after the reorganization in 1996. Thus in 1995/96 the average unmeasured Scottish household (domestic) bill for water and sewerage services was GBP107 (US$212) annually and the corresponding figure for customers in England and Wales was GBP208 (US$412). By 2002/03 the situation had reversed and the average unmeasured household bill for consumers in Scotland had increased to GBP248 (US$491), while in England and Wales it was GBP236 (US$467).[50] Both the speed of the rise in domestic charges in Scotland, and the fact that the gap was closed, are notable. Also important is the observation that the impact of increased charges was not evenly felt across the country. A policy of inter-regional or geographical charge harmonization[51] ensured that consumers in areas previously enjoying particularly low charges suffered the steepest rises, effectively cross-subsidizing consumers in high-charging areas. Thus while bills for consumers in the Western Isles, Orkney and Shetland have roughly trebled in absolute terms since 1996, those for consumers in the Forth Valley area have increased by a factor of six. Cross-subsidization on this scale has been defended, politically, on the grounds of regional and social equity.

In stark contrast to England and Wales where the government and the economic regulator proved reluctant to sanction explicit financial support for low-income households, low-income consumers in Scotland have enjoyed two separate packages of temporary or transitional financial support funded by central government. First, a transitional sewerage relief grant (TR) running for three years from 1996/97,[52] provided relief for domestic consumers who, for the first time, faced meeting the costs of sewerage services directly.[53] Secondly, a scheme of relief offered to households in receipt of Council Tax Benefit whose charges were above a qualifying threshold.[54]

This most recent scheme, however, regarded by the government[55] as a means of supplementing the support already offered through the progressive Council Tax charging arrangements,[56] enjoyed rather modest funding, and was poorly targeted. Thus while those already in receipt of Council Tax Benefit qualified for support, this support was not automatically extended to Income Support claimants. Furthermore, in terms of absolute numbers of households benefiting from the scheme the relatively high threshold meant that in 2002/03 more Band E households received assistance than those occupying Band A properties. In the scheme's favour was its relative administrative simplicity whereby local authorities identified eligible households and made automatic reductions in bills. Undoubtedly, it benefited some low-income households particularly in the north of Scotland.

Concerns over the efficacy of the second transitional relief scheme and the wide-ranging public debate over the question of support for low-income and other vulnerable households[57] coincided with the government's[58] consultation on the principles of charging (Scottish Executive 2004). The Executive's response was to seek to regularize and make permanent a new form of relief linked to the Council Tax benefit system. To this end, in its statement on 'The Principles to be Applied in Charging for Public Water and Sewerage Services in Scotland 2006–10' (Scottish Executive 2005) it announced a new scheme in which the 25 per cent discount on water and sewerage bills would continue to be granted to all single-adult households irrespective of the Council Tax valuation band of the property occupied or eligibility for Council Tax benefit. Crucially, eligibility for the 25 per cent discount was extended to households with two or more adults in receipt of Council Tax benefit. The cost of the extension was met partly through the abolition of discounts on water charges for second homes and other empty dwellings. Under the new scheme some customers in receipt of Council Tax benefit (primarily those occupying higher-banded properties) received less generous reductions in charges than they did under the transitional arrangements. However, those low-income households in receipt of Council Tax benefit and previously not eligible, or eligible for only a limited reduction in their water charges, received more assistance. The new arrangements came into force on 1 April 2006.

## Comparing Scotland with England and Wales

This description of policy initiatives in relation to affordability has highlighted the quite marked differences in approach pursued in the different jurisdictions. In terms of government and regulatory policy it is clearly the case that greater priority has been given to social equity concerns in Scotland. On more than one occasion the Scottish Executive has taken the initiative to offer direct support to low-income households. In England and Wales Ofwat has shown great reluctance to endorse measures offering a degree of direct financial support or relief to low-income households.

The question then arises: how have consumers fared under the two sets of arrangements? What empirical evidence may be assembled to assess whether water and sewerage services have become more or less affordable for low-income households across time? In the next section we present a calibration exercise to analyse changes in affordability for households in general, and low-income households in particular.

### *Calibration*

In prosecuting its political agenda through legislation the post-1997 Labour government has sought, as a matter of routine, to measure progress in achieving particular objectives, and to publish quantitative and qualitative information regularly.

On water and sewerage affordability there was no 'benchmark' or 'standard' from which measurements of improvement or deterioration could be taken. Instead a simple calibration statistic, created as one of a number of indicators of sustainable development under the previous Conservative administration, was available. This statistic was the percentage of gross or net household income spent on water and sewerage services as a proportion of all income. A decision was taken to continue to track this indicator over time (Table 3.8), which implied a particular understanding of 'affordability' within government, namely that the higher the proportion of household income spent on water and sewerage services, the less affordable the services are to the household. In other words the proportion of a household's income or budget spent on the service is negatively correlated with affordability.

The importance of the distinction between calibration and benchmarking in relation to water affordability should be emphasized. This point has been well made in the extensive literature on minimum income

*Table 3.8* Water affordability illustrative indicator (England and Wales)

| | *Proportion of households spending more than 3% of their income on water and sewerage charges (England and Wales)* |
|---|---|
| 1995/96 | 15 |
| 1996/97 | 14 |
| 1997/98 | 15 |
| 1998/99 | 15 |
| 1999/00 | 15 |
| 2000/01 | 11 |
| 2001/02 | 10 |
| 2002/03 | 9 |

*Source*: DEFRA 2004a, Quality of Life Counts Update 2004, Indicator Q3.

standards,[59] which itself informed UK government initiatives such as the design of policies to reduce child poverty. To date, no studies designed to establish affordability benchmarks for water have been undertaken in the United Kingdom.[60] Indeed Veit-Wilson (2004)[61] notes the existence of only one official UK study of the adequacy of benefits rates in general. Thus, while the term 'affordability' has come to be calibrated, and therefore understood in terms of the percentage of gross or net household income spent on water and sewerage services as a percentage of all income, without an appropriate affordability benchmark there are, in strict terms, no grounds for judging whether charges are in fact affordable or not.

Calibration is, however, possible. For this purpose we employ British microeconomic survey data at the household level – the Family Resources Survey (FRS).[62]

*Calibration using Family Resources Survey data.* The FRS contains data relating to water and sewerage charges paid by a cross-section of households in various years. The fact that this is a cross-sectional survey rather than a panel means that particular care is needed in comparing results between years or extrapolating beyond the particular time periods selected. More positively, the FRS benefits from the inclusion of McClements[63] scales permitting the calculation of estimates properly equivalized to reflect household size and composition.

In Table 3.9 the mean percentage of gross household income spent on water and sewerage charges by income decile is given for 1997/98 and 2003/04 for Scotland and England and Wales separately. Both years

*Table 3.9* Mean percentage of gross household income spent on water and sewerage charges by income decile, 1997/98 and 2003/04

| *Income decile* | *Mean % gross household income spent on water and sewerage charges by income decile* | | | |
|---|---|---|---|---|
| | *Scotland* | | *England and Wales* | |
| | *1997/98* | *2003/04* | *1997/98* | *2003/04* |
| 1 (low) | 1.3 | 2.8 | 3.5 | 2.7 |
| 2 | 0.9 | 1.9 | 2.5 | 2.0 |
| 3 | 0.7 | 1.6 | 2.1 | 1.6 |
| 4 | 0.7 | 1.5 | 1.8 | 1.4 |
| 5 | 0.6 | 1.3 | 1.5 | 1.2 |
| 6 | 0.6 | 1.2 | 1.3 | 1.0 |
| 7 | 0.5 | 1.1 | 1.1 | 0.9 |
| 8 | 0.4 | 1.0 | 0.9 | 0.7 |
| 9 | 0.4 | 0.8 | 0.7 | 0.6 |
| 10 (high) | 0.3 | 0.5 | 0.5 | 0.3 |

*Source*: FRS 1997/1998 and 2003/2004.
*Note*: Equivalized Income (cells based on under five observations are excluded).

fall between Periodic Price Reviews in England and Wales, and come more than a year after episodes of industrial restructuring in Scotland. All income estimates in the analysis were equivalized using the McClements scale to adjust for household size and composition. Gross income estimates were employed,[64] with the latter being defined according to the pattern of the Government's Households below Average Income publication (DWP 2004b).

The large price rises faced by domestic customers in Scotland following the 1996 reorganization of the industry are reflected in the figures. For England and Wales the change is less marked – however, of particular note is the fall in the charge burden for households in the lowest income decile. Reasons for this include industry initiatives such as the extension of domestic metering, but, more significantly, changes to the UK tax and benefits system, which raised the real incomes of those towards the bottom of the income distribution.[65] The latter clearly applied to Scottish households as well. However, the effect of this is masked by the effect of rapidly rising charges in absolute terms for Scottish consumers over this period.

Developing the analysis we follow the pattern of Sawkins and Dickie (2005) by analysing charges according to household type. In Table 3.10

*Table 3.10* Household water and sewerage charges by household composition

| *Household composition* | *1997/98* | | *2003/04* | |
|---|---|---|---|---|
| | *Mean weekly household water and sewerage charge (GBP)* | *Mean % gross weekly household income spent on water and sewerage* | *Mean weekly household water and sewerage charge (GBP)* | *Mean % gross weekly household income spent on water and sewerage* |
| *Scotland* | | | | |
| Single person without children | 1.4 | 0.3 | 3.8 | 0.7 |
| Couple without children | 2.0 | 0.4 | 5.9 | 0.9 |
| Three or more adults, no children | 2.1 | 0.5 | 6.1 | 1.1 |
| Single person with children | 1.4 | 0.6 | 3.8 | 1.2 |
| Couple with children | 2.2 | 0.5 | 6.5 | 1.2 |
| Three or more adults with children | 2.2 | 0.6 | 6.3 | 1.3 |
| Single pensioner | 1.4 | 0.5 | 4.0 | 1.2 |
| Pensioner couple | 2.1 | 0.7 | 6.1 | 1.6 |
| All households | 1.8 | 0.5 | 5.0 | 1.0 |
| *England and Wales* | | | | |
| Single person without children | 3.6 | 0.7 | 3.8 | 0.6 |
| Couple without children | 4.5 | 0.8 | 4.6 | 0.6 |
| Three or more adults, no children | 4.8 | 1.1 | 5.1 | 0.9 |
| Single person with children | 4.1 | 1.7 | 4.6 | 1.4 |
| Couple with children | 4.8 | 1.1 | 5.0 | 0.9 |
| Three or more adults with children | 5.0 | 1.4 | 5.2 | 1.1 |
| Single pensioner | 3.8 | 1.5 | 3.6 | 1.0 |
| Pensioner couple | 4.6 | 1.5 | 4.5 | 1.3 |
| All households | 4.4 | 1.1 | 4.6 | 1.1 |

*Source*: FRS (1997/98, 2003/04).
*Note*: Equivalized Income. At the time of writing the US$:GBP exchange rate was US$1.98 = GBP1.

*Table 3.11* Household water and sewerage charges by household composition (lowest income decile)

| *Household composition* | *1997/98* | | *2003/04* | |
|---|---|---|---|---|
| | *Mean weekly household water and sewerage charge (GBP)* | *Mean % gross weekly household income spent on water and sewerage* | *Mean weekly household water and sewerage charge (GBP)* | *Mean % gross weekly household income spent on water and sewerage* |
| *Scotland* | | | | |
| Single person without children | 1.3 | 1.1 | 3.4 | 2.4 |
| Couple without children | 1.6 | 1.6 | 4.8 | 3.4 |
| Three or more adults no children | 2.2 | 1.8 | 5.5 | 3.6 |
| Single person with children | 1.4 | 1.1 | 3.5 | 2.1 |
| Couple with children | 1.9 | 1.8 | 4.9 | 3.3 |
| Three or more adults with children | 1.8 | 1.5 | 4.6 | 2.7 |
| Single pensioner | 1.4 | 1.1 | 4.1 | 2.7 |
| Pensioner couple | 2.0 | 1.7 | 5.7 | 3.5 |
| All households | 1.9 | 1.5 | 4.3 | 2.8 |
| *England and Wales* | | | | |
| Single person without children | 3.4 | 3.3 | 3.7 | 2.6 |
| Couple without children | 4.3 | 4.1 | 4.4 | 3.2 |
| Three or more adults no children | 4.2 | 3.8 | 4.2 | 2.9 |
| Single person with children | 4.2 | 3.4 | 4.6 | 2.8 |
| Couple with children | 4.4 | 4.0 | 4.4 | 3.1 |
| Three or more adults with children | 4.6 | 4.3 | 4.9 | 3.4 |
| Single pensioner | 3.4 | 2.9 | 3.4 | 2.1 |
| Pensioner couple | 4.2 | 3.5 | 4.2 | 2.6 |
| All households | 4.6 | 4.3 | 4.9 | 3.4 |

*Source*: FRS (1997/98, 2003/04).
*Note*: Equivalized Income (cells based on under five observations are excluded).

the analysis is presented and indicates both a convergence in charge burden between Scotland and England and Wales over the period and an improvement in the position of single pensioners in England and Wales; due presumably to changes in the tax and benefits system combined with the ready availability of a metering option.

Disaggregating these results further we may analyse the position of households in the lowest income decile only. This revealing exercise (Table 3.11) shows once more the large increase in household income spent on water and sewerage in Scotland for all groups. In relative terms, those carrying the greatest burden are three or more adult households with no children, pensioner couples and couples with and without children. Single people without children are apparently better placed north of the border where single person discounts for charges (via the Council Tax system) are available.

*Comparison: Scotland versus England and Wales*

The quantitative evidence presented above suggests convergence between Scotland, England and Wales over time in terms of the affordability measure. Thus having outlined differences in policy emphases, nuanced approaches to the questions of access and affordability, differing ownership and regulatory arrangements, our simple calibration exercise suggests that, overall, the position of Scottish household consumers in relation the affordability of water and sewerage charges appears similar to that of their counterparts in England and Wales. In terms of regulation and government policy, however, greater emphasis appears to have been given to issues of social equity in Scotland, particularly over the period of the industry's reorganization, and consequent large price rises, post-1996. This stands in contrast to the experience of customers, particularly those on low incomes, in the early post privatization period in England and Wales.

## Conclusions

During the last 30 years there has been a reorientation of industrial and regulatory policy with respect to the water and sewerage industry in Great Britain in which policies prioritizing economic equity have gradually displaced or modified those prioritizing social equity. This change, discernible for example in relation to charging policy, began and took hold quickly, in England and Wales. In Scotland, instances of direct government intervention to mitigate some of the more politically unacceptable consequences of this change were more numerous.

Throughout Great Britain there remains a shared understanding at both national and local levels of the importance of access to basic water and sewerage services to the maintenance of the fabric of civil society. As long as UK governments continue to advocate policies designed to promote social inclusion in general, there is little doubt that both public and private sector water supply organizations will be involved in some way in their delivery.

Despite marked differences in ownership – public in Scotland, private in England and Wales – and more subtle differences in legal and regulatory arrangements, we find no pronounced evidence to suggest that, currently, low-income or other vulnerable households are treated more or less favourably in a systematic way in any one particular jurisdiction. However, Scotland seems to have more social equity concerns.

Notwithstanding the regulatory and social security protection for low-income and other vulnerable households, rising levels of water-related household debt suggest that these protections are, currently, imperfect.

## Notes

1. Thus a National Health Service was established and industries such as coal, rail, gas and steel were taken into public ownership. In the water industry the number of private sector operators dwindled as local authorities took over responsibility for service delivery across most, but not all, of the country.
2. Most notably from within the Conservative Party led by Mrs Margaret Thatcher.
3. An early discussion of the rationale for the UK privatization programme is presented by Kay and Thompson (1986). More comprehensive analyses are offered in Vickers and Yarrow (1988), Armstrong *et al.* (1994) and, most recently, for the English and Welsh water industry in Bakker (2003).
4. Penning-Rowsell and Parker (1983: 170).
5. The analysis does not extend to the fourth constituent of the United Kingdom, Northern Ireland, as at present the costs of domestic service delivery are met primarily through an allocation from a general consolidated property-based tax fund. It is therefore not possible to identify accurately charges for water and sewerage attributable to individual household units. This undermines empirical analysis.
6. A description of the twentieth-century development of the English and Welsh water industry may be found in chapter 5 of Hassan *et al.* (eds) (1996) and chapter 11 of Vickers and Yarrow (1988).
7. The Regional Water Authorities came into existence on 1 April 1974.
8. The creation of the RWAs was intended to allow the exploitation of economics of scale and scope in service provision and the promotion of greater pollution control.
9. Under the Water Act 1989.

10. Ofwat is a non-ministerial government department, and therefore not subject to direction from ministers. It is accountable to Parliament, provides evidence for Parliamentary Select Committees and provides an annual report to the Secretary of State and the First Minister of Wales.
11. The Ofwat title was retained.
12. The role of the existing Central Scotland Water Development Board, in developing bulk supplies to regions of southern Scotland, was preserved by this institutional restructuring.
13. The first Water Industry Commissioner for Scotland (Alan Sutherland) took up his post on 1 November 1999.
14. The criteria included allocative (economic) efficiency, equity, financial requirements, public health, environmental efficiency, consumer acceptability and understanding and administrative costs. It was suggested that energy and employment, which had appeared in the 1987 list, would probably be omitted in the late 1990s (OECD 1999: 17).
15. OECD (1999: 19).
16. Bakker (2001: 158).
17. Synnott (1985: 70).
18. Water Industry Act 1991, section 37.
19. Water Industry Act 1991, section 2 (3) (a) (i).
20. Reviews of the water charging and abstraction licensing schemes were conducted under the auspices of the DETR (1998a, 1998b, 1998c, 1999a, 1999b). A broader review of utility regulation was conducted under the auspices of the DTI (DTI 1998a, 1998b).
21. Previously sewerage costs had been met out of general tax revenues.
22. That is in terms of physical connections being made.
23. Networks of mains and sewers are generally rather small in scale. No national network exists, for example, although within regions such as that covered by Yorkshire Water schemes have been devised to move large quantities of water around the area.
24. For example, the Water Industry Act (1991) discussed above.
25. Details are given in DSS/Benefits Agency (1999).
26. No other (national) social security benefit may currently be claimed in respect of these charges; in particular Council Tax and Housing Benefit do not apply.
27. In Scotland, regional charge harmonization was introduced.
28. Approximately US$3.27.
29. In evidence to the House of Commons Environment, Food and Rural Affairs Committee (2003), paragraph 37.
30. 'The Gini coefficient is a popular measure of income inequality that condenses the entire income distribution into a single number between zero and one: the higher the number the greater the degree of income inequality' (Brewer *et al.* 2007: 18).
31. Water Act 1989, section 7.
32. Condition H of the company licence.
33. Generally, a customer could only be disconnected after the company had obtained a court judgement for the unpaid charges.
34. Ofwat Annual Report (1996: 19).
35. The Director General supported the principle of universal domestic metering but regarded a rapid change as uneconomic. Metering should therefore be

targeted, spread progressively and installed when requested by consumers (Ofwat 1991: 4).

36. Notably Anglian Water.
37. Save the Children (1996).
38. House of Commons Official Report, 10 December 1993, Vol. 234, c 395.
39. http://www.healthmatters.org.uk/issue14/dysentery. *Healthmatters* is an independent quarterly magazine covering current issues in healthcare and public health policy.
40. *Healthmatters*, Issue 18, summer 1994, p. 4.
41. Cited in Bakker (2001: 152).
42. Cholderton, Mid Southern, Southeast, Southwest and Wessex.
43. For example, in September 2001 Dee Valley Water applied for an interim determination for reasons which included the effect of the disconnection ban on its costs and ability to recover debt. Ofwat accepted that its costs and level of debt had both risen.
44. Statutory Instrument 1999, No. 3441. Note these regulations apply only to England. Water and sewerage are devolved responsibilities of the National Assembly for Wales.
45. House of Commons Environment Food and Rural Affairs Committee 2003, para. 39, p. 13.
46. Ofwat (2001) RD (Letter to Regulatory Directors) 12/01 (Birmingham: Ofwat).
47. Non-volume-related charges for domestic water are still the norm in England and Wales as well as Scotland.
48. Properties were valued and allocated to one of eight Council Tax bands A to H. Charges were levied in fixed proportion to the Band D charge.
49. Domestic metre penetration in Scotland was, and remains, extremely low.
50. WCCP (2003a: 7).
51. Initially within the North, East and West of Scotland Water Authority areas and since the creation of Scottish Water across Scotland.
52. The grant was GBP89.7 million in 1996/7, GBP59.7 million in 1997/8 and GBP29.6 million in 1998/9 (WCCP 2003a: 16).
53. Prior to 1996 sewerage costs had been met through general Council Tax revenues.
54. Thresholds were: GBP180 in 2001–02, GBP198 in 2002–03 and GBP220 in 2003–04. The total cost of the scheme was GBP24 million over 3 years.
55. The Scottish Executive.
56. Such as single-person discounts and the progressive weighting within the charging structure.
57. WCCP (2003a).
58. The Scottish Executive.
59. See, for example, US work by Citro and Michael (1995), and an international survey by Veit-Wilson (1998).
60. In contrast a Fuel Poverty benchmark does exist. See DEFRA (2001).
61. Veit-Wilson (2004, Appendix A, Para IV).
62. Family Resources Survey data, collected by the Department of Social Security and the Department for Work and Pensions and Family Expenditure Survey data, collected by the Department of Employment and the Central Statistical Office were obtained through the UK Data Archive. © Crown copyright material is reproduced by permission of the Controller of Her Majesty's Stationery

and the Queen's Printer for Scotland. Neither the original data creators, nor the depositors, nor the copyright holders, nor the UK Data Archive bear any responsibility for analysis and interpretation contained in this paper.
63. McClements (1977).
64. Gross income estimates have the virtue of being 'computationally clean'. This means there is no need to determine what deductions should be made in order to arrive at a net figure.
65. DWP (2004b).

## References

Armstrong, M., S. Cowan and J. Vickers (1994) *Regulatory Reform: Economic Analysis and British Experience* (Cambridge, MA: MIT Press).
Bakker, K. (2003) *An Uncooperative Commodity: Privatizing Water in England and Wales* (Oxford: Oxford University Press).
Bakker, K.J. (2001) 'Paying for Water: Water Pricing and Equity in England and Wales', *Transactions of the Institute of British Geographers*, 26(2), 143–64.
Brewer, M., A. Goodman, A. Muriel and L. Sibieta (2007) *Poverty and Inequality in the UK: 2007*. IFS Briefing Note No. 73, Institute for Fiscal Studies. http://www.ifs.org.uk/bns/bn73.pdf, accessed on 5 June 2007.
British Medical Association (1994) *Water – A Vital Resource* (London: British Medical Association).
Centre for the Study of Regulated Industries (1994) *The UK Water Industry Charges for Water Services 1994/95* (London: CIPFA).
Citro, C. and R. Michael (eds) (1995) *Measuring Poverty: A New Approach* (Washington, DC: National Academy Press).
Department for Environment, Food and Rural Affairs (DEFRA) (2004a) *Quality of Life Counts Update 2004* (London: DEFRA).
Department for Environment, Food and Rural Affairs (DEFRA) (2001) *The UK Fuel Poverty Strategy* (London: DEFRA).
Department for Work and Pensions (2004a) *The Abstract of Statistics 2003 Edition* (London: Information and Analysis Directorate, Information Centre, Department for Work and Pensions).
Department for Work and Pensions (2004b) *Households Below Average Income 2002/3* (London: Department for Work and Pensions).
Department for Work and Pensions, Office for National Statistics. Social Survey Division and National Centre for Social Research (2005) *Family Resources Survey, 2003–2004* [computer file] (Colchester, Essex: UK Data Archive [distributor], April, SN: 5139).
Department of the Environment, Transport and the Regions (DETR) (1998a) *Water Charging in England and Wales – A New Approach: Consultation Paper* (London: Department of the Environment, Transport and the Regions).
Department of the Environment, Transport and the Regions (1998b) *Water Charging in England and Wales: Government Decisions Following Consultation* (London: Department of the Environment, Transport and the Regions).
Department of the Environment, Transport and the Regions (1998c) *The Review of the Water Abstraction Licensing System in England and Wales: Consultation Paper* (London: Department of the Environment, Transport and the Regions).

Department of the Environment, Transport and the Regions (1999a) *Taking Water Responsibly: Government Decisions Following Consultation on Changes to the Water Abstraction Licensing System in England and Wales* (London: Department of the Environment, Transport and the Regions).

Department of the Environment, Transport and the Regions (1999b) *Water Industry Act 1999: Consultation on Regulations* (London: Department of the Environment, Transport and the Regions).

Department of Social Security, Office for National Statistics Social Survey Division, Social and Community Planning Research, Family Resources Survey, 1997–1998 [computer file], 2nd Edition (Colchester, Essex. The Data Archive [distributor], 22 September 2000, SN: 4068).

Department of Social Security/Benefits Agency (1999) *Income Support Guide IS20 from November 1999* (London: Benefits Agency).

Department of Trade and Industry (1998a) *A Fair Deal for Consumers: Modernising the Framework for Utility Regulation* (London: Department of Trade and Industry).

Department of Trade and Industry (1998b) *A Fair Deal for Consumers: Modernising the Framework for Utility Regulation: Response to Consultation* (London: Department of Trade and Industry).

Fitch, M. (2002) *Water Poverty in England and Wales*. Working Paper (Leicester: Centre for Utility Consumer Law, University of Leicester).

Fitch, M. (1998) *Water Charities*. Working Paper 6/98 (Leicester: Centre for Utility Consumer Law, University of Leicester).

Hassan, J., P. Nunn, J. Tomkins and I. Fraser (eds) (1996) *The European Water Environment in a Period of Transformation* (Manchester: Manchester University Press).

*Healthmatters* (1994), Issue 18, Summer.

*Healthmatters* (1993), Issue 14, Summer.

Herbert, A. and E. Kempson (1995) *Water Debt and Disconnection* (London: Policy Studies Institute).

House of Commons Environment, Food and Rural Affairs Committee (2003), *Water Pricing. First Report of Session 2003–2004*, HC121 (London: TSO).

Kay, J.A. and D.J. Thompson (1986) 'Privatisation: a Policy in Search of a Rationale', *Economic Journal* 96, 18–32.

Kempson, E. and F. Bennett (1997) *Local Living Costs: Variations in the Costs Borne by Low Income Households* (London: Policy Studies Institute).

McClements, L. (1977) 'Equivalence Scales for Children', *Journal of Public Economics* 8, 191–210.

Organisation for Economic Co-operation and Development (OECD) (1999) *Household Water Pricing in OECD Countries* (Paris: OECD).

Organisation for Economic Co-operation and Development (OECD) (1987) *Pricing of Water Services* (Paris: OECD).

Ofwat (various) Annual Reports (London: HMSO).

Ofwat (2005) *Tariff Structure and Charges 2005–2006 Report* (Birmingham: Ofwat).

Ofwat (2000) *Tariff Structure and Charges 2000–01 Report* (Birmingham: Ofwat).

Ofwat (1997) *1997–98 Report on Tariff Structure and Charges* (Birmingham: Ofwat).

Ofwat (1993) *The Distributional Effects of Different Methods of Charging Households for Water and Sewerage* (Birmingham: Ofwat).

Ofwat (1992) *MD76 Guidelines on Debt and Disconnection* (Birmingham: Ofwat).

Ofwat (1991) *Paying for Water the Way Ahead* (Birmingham: Ofwat).

Ofwat (1990) *Paying for Water. A Time for Decisions* (Birmingham: Ofwat).
Penning-Rowsell, E.C. and D.J. Parker (1983) 'The Changing Economic and Political Character of Water Planning in Britain', *Progress in Resource Management and Environmental Planning* 4, 169–99.
Save the Children (1996) *Water Tight: The Impact of Water Metering on Low-Income Families* (London: Save the Children).
Sawkins, J.W. and V.A. Dickie (2006) *Social Policies and Private Sector Participation in Water Supply: The Case of Great Britain.* Programme on Markets, Business and Regulation (Geneva: UNRISD).
Sawkins, J.W. and V.A. Dickie (2005) 'Affordability of Household Water and Sewerage Services in Great Britain', *Fiscal Studies* 26(2), 225–44.
Scottish Executive (2005) *The Principles to be Applied in Charging for Public Water and Sewerage Services in Scotland 2006–2010* (Edinburgh: Scottish Executive).
Scottish Executive (2001) *Dwellings Connected to Public Water Mains and Public Sewers* (Edinburgh: Scottish Executive).
Synnott, M.F. (1985) *The Relationship between the Regional Water Authorities and Local Planning Authorities.* Unpublished doctoral thesis (London: Department of Geography, University of London, London School of Economics).
Veit-Wilson, J. (2004) *Memorandum Submitted to House of Commons Select Committee on Work and Pensions* (London: TSO).
Veit-Wilson, J. (1998) *Setting Adequacy Standards: How Governments Define Minimum Incomes* (Bristol: Policy Press).
Vickers, J. and G. Yarrow (1988) *Privatization: An Economic Analysis* (Cambridge, MA: MIT Press).
Water Authorities Association (1988a) *Waterfacts '88* (London: Water Authorities Association).
Water Authorities Association (1988b) *National Performance Ratios and Statistics 1983/84 to 1987/88* (London: Water Authorities Association).
Water Companies' Association (1989) *Water Companies: The Facts, the Figures, 1989 Edition* (London: Water Companies' Association).
Water Customer Consultation Panels (WCCP) (2003a) *Affordability of Scottish Household Water and Sewerage Charges* (Stirling: WCCP).
Water Customer Consultation Panels (WCCP) (2003b) *Affordability of Scottish Household Water and Sewerage Charges: Supplementary Report* (Stirling: WCCP).
Water Services Association (1989) *Waterfacts '89* (London: Water Services Association).

# 4
# Colombia

*Andrés Gómez-Lobo and Marcela Meléndez*

## Introduction

Private sector participation in the provision of water and sanitation services in Colombia has its origin in the 1991 Constitution that authorized the government to delegate the provision of public services to private sector providers while retaining responsibility for regulation, supervision and control, and in the enactment of Law 142 of 1994, the Public Utilities Law of Colombia, which regulated the procurement of public services by the private sector. The first private sector participation (PSP) experience in the water industry involving delegation of service provision occurred in 1994, with the award of a management contract to *Aguas de Barcelona* in the city of Cartagena, although minority private share ownership had already been introduced earlier in the cities of Barranquilla, Florencia and Montería. During the first decade of the current century, PSP in the Colombian water sector has expanded significantly, with the award of at least 19 additional contracts in other localities. There is a wide diversity in scope of these experiences, ranging from management contracts to outright concessions that involve investment commitments. In 2006, close to 10 per cent of the water supply companies in Colombia were either in private hands or in those of mixed private–public ownership. This figure, however, understates the real extent of PSP in water in Colombia since the private sector is less involved in the operation of companies in smaller localities. Thus, as a share of population supplied, the importance of the private sector is larger than 10 per cent (19 per cent by some sources – Owen 2006). This shows that the private sector is an important and growing agent in the Colombian water sector.

Recognizing the importance of adequate water supply and sanitation for the alleviation of poverty, this chapter investigates the impact of PSP on the poor and how social policies are designed to help them. We find that PSP has had either a neutral or positive effect on access, and no effect on affordability. The results on affordability are quite surprising given that prior research in other parts of the world (some of which is contained in other chapters in this book) shows that privatization is associated with a rise in tariffs, due presumably to the reduction of implicit public subsidies or to higher investment and quality targets. Thus, we would expect that affordability problems for the poor would be higher in areas with privately operated water systems. However, the results do not confirm this hypothesis. On the contrary, they indicate that there is no difference in the affordability problems faced by households living in areas served by a private provider compared to those served by a public or non-profit provider.

We explore the possible role of social policies applied in the sector that may have contributed to making private sector participation more acceptable to the poor. It appears that the particular subsidy scheme used in Colombia to reduce the financial burden of utility bills on poorer households is a contributing factor. This is particularly so when we consider that the errors of exclusion of this subsidy – poor deserving households who do not receive the benefit – are extremely low, at least among connected households.

Therefore, the main policy conclusion that emerges from this study is that in the presence of appropriate social policies, PSP does not necessarily imply that the welfare of poorer households is negatively affected. The impact of reforms on the poor will depend on many factors, including how the reform is structured, but particularly on the complementary social policies that are implemented to help the poor.

However, we also find that in the particular case of the Colombian water sector, the subsidy scheme is overly generous, with significant leakages to non-deserving households (high errors of inclusion). In addition, many poor households are not connected and therefore do not benefit from the subsidy scheme. The subsidy may also be creating barriers for further private sector participation due to the particular form in which it is implemented. The challenge for Colombia therefore is to improve the targeting properties of the subsidy without compromising the social benefit that it currently provides.

This chapter is organized as follows. The next section presents a brief history of the Colombian water sector, and characterizes its general regulatory framework, including institutional arrangements, and tariff-setting procedures. It also presents some general statistics of access to water and affordability. Then a description of the different PSP modalities in the Colombian water sector is given. Subsequently, we present some empirical evidence about the impacts of PSP on poverty-related issues in Colombia. In the final section we discuss the subsidy scheme used in Colombia to make water more affordable to the poor, its targeting properties, and its potential role in explaining our empirical results. The chapter concludes with some policy recommendations.

## The Colombian water sector

### Legal and institutional framework

The 1991 Constitution identified public utilities as one of the core services that contribute to the well-being of the population. It reiterated the ultimate responsibility of the state to ensure the provision of these services to the citizens (Article 365), and its obligation to supervise and control their provision (Article 334). It also assigned an important role to the private sector by stating that these services may be provided directly by the state or *delegated to the private sector or community based organizations* (Article 365).

Law 142/94 is a Public Utilities Law that covers all sectors within a consistent and unifying framework. It promoted the adoption of cost-recovery principles for utilities charges and established limits on the extent of cross-subsidization between customers. It also provided the institutional framework under which public utilities sectors currently operate. It created the Superintendence for Public Services (SSPD), which was to be in charge of ensuring the adequate control and supervision of the public utilities, and defined the functions of three Regulatory Commissions – one for water and sanitation (CRA), another for electricity and gas (CREG) and a third one for telecommunications (CRT).

In Colombia, the line Ministries are responsible for policy formulation, as well as for the granting of concessions. In the case of the water and sanitation sector, the line ministry is the Ministry of Environment, Housing and Territory Development (MMAVDT for its acronym in Spanish). The high level of decentralization in Colombia, however, places significant limits on the authority of the MMAVDT. As is common in many other countries, water and sanitation services in Colombia are under municipal responsibility. Municipal governments are responsible for guaranteeing service provision and have the power to tax services and to define service areas. They are also responsible for territorial planning issues. Central government retains the responsibility for supervising the *ex-post* performance of all utilities nationwide and has the obligation to intervene in the management of utilities found to be in financial difficulties. This is carried out by SSPD, who supervises the performance of the public services providers and monitors their compliance with service and safety standards and other regulations issued by CRA.[1]

CRA defines tariff-setting methodologies based on standard formulas and investment plans presented by the operators and sets quality and technical standards to be followed by the utilities. Its two central functions are the regulation of monopoly power and the promotion of competition. Since the MMAVDT Minister presides over this regulatory commission, it is imperative to get his or her approval before any decision is taken by CRA. Finally, CRA does not have responsibility over environmental regulation, which is handled by decentralized environmental authorities.

### Access to water services

This section presents the situation of access to water services in Colombia using data from the Living Standards Measurement Surveys of 1997 and 2003. Table 4.1 shows the distribution of households in urban and rural areas, with households classified by expenditure per capita quintiles.[2] This information is important in understanding poverty issues and access to water in Colombia. The table shows that the population is concentrated in the urban areas (75 per cent of all households). While urban areas concentrate most of the poor in number, the poorest 20 per cent of households are predominantly in rural areas and 72 per cent of rural population is classified as poor.

Access to water is still a major problem in Colombia, although it is mostly confined to rural areas. Taking the more flexible definition of the United Nations,[3] we can see that in 2003 only 78 per cent of the

*Table 4.1* Urban/rural household distribution by expenditure per capita quintile, 2003

| | *Urban* | | *Rural* | |
|---|---|---|---|---|
| | *No.* | *%* | *No.* | *%* |
| Q1 | 962,669 | 43.0 | 1,276,488 | 57.0 |
| Q2 | 1,542,172 | 68.9 | 697,505 | 31.1 |
| Q3 | 1,802,005 | 80.5 | 435,934 | 19.5 |
| Q4 | 2,022,464 | 90.3 | 217,524 | 9.7 |
| Q5 | 2,116,122 | 94.6 | 121,225 | 5.4 |
| Total | 8,445,432 | 75.4 | 2,748,676 | 24.6 |

*Source*: ECV (2003), Departamento Nacional de Estadística, DANE.

poorest households had access to water at a national level (Table 4.2).[4] In the case of piped connections in exchange for payment the situation is not very different. However, while there is quasi-universal coverage in urban areas, a substantial number of the rural households (especially the poorest) still do not have piped connections.

Table 4.3 shows that not all households with access to piped water have continuous service (24 hours a day, seven days a week). We observe that,

*Table 4.2* Access to water (according to United Nations and access to piped connections with payment)

| *Year* | *Quintile* | *Access (United Nations)* | | | *Piped (connections with payment)* | | |
|---|---|---|---|---|---|---|---|
| | | *Urban* | *Rural* | *Total* | *Urban* | *Rural* | *Total* |
| 1997 | Q1 | 94.4 | 43.4 | 62.7 | 94.4 | 40.8 | 61.1 |
| | Q2 | 96.9 | 54.9 | 83.0 | 96.9 | 52.6 | 82.2 |
| | Q3 | 99.2 | 62.8 | 92.2 | 99.1 | 58.1 | 91.2 |
| | Q4 | 98.8 | 65.5 | 95.2 | 98.8 | 63.1 | 94.9 |
| | Q5 | 99.4 | 82.4 | 98.9 | 99.4 | 78.9 | 98.7 |
| 2003 | Q1 | 97.5 | 63.6 | 78.2 | 93.9 | 48.1 | 67.8 |
| | Q2 | 98.8 | 70.6 | 90.1 | 96.7 | 56.0 | 84.1 |
| | Q3 | 99.1 | 72.3 | 93.9 | 98.1 | 59.2 | 90.5 |
| | Q4 | 99.4 | 76.2 | 97.1 | 98.5 | 65.6 | 95.3 |
| | Q5 | 99.2 | 63.6 | 97.2 | 98.6 | 53.9 | 96.2 |

*Note*: acceptable solutions for water are: household connection, well, and public fountain.
*Source*: ECV (1997, 2003), Departamento Nacional de Estadística, DANE.

*Table 4.3* Connected households with uninterrupted water service

| | | *Water (%)* | | |
|---|---|---|---|---|
| | | *Urban* | *Rural* | *Total* |
| 1997 | Q1 | 61.8 | 70.7 | 65.5 |
| | Q2 | 71.3 | 62.5 | 69.5 |
| | Q3 | 73.2 | 63.1 | 72.0 |
| | Q4 | 77.0 | 66.5 | 76.3 |
| | Q5 | 84.1 | 74.3 | 83.8 |
| 2003 | Q1 | 63.0 | 60.0 | 61.8 |
| | Q2 | 68.7 | 60.7 | 67.1 |
| | Q3 | 75.7 | 63.3 | 74.2 |
| | Q4 | 78.6 | 63.9 | 77.6 |
| | Q5 | 83.2 | 67.5 | 82.7 |

*Source*: ECV (1997, 2003), Departamento Nacional de Estadística, DANE.

*Table 4.4* Households by quality characteristics of piped water (percentage), 2003

| | | *Urban* | *Rural* | *Total* |
|---|---|---|---|---|
| Q1 | Sediments | 11.3 | 14.9 | 13.3 |
| Q2 | | 9.0 | 14.7 | 10.7 |
| Q3 | | 8.8 | 13.9 | 9.8 |
| Q4 | | 7.2 | 17.1 | 8.2 |
| Q5 | | 8.0 | 22.1 | 8.7 |
| Q1 | Bad taste | 7.0 | 10.2 | 8.8 |
| Q2 | | 6.1 | 8.0 | 6.7 |
| Q3 | | 4.3 | 8.1 | 5.1 |
| Q4 | | 4.6 | 7.1 | 4.9 |
| Q5 | | 3.8 | 25.2 | 5.0 |
| Q1 | Bad smell | 5.1 | 6.2 | 5.8 |
| Q2 | | 3.6 | 3.6 | 3.6 |
| Q3 | | 3.2 | 6.2 | 3.8 |
| Q4 | | 2.8 | 4.6 | 2.9 |
| Q5 | | 2.9 | 20.7 | 3.8 |
| Q1 | Bad colour | 11.9 | 16.5 | 14.6 |
| Q2 | | 10.9 | 17.0 | 12.8 |
| Q3 | | 11.1 | 16.5 | 12.1 |
| Q4 | | 11.1 | 17.4 | 11.8 |
| Q5 | | 9.9 | 40.7 | 11.6 |
| Q1 | None of the above | 76.6 | 69.3 | 72.4 |
| Q2 | | 79.0 | 71.5 | 76.6 |
| Q3 | | 80.7 | 73.0 | 79.2 |
| Q4 | | 81.6 | 68.5 | 80.3 |
| Q5 | | 81.3 | 45.3 | 79.4 |

*Source*: ECV (2003), Departamento Nacional de Estadística, DANE.

in general, the quality of service in terms of continuity has declined over the period 1997–2003. Table 4.4 provides another view of water service quality in Colombia. These figures are only available for 2003. They show that service quality is quite poor for a considerable share of households in all income quintiles, and especially for those located in rural areas.

According to the SSPD, in 2005 there were 7.6 million people who were still being supplied with water that was unfit for human consumption (Owen 2006). The majority of the people affected (6.7 million of the 7.6 million) were generally living in areas where the system covered less than 10,000 residents.

While improvements in terms of access have been made, there is still a long way to go, and water quality is still a major challenge in Colombia.

## PSP in the Colombian water sector[5]

There are two clearly defined stages in the PSP in the water and sanitation sector in Colombia. The first stage, between 1991 and 1997, consisted first in the formation of mixed public–private companies to administer and operate water and sanitation services and, later, in individual municipalities awarding contracts to private operators. Table 4.5 presents a summary of the main PSP experiences during this first stage of PSP in the water sector. The second stage, from 1997 onwards, involved a more structured approach, with the central government playing a vital role in structuring and funding these processes.

*Table 4.5* Main PSP experiences before 1997

| *Municipality* | *Population 1995* | *Type of PSP* | *Year* |
|---|---|---|---|
| Tunja | 113,454 | Concession | 1996 |
| Palmira | 255,303 | Municipal/Private partnership | N/A |
| Neiva | 289,516 | Municipal/Private partnership | 1996 |
| Cartagena | 780,527 | Municipal/Private partnership | 1995 |
| Santa Marta | 329,556 | N/A | N/A |
| Montería | 303,468 | Minority share ownership | 1994 |
| Florencia | 112,737 | Minority share ownership | 1991 |
| Barranquilla | 1,126,729 | Minority share ownership | 1991 |

*Source*: CONPES (1997), National Planning Department and DANE.

One example of the first stage of development was the creation in 1991 of a public share company in Barranquilla to operate the water and sanitation infrastructure. Private ownership started at 11 per cent of the shares and increased later to 50 per cent. Following this experience other cities (Montería, Florencia, and Santa Marta) adopted similar PSP models.

Cartagena involved a private operator in its mixed ownership company in 1994. This operator was responsible for managing and operating the water and sewerage services in the city and was committed to investing US$9.67 million, to match the investments committed by the regional authorities. The explicit objective of this contract was to increase coverage rates to 92 per cent in water and 90 per cent in sanitation.[6]

In Chipichape in 1994 a completely private company was established to operate and manage the water and sewerage services. This company bills customers for water and sewerage services and then pays the

Municipal Company of Cali (EMCALI), the owners of the infrastructure, a transport fee for using the water and sewerage mains and for the disposal of wastewater.

This first stage was characterized by a rather haphazard and piecemeal approach to PSP. A review by the National Committee on Social and Economic Policy (CONPES 1997) identified several problems with the way in which PSP was undertaken by different municipalities during this period. These problems were:

- The goals of each process were not clearly specified and the coverage targets set were not based on the real capacity of generating funds from tariff charges.
- The scope and limits of PSP were not clearly defined.
- No evaluations were made of the state of the infrastructure, the investments required to improve it, and the funding capacity from tariffs and other sources.
- Tendering of these contracts was not done in a competitive manner. Although the Constitution and the Public Services Law 142/1994 required a competitive process to involve the private sector in the management and operation of water and sewerage services, Municipalities did not specify clearly the selection criteria for potential operators and the time given to companies to prepare their bids was considered very short. In seven examples analysed by Ochoa (1996), potential bidders had at most four months to present a bid, with the extreme case of 19 days in the case of Barranquilla. In three of the seven cases only one bid was received.

In response to these problems, in 1997 the national authorities developed the Management Modernization Programme (Programa de Modernización Empresarial, or PME). This initiative was aimed at promoting PSP in the water sector, but on a more technically sound basis. The policy was implemented by the MMAVDT and provided the municipalities with technical, legal and financial advice in structuring a reform process of their water and sanitation services that included the participation of the private sector.

Under the PME, a municipality receives technical advice and co-financing for the hiring of consultants in order to structure a reform process in which tariff levels, investment commitments and coverage targets are mutually consistent. If the municipality intends to keep tariffs at a low level, funding additional investments would be difficult. In this case, the municipality would have no choice but to tender a management contract where the private sector is not required to undertake investments. If tariff levels are sufficiently high to fund some investment, then a concession-type contract with the private operator assuming some investment commitments could be contemplated.

Some investment needs can also be financed through the central government budget if municipalities chose to undertake reforms within the framework of the PME programme. Specific targets for the improvement of services to low-income households are also a central feature of the reforms structured under PME.

Other features of the PME programme include the creation of autonomous operating companies in the participating municipalities and a commercial orientation of management and services. In addition, under PME the central authorities explicitly promote the association of neighbouring municipalities in a given reform process with the objective of exploiting economies of scope and scale in the operation of services by tendering contracts over a more aggregate geographical area than just a municipality.

Contracts are competitively tendered and the duration of contracts varies from 10 to 30 years. The tendering variable is either the price bidders are willing to pay for each share of the company or the tariff offered to users.

From its creation in 1997 to early 2003, 19 contracts have been tendered under the PME framework.[7] Given that some contracts cover more than one municipality, the number of municipalities involved is larger. A summary of these contracts is presented in Appendix 4.1. In practice almost all contracts tendered to date have mixed public–private investment commitments with US$152 million of the total US$355 million required investment being funded by the private sector (equivalent to 43.8 per cent of total) and benefiting 1.8 million individuals. The rest of the investment program is funded from national government funds or municipal funds.

Table 4.6 presents the information available from the National Planning Department (DNP) regarding the institutional structure and ownership of water providers in 2005. From this table we can see that 89 providers – nearly 10 per cent of the total – have some form of PSP, including those companies that have a concession or contract under the PME framework.[8]

From this information we can conclude that there are at least three types of PSP schemes in operation in Colombia. First, a municipality may have tendered a contract under the PME framework. It is most probable that these contracts were tendered after 1997.[9] Secondly, a municipality

*Table 4.6* Types of water providers in Colombia, 2005

| *Type of organization* | *Number* |
|---|---|
| Private company | 62 |
| Mixed property company | 27 |
| Municipal company | 1 |
| State-owned company | 196 |
| Organization within municipality | 188 |
| Share company wholly owned by public sector | 12 |
| Other (authorized organizations and others) | 369 |
| Total | 855 |

*Source*: National Planning Department (DNP) of Colombia.

may have followed an independent process and have a mixed ownership company. Thirdly, a municipality may have followed an independent process and have a totally private operator providing services within its coverage area. We have to bear in mind that there are some municipalities where there is more than one operator, some with PSP and others without.

## Empirical evidence about the impact of PSP on poverty-related issues in Colombia

Gómez-Lobo and Meléndez (2007) use two years of the Living Standards Households surveys (1997 and 2003) and econometric techniques from the modern policy evaluation literature to identify the impacts of PSP in the Colombian water sector on access, quality and affordability. In this section we present that part of the research that explores the impact of PSP on access and affordability. Our variables of interest are: (a) whether a household has a connection to piped water supply; and (b) whether the monthly water bill (excluding sewerage) is above 3 per cent of monthly household expenditure. Since the main interest is the impact of PSP on low-income households, observations are disaggregated according to expenditure per capita deciles.[10] Households in the first four deciles are considered poor.

Table 4.7 presents some summary statistics. As previously shown, at the national level there has been an important increase in the percentage of households connected to piped water. Although this increase in coverage has benefited households across the whole income distribution, it has been strongest among the lowest deciles. This is to be expected since

*Table 4.7* Summary statistics by expenditure per capita deciles (percentage)

| *Decile* | *Proportion of households with a water connection* | | *Expenditure on water as a proportion of total household expenditure* | |
|---|---|---|---|---|
| | *1997* | *2003* | *1997* | *2003* |
| 1 | 54 | 62 | 4.9 | 4.8 |
| 2 | 69 | 74 | 2.7 | 2.9 |
| 3 | 78 | 82 | 2.1 | 2.5 |
| 4 | 87 | 87 | 2.0 | 2.4 |
| 5 | 91 | 89 | 1.7 | 2.2 |
| 6 | 91 | 92 | 1.7 | 2.0 |
| 7 | 94 | 95 | 1.7 | 1.9 |
| 8 | 96 | 96 | 1.4 | 1.6 |
| 9 | 98 | 95 | 1.4 | 1.4 |
| 10 | 99 | 98 | 1.2 | 1.2 |

*Sources*: ECV (1997, 2003), Departamento Nacional de Estadística, DANE.
*Notes*: All statistics are the average of each variable in each equivalent expenditure decile. Survey weights were used to estimate averages in each case.

the higher-income households already had high coverage rates. Affordability is still an important issue given that households in the lowest expenditure decile devote, on average, 5 per cent of their expenditure to water bills. We also observe that the proportion of expenditure devoted to water bills decreases as income increases.

The above figures do not reveal the impact of PSP in the water sector per se. From a methodological point of view, identifying the impact of PSP is not trivial. In the first place, the Living Standards survey is representative at the national level and may not be representative at the municipal level. Therefore, it may be erroneous to form a pseudo panel of municipalities and compare the average of each variable between municipalities with and without PSP or compare the 'before and after' effect of those municipalities that introduced PSP between 1997 and 2003. In order to robustly identify the different effects of private ownership versus public ownership, making sure that the results obtained are not due to systematic differences in the household and municipal characteristics of each observation, Gómez-Lobo and Meléndez (2007) use several econometric estimation techniques and different sub-samples of data.

One estimation method consists simply in a cross-section regression using the 2003 data, with a dummy variable taking a value of one if the household resides in a municipality with PSP that year.[11] The coefficient associated with this dummy variable gives an indication of the effect of

PSP on the dependent variable. This estimation method has the potential drawback that municipalities that introduced PSP may in some way be different from municipalities that did not introduce PSP. Thus, the coefficient may be picking up effects of these other characteristics rather than the effect of PSP per se. In order to avoid this problem, the next two estimation methods use data from the 1997 as well as the 2003 waves of the survey. A difference in difference (DID) estimator is used to compare the change in the variable of interest between 1997 and 2003 for treated municipalities (with PSP) to the change during the same period for non-treated municipalities (without PSP). The first application of this method uses the full sample of municipalities while the second application drops from the sample municipalities with non-PME type contracts.[12] The final estimation method used is a *propensity score-matching* estimator.[13] This type of matching estimator compares the outcome of one household that was treated with one (or several) untreated 'similar' households. Similarity in this context refers to having common characteristics.

Each estimation method is used on different sub-samples of the data. The first sub-sample includes household observations from all municipalities available in the survey. The second sub-sample drops all of the observations from the largest cities (Bogotá, Cali and Medellín) and the third sub-sample drops all of the observations that belong to the largest municipality in each department, thus leaving observations from the relatively smaller municipalities in each region. The main reason for such sample selection was to use homogenous data, thus making the treatment and control groups more comparable.

We summarize the results of Gómez-Lobo and Meléndez (2007) for the access and affordability variables in Tables 4.8 and 4.9. Since the main interest is in the effects of PSP on the poor, the results are presented for both the full sample of households and the subset of households in the first four deciles of the income distribution. To simplify the presentation, for each model we show only the sign of the parameter relating to the presence of PSP when this coefficient is statistically different from zero. A positive (+) sign implies that the estimated coefficient is positive and statistically different from zero. A negative (−) sign implies that the estimated coefficient is negative and statistically different from zero, while a blank implies that the estimated coefficient is not statistically different from zero.[14]

### Water connections

The results on the impact of PSP on access depend upon the method of estimation (Table 4.8). A simple linear regression using 2003 data

*Table 4.8* Impact of PSP on water coverage rates

| | | *All municipalities in the data Medellín and Bogotá* | *All municipalities except Cali, in each department* | *All municipalities excluding largest* |
|---|---|---|---|---|
| Simple regression using 2003 data only | Decile 1–10 | + | + | + |
| | Decile 1–4 | + | + | + |
| Difference in difference estimator using 1997 and 2003 data | Decile 1–10 | | | + |
| | Decile 1–4 | | | + |
| Difference in difference dropping municipalities with PSP but not PME | Decile 1–10 | + | + | + |
| | Decile 1–4 | | + | + |
| Propensity score matching using 2003 data | Decile 1–10 | + | + | + |
| | Decile 1–4 | + | | |

*Source*: Gómez-Lobo and Meléndez (2007).

indicates that for both the full sample of observations and the poorer households sample, water connection rates in municipalities with PSP are higher than in non-PSP municipalities. However, results obtained using DID estimators indicate that PSP does not have a statistically significant effect on water coverage, except when the sample is restricted to the relatively smaller municipalities. In this last case there is a positive and significant effect on coverage rates on both the full sample and the poorer households sample.

When the DID estimator is used dropping all municipalities that had non-PME PSP at some date, almost all the estimated coefficients secure positive and significant results, for both the full households sample and the poorer households sample. In this case, observations in PME municipalities are being compared with observations in municipalities that never had any type of PSP.

Finally, the propensity-score estimator indicates a positive and significant effect of PSP. When the sample is restricted to the poorer households, however, in two of the three cases there is no statistically significant effect.

The results for water connections can, then, be summarized as follows. In general, there seems to be a positive or neutral impact of PSP on coverage rates, although in some cases there is no discernible effect. This last result may be due to the fact that coverage rates in urban areas were already quite high in 1997, even for poorer households. Results from the labour supply literature seem to suggest that the difference in difference estimator is more robust than the other estimators (see Blundell and Costa-Diaz 2002). Therefore, we can put somewhat more emphasis on the results from DID estimation. They imply that there is either no effect of PSP on water connection rates or a positive effect if only the smallest municipalities are considered. There were no cases in which PSP was found to have a negative effect on water coverage rates.

### Affordability

Once again, results vary across estimation methods (Table 4.9). The linear regression with 2003 data and the first DID estimator show a positive and significant impact of PSP on affordability in five out of the six cases when all households are included. This implies that in municipalities that had PSP, a larger fraction of households paid water bills that were above 3 per cent of monthly household expenditure. However, when the sample is restricted to the poorer households, the effect of PSP on affordability is not statistically significant and this effect disappears.

If only PME municipalities are compared with non-PSP municipalities, the impact of PSP is negative and statistically significant, for both the full and the restricted samples. This implies that PME municipalities were associated with lower water bills to total expenditure than municipalities that never had private sector participation.

*Table 4.9* Impact of PSP on affordability

| | | *All municipalities in the data* | *All municipalities except Cali, Medellín and Bogotá* | *All municipalities excluding largest in each department* |
|---|---|---|---|---|
| Simple regression using 2003 data only | Decile 1–10 | + | + | |
| | Decile 1–4 | | | |
| Difference in difference estimator using 1997 and 2003 data | Decile 1–10 | + | + | + |
| | Decile 1–4 | | | |
| Difference in difference dropping municipalities with PSP but not PME | Decile 1–10 | – | – | |
| | Decile 1–4 | – | – | – |
| Propensity score matching using 2003 data | Decile 1–10 | | – | – |
| | Decile 1–4 | | | |

*Source*: Gómez-Lobo and Meléndez (2007).

With the propensity-score matching estimator the PSP variable is found in general to have no effect on affordability among the poor.

Overall, these results suggest that PSP is not associated with higher affordability problems for poorer households. As measured by the proportion of poor households that pay more than 3 per cent of their monthly income on water bills, there is no statistically measurable effect of PSP on the poor.[15] However, there is evidence from two of the estimation methods that PSP did increase the number of households facing an affordability problem when the full sample is used. Thus, it seems that PSP did increase tariffs, but this principally affected the wealthier households. This last result is probably due to the subsidy scheme used in Colombia to protect poor households from high utility service bills, an issue that will be discussed further below. Although PSP brings about higher bills as a proportion of expenditure, households in the lower deciles receive a subsidy that helps to neutralize this effect.

## Utility subsidies in Colombia

To what extent are the results of PSP concerning affordability the result of the particular water subsidy scheme used in Colombia? First we describe the subsidy scheme and present an analysis of its targeting properties. We then return to this question and discuss the implications of the subsidy scheme for the water sector and PSP in particular.

In order to address the financial hardship related to utility bills for poor households, a system of cross-subsidies is used in Colombia whereby the poorest households pay a tariff below the average cost of provision, while the higher-income households and the industry and retail sectors pay a surcharge or 'contribution' to finance the subsidies granted. These cross-subsidies have existed for a long time. However, Law 142 of 1994 formalized these cross-subsidies, setting limits to the amount of the surcharge and the subsidy for different types of dwellings.

The tool to target subsidies in Colombia is the socioeconomic stratification of dwellings, a system by which all dwellings are categorized into one of the six groups according to observable characteristics. Dwellings that are identified to be the poorest correspond to category one. In category six, at the other extreme of the distribution, are the dwellings identified as the wealthiest. According to the 1994 law, the maximum subsidy over the subsistence consumption level is 50 per cent for category one, 40 per cent for category two and 15 per cent for category three. In addition, the maximum contribution over the total consumption of categories five and six and of non-residential consumers should be

20 per cent. The neutral tariff rate must reflect the cost recovery principle of service provision.

The cross-subsidies are internal to each operator. In principle, those utilities that generate surpluses must transfer them to 'solidarity and income redistribution funds', which are funds managed by central authorities that are supposed to distribute surcharge surpluses across regions in order to cover operating losses. In practice, surpluses are rarely transferred and local deficits are funded entirely by national or local governments.

### Evaluation of the water subsidy

Using the household socioeconomic category and the water expenditure data available from the Living Standards survey of 2003, as well as water prices from the corresponding water providers,[16] obtained through the Superintendence of Public Services, Casas, Medina and Meléndez (2005) evaluate the subsidy system in two dimensions: focalization (or targeting properties) and the impact on affordability (see Table 4.10). The sample used in this evaluation is composed of 62 per cent of the households connected to water in the urban areas of Colombia in 2003.[17]

There are several approaches to evaluating the focalization properties of a subsidy. One common approach is to calculate *the errors of inclusion* and *exclusion*. The *error of inclusion* is equal to the share of households that should not be receiving a subsidy but in practice do receive it. It is an indicator of the leakage of national resources to non-deserving households. The *error of exclusion,* on the other hand, is equal to the share of households that should be subsidized based on their poverty level and are not receiving a subsidy. There is usually a trade-off between the errors of inclusion and exclusion as discussed in Gómez-Lobo and Contreras (2003). Another approach is to use a relative distribution curve (also known as a Lorenz curve) and calculate its associated Gini coefficient. The Gini coefficient varies between −1 and 1, with negative values implying a more progressive distribution of benefits.

Casas *et al.* (2005) find that the inclusion and exclusion errors are 58 per cent and 0.3 per cent respectively (see Table 4.10). This shows that although the poorest are not excluded from the subsidy scheme, a large amount of resources goes towards subsidizing consumption for households that do not belong to the poorer segments of the population. In other words, such subsidies could be considered as universal. In the first nine income deciles well over 90 per cent of households receive a subsidy while 65 per cent of households in the richest decile also receive this benefit. Not surprisingly, the Gini coefficient for this water subsidy is of

*Table 4.10* Evaluation of the subsidy system – the case of water

| *Variable* | *D1* | *D2* | *D3* | *D4* | *D5* | *D6* | *D7* | *D8* | *D9* | *D10* | *Total* |
|---|---|---|---|---|---|---|---|---|---|---|---|
| *Focalization* | | | | | | | | | | | |
| Percentage of households receiving subsidy (%) | 98.6 | 99.6 | 98.7 | 99.5 | 98.5 | 98.7 | 97.7 | 96.2 | 91.4 | 64.6 | |
| Distribution of subsidized households across deciles (%) | 6.0 | 7.8 | 8.5 | 10.1 | 10.5 | 11.7 | 11.4 | 12.2 | 12.1 | 9.6 | |
| Distribution of subsidies across deciles (%) | 7.0 | 9.5 | 10.6 | 11.5 | 12.5 | 11.7 | 11.1 | 11.2 | 9.3 | 5.6 | |
| Average subsidy (US$2003) | 3.22 | 3.39 | 3.43 | 3.14 | 3.30 | 2.78 | 2.68 | 2.53 | 2.11 | 1.60 | |
| Average contribution (US$2003) | 8.78 | 3.87 | 3.02 | 4.98 | 3.70 | 5.01 | 3.66 | 5.67 | 4.89 | 6.86 | |
| Errors of inclusion (%) | | | | | | | | | | | 58.0 |
| Errors of exclusion (%) | | | | | | | | | | | 0.3 |
| Quasi-Gini coefficient | | | | | | | | | | | –0.01 |
| *Affordability* | | | | | | | | | | | |
| Average household expenditure in water as a share of total income (with subsidy) (%) | 9.5 | 3.7 | 3.1 | 2.6 | 2.3 | 2.0 | 1.8 | 1.6 | 1.4 | 1.0 | |
| Average household expenditure in water as a share of total income (without subsidy) (%) | 14.7 | 6.1 | 4.9 | 4.1 | 3.4 | 2.9 | 2.5 | 2.1 | 1.6 | 1.0 | |
| Average subsidy as a share of income (%) | 8.1 | 2.5 | 1.8 | 1.5 | 1.2 | 0.9 | 0.7 | 0.5 | 0.4 | 0.2 | |

*Source*: ECV (2003), Superintendence of Public Services and calculations by the authors.

−0.01 indicating lack of progressiveness in the subsidy distribution (see Table 4.10). A value of this coefficient close to zero implies that the subsidy is distributed proportionally among the population and therefore does not improve income distribution.

Therefore, the water subsidy in Colombia is not well targeted. Almost all households receive a subsidy, indicating that the scheme is more akin to a universal subsidy than a targeted subsidy. This occurs because most dwellings are classified in one of the three socioeconomic categories liable to receive benefits. The dwelling classification used in Colombia is not discriminating well between poor and non-poor households and should be revised.[18]

On the other hand, the subsidy scheme does indeed reduce the financial burden of water bills in poor households. For example, as a result of the subsidy the average bill for households in the fourth decile falls from 4.1 per cent to 2.6 per cent of household income (see Table 4.10). Although the subsidy is not enough to make water bills fall below the 3 per cent threshold used as the criteria to evaluate affordability when analysing the impact of PSP for the first to third deciles, it does significantly reduce the financial burden on poor households. This provides additional justification as to why additional national resources should be directed to the poorest and why the dwelling classification needs to be revised.

### The subsidy scheme and PSP

We presented evidence indicating that PSP has not made the services less affordable to poorer households and that the negative impacts of PSP on affordability in Colombia seem to be restricted to wealthier households. The fact that PSP does not seem to have affected the water bills of poorer households in Colombia suggests that the generous subsidy scheme in place has served to cushion the potential negative impact of the rising tariffs.

## Conclusions

In this chapter we explored the impact of PSP on the water sector in Colombia, in terms of access to water services and affordability, especially for the poorer segments of the population. We showed that although PSP has been taking place in Colombia since 1991, concerted efforts to promote PSP by local and central authorities only began in 1997. Since then, PSP has been growing in the country and it currently serves around 15 per cent of the urban population. As in other developing countries, access to piped water supply is a major problem in Colombia, especially for large segments of the rural population.

We show that the overall impact of PSP seems to be neutral or somewhat positive with regards to access to piped water.[19] With regards to the affordability of the service, as measured by the proportion of poor households that expend more than 3 per cent of their monthly income on water bills, there seems to be no apparent impact of PSP on the poor. We do find negative impacts if we take a larger sample but a neutral or positive impact is found if we only consider the poorest households. This result suggests that the water subsidy scheme is probably shielding poor households from the financial consequences that may be associated with PSP.

An overview of the subsidy system in place shows an effort on the part of the government to ensure water and sanitation services at prices affordable to the poorest households. It also shows, however, a significant amount of resources going to households that may not need them, at the cost of a deficit that places stress on the cash flows of public and private service providers and probably discourages private investments.

The policy implications are important. The case of Colombia shows that PSP does not necessarily imply higher affordability problems for the poor. It all depends on the complementary social policies that are implemented along with reforms. Thus, more effort should be directed towards designing effective social policies in the utility sectors when discussing water sector reform. While the spirit of the subsidy scheme in Colombia is to ensure that households that cannot afford to pay the full price for the basic services will still have access to them, in practice a significant amount of subsidy benefits are going to households that may not need them. This is because of the weakness of the targeting instrument used in Colombia that is based on a socioeconomic categorization of dwellings.

In addition, non-connected households – which account for between 13 per cent and 38 per cent of households in the lowest four income deciles (see Table 4.7) – do not receive any benefit from the subsidy scheme. Since most households are classified in the first three categories, reform needs to be taken in order to better utilize resources to increase coverage for those who do not have access.

Another concern with the subsidy scheme relates to the mechanism used to finance these benefits. The water and sanitation sector in Colombia is extremely segmented, and local in character. Therefore, providers in areas in which there are few or no contributors to the subsidy scheme operate under permanent deficits. Delays from the national and subnational governments to cover these deficits place pressure on their cash flows, thus limiting investment capacity in new connections or service quality improvements. It also discourages private sector participation in these systems.

Therefore, although the water subsidy used in Colombia has been useful as a social policy instrument to help poor households pay their water bills, it is far from perfect. Efforts should be made to improve the targeting properties of the scheme. The resources saved could then be used to subsidize currently unconnected households. The way the subsidy is financed should also be reviewed. Ideally, the cross-subsidy from contributors to beneficiaries should operate at a regional or national level rather than at the local level, as it does at present. This would require a central authority to collect user surcharge contributions from all operators in a region (or at the national level) and then distribute these resources according to the number of subsidy beneficiaries of each firm. The existing 'solidarity' funds could easily be used for this purpose.

## Notes

1. The Superintendence of Public Services (SSPD) issues opinions to the Regulatory Commission and the line ministry regarding the performance of service providers and their compliance with sector laws and regulations. It also investigates irregularities, conducts inspections, penalizes companies that fail to comply with the rules, and has the authority to intervene and liquidate non-performing public enterprises. It also acts as an appeals body for consumer complaints against service providers. Finally, SSPD also has an enforcement role with respect to the utility subsidy scheme to be described further below. It certifies the dwelling categories of residential users in the allocation of subsidies, and ensures that, based on this categorization, the subsidies reach the poor. The President appoints the Superintendent.
2. We use expenditure to classify households in terms of income distribution. The results are very similar if income is used. We use equivalent scales to calculate the expenditure per capita. Every member of the household 18 years old or more has a weight of one, while members under 18 years old have a weight of 0.5.
3. Under this definition, a household is considered to have access to water if it has a connection in its dwelling, or access to a well or public fountain.
4. We do not have an explanation of why in some quintiles coverage rates fall between 1997 and 2003. This may be due to a real fall in these rates, or to statistical errors due to different sample size and geographical coverage of each survey. This issue will be further discussed below.
5. This section is based on CONPES (1995, 1997 and 2003).
6. Since we do not have municipal-level coverage rates we cannot evaluate whether or not these targets were met.

7. Four more contracts as well as two extensions to existing contracts have been signed since 2003 to date within the PME framework.
8. Fernández (2004) presents a somewhat different figure. According to his study, there were over 100 municipalities with private participation in the water sector in 2003, accounting for 15 per cent of the urban population.
9. There is one exception, the city of Cartagena. It had a contract with a private operator since 1995. However it later extended this contract under the PME framework.
10. Households without expenditure information were dropped from the database. As noted above, equivalent scales were used to calculate household expenditure per capita.
11. A more detailed technical discussion can be found in Gómez-Lobo and Meléndez (2007).
12. The information available was not clear as to when non-PME contracts were introduced in the relevant municipalities. Therefore, these municipalities were dropped from the sample in the third model estimated to evaluate whether this possible measurement was affecting the results.
13. See Rosenbaum and Rubin (1984, 1985) and also Heckman, Ichimura and Todd (1997).
14. Each model includes also a set of typical household, regional and municipal-level control variables. See Gómez-Lobo and Melendez (2007) for details.
15. Although not the subject of this book, it is important to note that Gómez-Lobo and Meléndez (2007) do find a positive result of PSP on continuity of service and sewerage connection rates, especially among poor households.
16. Water prices are two-part tariffs composed of a fixed part, and two variable portions, one applying to the first 20 cubic metres consumed, and another applying to water usage beyond that threshold.
17. Not all water providers report to the Superintendence of Public Services, as they should, so price data are not available for the full sample of urban households. Rural households are not included in this exercise because there is no information about their socioeconomic category in the survey.
18. Gómez-Lobo and Contreras (2003) find similar results using the 1997 survey for Colombia.
19. As shown in Gómez-Lobo and Meléndez (2007), the benefits of PSP are clearer in the case of sewerage connection rates and continuity of service.

## References

Andres, L. (2004) *The Impacts of Privatization on Firms in the Infrastructure Sector in Latin American Countries*. Mimeo (Chicago, IL: University of Chicago).

Andres, L., V. Foster and L. Guasch (2006) *The Impact of Privatization on the Performance of the Infrastructure Sector: The Case of Electricity Distribution in Latin American Countries*. World Bank Policy Research Working Paper 3936 (Washington, DC: World Bank).

Blundell, R. and M. Costa-Diaz (2002) 'Alternative Approaches to Evaluation in Empirical Microeconomics', The Institute for Fiscal Studies and Department of Economics, ucc, CEMMAP Working paper CWP 10/02.

Blundell, R., C. Meghir, M. Costa Dias and J. Van Reenen (2004) 'Evaluating the Employment Impact of a Mandatory Job Search Program', *Journal of the European Economic Association* 2(4), June, 569–606.

Casas, C., P. Medina and M. Meléndez (2005) 'Subsidios al consumo de los servicios públicos en Colombia ¿Hacia donde movernos?', *Coyuntura Social*, No. 33.

Cardenas, M. and M. Meléndez (2004) *Provisión de servicios públicos e infraestructura en zonas marginadas y no interconectadas*. Background paper for the World Bank's Recent Developments in Infrastructure (REDI) project, manuscript, Fedesarrollo.

Clarke, G., K. Kosec and S. Wallsten (2004) *Has Private Participation in Water and Sewerage Improved Coverage? Empirical Evidence from Latin America*. World Bank Policy Research Paper No. 3445, November (Washington DC: World Bank).

CONPES (1995) *Participación del sector privado en infraestructura física*. Documento CONPES 2775 (Bogotá, Colombia: CONPES).

CONPES (1997) *La participación privada en agua potable y saneamiento básico: Política y estrategia*. Documento CONPES 2912 (Bogotá, Colombia: CONPES).

CONPES (2003) *Importancia estratégica del programa de Modernización Empresarial en el Sector de Agua Potable y Saneamiento Básico*. Documento CONPES 3253 (Bogotá, Colombia: CONPES).

Estache, A. (2005) *Privatization in Latin America: The Good, the Ugly and the Unfair*, Mimeo (Washington, DC: World Bank).

Fernández, D. (2004) *Recent Economic Developments in Infrastructure (REDI) in the Water Sector – Colombia, Final Report*. February (Washington, DC: World Bank).

Galiani, S., P. Getler and E. Schargrodsky (2005) 'Water for Life: the Impact of the Privatization of Water Services on Chile Mortality', *Journal of Political Economy*, 113(1), 83–120.

Gómez-Lobo, A. and D. Contreras (2003) 'Water Subsidy Policies: a Comparison of the Chilean and Colombian Schemes', *The World Bank Economic Review* 17(3), 391–407.

Gómez-Lobo, A. and M. Meléndez (2007) *Social Policy, Regulation and Private Sector Participation: The Case of Colombia*. Working Paper (Geneva: UNRISD).

Heckmen, J., H. Ichimura and P. Todd (1997) 'Matching as an Econometric Evaluation Estimator', *Review of Economic Studies* 64, 605–54.

Leuven, E. and B. Sianesi (2003) PSMATCH2: Satat Module to Perform Full Mahalanobis and Propensity Score Matching, Common Support Graphing and Covariate Imbalance Testing'. http://ideas.repec.org/c/boc/bocode/s432001.html. Version 3.0.0.

Ochoa, F. (1996) 'Evaluación de la Participación Privada en Acueducto y Alcantrillado', Ministeria de Economía, Dirección Nacional de Planificación and Comisión Regulatorio de Aqua, Bogotá, November.

Owen, D.L. (2006) *Pinsent Masons Water Yearbook, 2006–2007* (London: Masons Solicitors).

Rosenbaum, P. and D.B. Rubin (1984) 'Reducing Bias in Observational Studies using Subclassification on the Propensity Score', *Journal of the American Statistical Association* 79, 516–24.

Rosenbaum, P. and D.B. Rubin (1985) 'Constructing a Control Group Using Multivariate Matched Sampling Methods that Incorporate the Propensity Score', *The American Statistician* 39(1), 33–8.

*Appendix 4.1* Summary of contracts tendered until 2003 under the PME framework

| *Contract*[1] | *Population (×1,000)* | *PSP type* | *Start date* | *Investments (US$ millions)* | | | |
|---|---|---|---|---|---|---|---|
| | | | | *Total* | *Nat.* | *Mun.* | *Pri.* |
| ASOAGUA (La Guajira): Barrancas, Distracción, El Molino, Villanueva | 42.7 | Operation with investment (12 years) | Nov. 2000 | 0.8 | 0.3 | 0.3 | 0.2 |
| ASOSASA (Atlántico): Sabana grande y Santo Tomás | 44.0 | Operation with investment (10 years) | Jun. 2002 | 4.6 | 0.8 | 3.4 | 0.4 |
| Buenaventura (Valle del Cauca) | 350.0 | Management and operation (20 years) | Jan. 2002 | 62.0 | 15.0 | 19.0 | 28.0 |
| Cumaral (Meta) | 9.2 | Construction–operation (10 years) | Jan. 2002 | 1.5 | 0.7 | 0.5 | 0.3 |
| El Charco (Nariño) | 5.3 | Management and operation | Jan. 2002 | 1.6 | 0.7 | 0.6 | 0.3 |
| Guapi (Cauca) | 14.0 | Management and operation (20 years) | Jan. 2002 | 1.0 | 0.2 | 0.4 | 0.4 |
| Istmina (Chocó) | 13.5 | Management and operation (12 years) | Oct. 2001 | 1.7 | 0.1 | 0.1 | 1.5 |
| Maicao (Guajira) | 100.0 | Concession (30 years) | Jan. 2001 | 51.3 | 6.8 | 16.5 | 28.0 |
| Montería (Córdoba) | 320.0 | Concession (20 years) | Jan. 2000 | 70.0 | 4.0 | 28.0 | 38.0 |
| Nátaga (Huila) | 1.8 | Construction–operation (10 years) | Apr. 2001 | 2.8 | 2.2 | 0.6 | – |
| Pondera (Atlántico) | 9.1 | Construction–operation (10 years) | Aug. 2002 | 1.2 | 0.6 | 0.7 | 0.0 |
| Puerto Carreño (Vichada) | 7.5 | Management and operation (20 years) | Jan. 2002 | 2.2 | 0.3 | 1.5 | 0.4 |
| Riohacha (Guajira) | 90.0 | Management and operation (20 years) | Nov. 2000 | 36.1 | 4.4 | 7.5 | 24.2 |
| San Juan Nepomuceno (Bolívar) | 27.0 | Management and operation (10 years) | Dec. 2001 | 3.0 | 0.4 | 2.6 | 0.0 |
| San Marcos (Sucre) | 32.75 | Operation with investment (15 years) | Jul. 2002 | 4.1 | 1.0 | 2.9 | 0.2 |
| Soledad (Atlántico) | 360.0 | Concesión (20 years) | Dec. 2001 | 43.2 | 2.0 | 28.0 | 13.2 |
| Tadó (Chocó) | 9.1 | Management and operation (12 years) | Oct. 2001 | 0.6 | 0.1 | 0.0 | 0.4 |
| Sincelejo-Corozal (Sucre) | 280.5 | Operation with investment (20 years) | Dec. 2002 | 61.0 | 1.9 | 6.1 | 17.0 |
| El Banco (Magdalena) | 51.7 | Operation with investment (16 years) | May 2003 | 6.4 | 1.8 | 4.5 | 0.05 |
| Total | 1,768.2 | | | 355.0 | 43.4 | 123.1 | 152.5 |

*Source*: CONPES (2003) and Ministry of Environment, Housing and Territorial Development (MAVDT).
*Note*: [1]Name of contract is followed by Department (in parenthesis) and by the municipalities involved.

# 5
# Brazil

*André Rossi de Oliveira*

## Introduction

As is the case in many other developing countries, the provision of water services in Brazil was very deficient in the 1950s and 1960s. There were different management models in place involving municipalities who provided water and sanitation services independently, while others formed consortia with neighbouring municipalities, and in some cases the state departments were in charge of the entire production process, including planning, construction and operation.

Recognizing the close link between economic and social development and access to basic public utility services, the military government in Brazil, which took power in 1964, decided to establish the promotion of universal water and sanitation services as one of its main priorities. The creation of the National Housing Bank (BNH) in 1964 was to serve as a vehicle for the implementation of this policy. Its initial mission was to implement an urban development policy, but this was later expanded to include an assessment of the situation of the water and sanitation sector in Brazil and the financing of its expansion.

In order to have access to the financial resources made available by BNH through the Sanitation Financial System (SFS), the municipalities were required to organize service provision in the form of autonomous departments or mixed ownership companies (Turolla 2002). This encouraged the municipalities to operate the water services, with only a few municipalities relinquishing operation of those services to the state.

This situation was changed, however, by the establishment of the National Sanitation Plan (Planasa) in 1971. The plan laid out investment schedules for the sector, as well as tariff, access to credit and other sector policies. It also promoted the creation of state water and sanitation companies (CESB, the acronym in Portuguese, will be used in the rest of the text), encouraging municipalities to grant long-term concessions to those companies in exchange for financial resources coming mostly from BNH. This centralization was justified on two grounds. The first was that there existed economies of scale in large metropolitan areas to be captured and there was a need to reduce planning costs. The second was the alleged need to introduce cross-subsidies, whereby more profitable regions would finance less profitable areas.

The incentives faced by the CESBs under Planasa were such that priority was given to construction and expansion plans, with a detrimental effect on management and operation (Rezende 1996). Loans from BNH, for instance, were not available for activities pertaining to companies' operations, but only for the expansion of infrastructure. As a result of such policies under Planasa, the coverage of water provision in urban areas in Brazil increased from 60 per cent in 1970 to 86 per cent in 1990, while coverage of sewage collection increased from 22 per cent to 48 per cent over the same period of time (Seroa da Motta 2004). On the other hand, lack of interest in the management and operations led to a deterioration of water and sewage systems, leading to high system losses.

By the late 1980s, the performance of the highly centralized Planasa system had deteriorated significantly and the system was abolished in 1988. At the same time, the Brazilian economy was undergoing a hyperinflationary process which led the government to keep companies' tariffs under tight controls in order to avoid fuelling inflation. Dwindling investments due to lack of appropriate financing (BNH ceased to exist in 1996 and this led to a sharp decrease in foreign capital inflow), political meddling and mounting debt service from previous loans suggested a gloomy future for the water and sanitation sector.

As a result, since the mid-1990s, Brazil has been experimenting with various forms of PSP such as concession contracts. In the urban areas, it is estimated that there are some 1,350 water and sewerage entities, of which 32 have been privatized (Owen 2006). Currently, 25 per cent of the population is served by the private sector and this figure could grow to 36 per cent within ten years.

The main objective in this chapter is to study past and present experiences with regard to the private provision of water services in Brazil and to assess the impact on access and affordability indicators. We will also try to analyse the social policies in place to help the poor. The chapter is divided into six sections. In the next section we provide a background account of the recent evolution of the sanitation sector in Brazil, with particular interest in the participation of private capital. We also present a literature review on the private provision of water services in Brazil.

The following section looks at social policies and regulation and describes in detail the specific programmes implemented in the country. There is then a discussion of some indicators of access to and affordability of water supply in Brazil. In the subsequent sections we bring the results from a plethora of estimations of different econometric models that attempt to measure the effects of private provision on access and affordability.

## The private provision of water services in Brazil

### Current developments in the water sector

As discussed above, the Planasa system was dismantled in 1988. Following its collapse, no consistent set of policies for the water and sanitation sector was put in place to fill the vacuum, a situation that has persisted to the present day. A law regulating the management of water resources in Brazil was passed by the Congress (Law 9.433, 8 January 1997). Any attempt to pass legislation specific to the water and sanitation sector has been difficult, mainly because of disputes between municipalities and states over the right to grant concessions.

The Constitution established that public services such as water and sanitation should be provided by the State either directly or through concessions, and also authorized municipalities to grant concessions. The Constitution and the 'Concessions Law' of 1995 (Law 8.987) seem to be ambiguous when it comes to establishing which level of government is responsible for the provision of water and sanitation services and who has the power to grant concessions. The Constitution gave the municipalities the right to grant concessions of public services of local interest, but recognized that the federal and state governments should guarantee the efficient and adequate regulation of water and sanitation services. These two provisions caused confusion over how to regulate water and sanitation services in municipal and metropolitan areas, in most cases part of the concession areas of regional companies.

The 'Concessions Law' also determined that the municipalities should have the power to grant concessions or provide the services themselves. However, it kept the door open for the regional companies (CESBs) to play a role by specifying that the municipalities could only renew concession contracts through public tenders, in which the regional companies could participate.

With the monetary stabilization achieved by the Brazilian economy through the 'Real Plan' (named after of the currency introduced in 1994), the water and sanitation companies tried to recuperate their investing capacity and align their revenues and costs. They were unsuccessful in this. As mentioned before, inappropriate management practices and lack of incentives for efficiency played a significant role in their failure. It should be noted that after investments in water reached their lowest level in the biennium of 1993–94, they recovered in 1998, but then immediately experienced another reduction. The improvements in the period 1994/98 can be attributed to weak fiscal controls, since public companies were allowed to borrow in order to make investments. The end result was a significant reduction in the primary fiscal surplus. When those controls were tightened up again and a sound primary surplus received high priority, investments in the sector suffered a deep reduction. The renewed effort to balance the budget led to the adoption of the 'Law of Fiscal Responsibility' in 2000. This law established limits on public indebtedness, both on direct administration and on companies where the government was the majority shareholder. Moreover, credit ceilings to public sector borrowing prevented the financial system from lending to public companies. Therefore, even when financial resources were available, service providers could not tap into them due to their public status.

In one attempt to restructure the sector, in 2001 the government submitted a legislative bill to Congress (known as PL 4.147), which tried to give water companies administrative and financial autonomy, establishing pricing principles and concession criteria. It also tried to establish the state rather than the municipalities, as the authority with the power to grant concessions in metropolitan areas. The idea was to ensure the financial viability of the state water companies by allowing them to keep, at least in part, their ability to reap scale economies. These gains should be available to finance cross-subsidies to poor municipalities within the area covered by the firm.

The pricing principles introduced by the bill were based on incentive regulation and, more specifically, on price cap and yardstick competition methods. The main objective was to promote efficiency and participation of private capital.

The bill ran into opposition from many stakeholders. The municipalities were opposed to it, principally because it tried to give the states power to grant concessions in metropolitan areas. There was also some resistance from people who were opposed to the idea of the privatization of public services. More precisely, some people questioned the introduction of the private sector in water, arguing that its profit-seeking motive was inconsistent with the provision of essential services such as water.

One of the major concerns of the government of President Lula da Silva, which came to power in January of 2003, was to restructure and restore investments in the water sector. The federal administration set up a task force within the Ministry of Cities to elaborate a draft bill outlining the new regulatory framework for the sector to be submitted to Congress. In a nutshell, the proposal suggests that the concession power should be assigned to municipalities when the service is of local interest and that pricing and concession procedures should both be regulated by autonomous authorities. It should come as no surprise that this proposal ran into the same kind of difficulties as that submitted by the previous administration, opposing those who support municipalities' powers against those who want to preserve the cross-subsidy system operated by state sanitation companies (Seroa da Motta and Moreira 2004).

After a long period of discussions and some modifications, the bill was approved by Congress and sanctioned by the president in January 2007. It establishes criteria for municipalities and states to access federal financing and establishes a council with participation from the civil society. These councils have leverage to influence municipalities' decisions regarding tariff setting and the termination of service because of non-payment. The bill does not clearly define powers of concession – a matter that apparently will have to be decided by the country's highest court. It does, however, establish that investments made by concessionaires will have to be reimbursed in case their contracts are unilaterally terminated by the municipalities.

This new bill may change the context of the Brazilian water and sanitation sector, which still reflects the guidelines laid out by Planasa in 1971. The sector is currently dominated by the regional companies, the CESBs, which still hold concessions from municipalities. The municipal provision of water and sanitation services is concentrated mainly in the states of São Paulo, Minas Gerais and Rio Grande do Sul, either through agencies under direct municipal control, autonomous agencies or municipal companies. There is a small number of cases corresponding to private companies currently holding partial or full municipal concessions.

## Private sector participation in the water sector in Brazil

In the northern region of Brazil, there are only two cities where water is supplied by private companies: Manaus (the capital of the state of Amazonas) and Novo Progresso (in the state of Pará). In the midwest, the states of Mato Grosso, Mato Grosso do Sul and Tocantins have involved PSP in the water sector. In the southeast region, PSP is concentrated primarily in the states of São Paulo and Rio de Janeiro, and also in Espírito

Santo and Minas Gerais. In the south, the states of Paraná and Santa Catarina have involved PSP.

There is considerable diversity in the forms of PSP in terms of financing and tariff structures. In some cases, companies include the entirety of the initial capital cost, while others rely on more complex financing schemes such as equity and debt to finance investment. The tariff structures are based on previous policies such as minimum consumption rates, increasing block-rate tariffs, and differentiated according to user groups. In some cases, price cap regulation is implemented. In most cases, concessions are the contractual instrument of choice. The municipalities in the state of Rio de Janeiro that involved PSP opted mostly for full concessions (including water and sewage), whereas the state of São Paulo preferred partial concessions.[1]

Those private firms that were awarded these concession contracts were principally construction companies involved in public infrastructure works. By entering into the water sector, these firms made a strategic choice to restore their core business which was being affected by the decline in public investment. There were a few cases of concessions being granted to consortia of domestic and international companies where the domestic partner was typically a construction company and the international partner was a company with experience in the water business (Parlatore 2000).

## Social policy and regulation

Despite its abundant natural and human resources and its great potential for economic development, Brazil faces many economic and social challenges. One of the biggest challenges facing the country is to reduce the growing levels of poverty and the increasing inequality. Figure 5.1 shows not only that a large portion of the Brazilian population is below the poverty line, but also that the poverty rate is very unequal across geographical regions. For example, poverty rates for 2003 in the north and northeast regions of around 50–60 per cent are much higher than those found in the midwest, southeast and southern regions which is between 20 and 30 per cent. Although poverty increased in most regions over the 1990s and the early years of the twenty-first century, a recent report by the United Nations shows that poverty has been stabilized or has started to decrease in some regions (United Nations Commission for Latin America and the Caribbean 2006).

The inequality in poverty rates across regions depicted above, however, is only one facet of socioeconomic inequality in Brazil. Brazil has one of

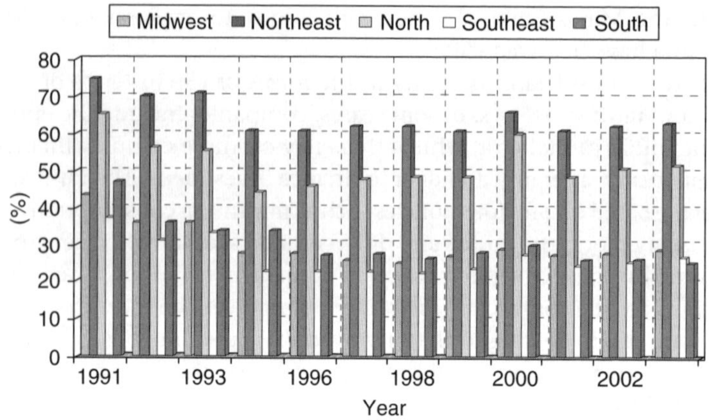


*Figure 5.1* Poverty rates by geographical region
*Sources*: IBGE – 1991 and 2000 demographic censuses; 1992–1999 and 2001–2003 PNADs.

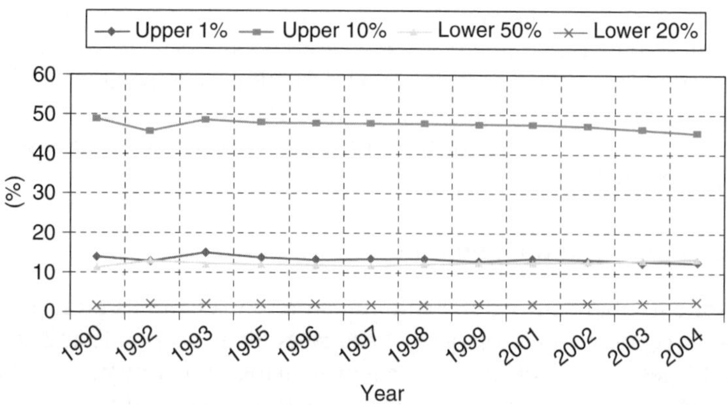


*Figure 5.2* Share of total income by income class
*Source*: IPEA (Institute for Applied Economic Research).

the highest levels of inequality (over 0.61 as measured by the Gini coefficient) to be found anywhere in the world. As can be seen in Figure 5.2, income distribution is also highly unequal. The richest 1 per cent of the population earn a higher percentage of total income than the poorest 20 per cent, and almost the same as the poorest 50 per cent. In addition, the richest 10 per cent earn almost half of the total income in Brazil – a situation that has scarcely improved at all over the past one and a half decades.

Social policies in Brazil have had the intention of addressing these dramatic socioeconomic disparities. For the water sector, public policy in the form of regulation or social policies was centralized by the federal government within the BNH until the late 1980s, which managed the 'Time of Employment Guarantor Fund'[2] (the acronym in Portuguese, FGTS, will be used from now on), a pension fund whose resources could be used to finance projects in the water sector, among other uses. As mentioned before, under the Planasa system those resources were used to encourage municipalities to hand over the provision of water and sewage services to the CESBs (the regional (state) sanitation companies) which would then receive loans at interest rates lower than market rates. In the 1970s–1980s social policy in the sector consisted of heavy investments in the expansion of water supply systems (sewage was not a priority), thereby increasing coverage, and a system of cross-subsidies put in place by the CESBs. The same tariff was applied to all of the different localities served by the company, irrespective of the cost of service provision. As a consequence, users in municipalities where the cost of service was less than the actual cost subsidized those where the provision of services was very high.

The Planasa system of cross-subsidies, low interest loans, (almost) unlimited resources and heavy investment resulted in an impressive expansion of water services coverage. However, this expansion was uneven across the regions. In general, municipalities that did not use the Planasa system, preferring instead to involve municipal companies or autonomous entities, did not fare as well as those that opted for the Planasa system. In addition, low-income families were excluded from the network, since projects financed by Planasa were in general required to yield a reasonable rate of return.

With the ending of BNH and Planasa, the social policies that were put in place over the years were also dismantled. However, some cross-subsidies remained. As a consequence, companies became increasingly inefficient and different parties started to claim rights over the surplus generated by subsidies in some regions where revenues were higher than costs. There was no coherent policy for the water sector to replace the Planasa system. Different ministries and federal government departments were successfully put in charge of designing such policies. There have been many initiatives aimed at increasing investments in low-income population areas and improving water services. The failure was largely the result of not having an integrated policy framework for the water sector. Different ministries, such as the Ministries of Cities, Health, Environment and National Integration, as well as those of Tourism, Defence and Agriculture, were all in charge of increasing investment in the sector. Below we outline some of the most important programmes that were put in place to increase investment in the water sector.

### Pro-Sanitation programme

The objective of this programme, created in 1995, was to promote the improvement of health and quality of life through actions in the water sector, in conjunction with other sectoral policies. It tried to help finance some public water companies to through FGTS. Projects related to this programme included the development of water supply and sanitation infrastructure and institutions. In 2005, Pro-Sanitation became part of the umbrella programme Sanitation for Everyone, which is discussed below.

### Pro-Sanitize programme

Pro-Sanitize, created in 1988, was the first initiative by the state aimed at increasing water supply and sanitation services for low-income families. The objective of the programme was to solve, in a self-sustainable manner, water problems in densely populated urban areas, usually occupied by low-income families, where water supply, sewage collection and treatment, solid waste disposal, drainage and other sanitation services were precarious.

The first stage of the programme, Pro-Sanitize I (1988–96), obtained a US$100 million loan from the World Bank, which amounted to 50 per cent of the programme's funding. Caixa Econômica Federal (a public bank) funded 25 per cent, with resources coming from FGTS, and the remaining 25 per cent came from local water companies and municipal and state governments. Instead of promoting the implementation of conventional water systems, with state of the art – and thus expensive – technologies, the programme invested in simpler systems which, despite their lower cost, used technologies tailored to the communities where they were implemented. In many places, families were grouped together in a sort of 'condominium', and as a result water supply and sewage collection systems were more efficient and less expensive.

The programme was very successful, having exceeded its initial targets. It made drinking water available to 900,000 people, compared with a target of 200,000, and sewage services available to one million people – exceeding the target of 700,000 people by more than 40 per cent.

Following the success of the Pro-Sanitize I programme, the government started the second stage of the programme in 2000, under the name Pro-Sanitize II (also known as the Project of Technical Assistance to Pro-Sanitize). This was funded by a loan of US$30.3 million from the World Bank (85 per cent of the total) and the remaining funds came from the Federal Government. It was managed by the National System of Basic Sanitation (SNSB is the acronym in Portuguese) and lasted until

15 December 2006. The programme provided technical assistance to projects designed to increase water coverage to low-income urban dwellers and poor communities in the outskirts of large cities, targeted 1–2 million people and fostered community involvement and technology adapted to local situations, much as had been the case with Pro-Sanitize I.

**Pro-Community – programme of improvements in communities**

The target group of this programme is families with monthly incomes lower than 12 minimum salaries.[3] They could obtain loans of up to R$5,000 (approximately US$2400)[4] at below-market interest rates for joint projects with public entities concerning construction and the improvement of facilities in the following areas: water supply, sewage, solid waste disposal, improvement of public ways, drainage, electricity distribution, sports and leisure. The programme was funded by FGTS and the federal budget and was managed by *Caixa Econômica Federal*.

**FCP/SAN – programme to finance private concessionaires of sanitation services**

This programme could be used only by private operators of water services, who were entitled to loans at special interest rates to finance projects that could increase coverage of water supply and sewage collection and treatment for low-income familes – namely those with monthly incomes of less than 12 minimum salaries (see note 3). The funding came from FGTS, but the private concessionaire had to match at least 25 per cent of the value of the loan. The *Caixa Econômica Federal* bank was in charge of managing the programme.

**Rural Sanitation Programme**

This programme was part of the 2005 federal government budget, and its objective is to increase coverage and improve the quality of 'environmental sanitation'[5] services in rural areas. The target population is people living in rural areas, especially those in settlements under land reform and localities with up to 2500 inhabitants, as well as communities from the ethnic minorities.

**Sanitation is Life Programme**

A programme of the National Department of Environmental Sanitation, the aim of this scheme is to assure fundamental human rights to access potable water and to life in a sanitary environment, in both cities and the countryside, through the provision of universal water and sewage services, the collection and treatment of solid waste, drainage systems in urban areas, and the control of reservoirs and vectors of transmittable diseases. The programme finances projects to increase the coverage of water supply, sewage and drainage services, as well as to increase efficiency of public water services. Funds come from the federal budget and international institutions.

### Sanitation for Everyone programme

Created in May 2005, this programme tries to replace all of the other programmes that have tried to increase coverage in water supply and used FGTS. One of the main differences of this initiative compared to the previous programmes was the involvement of the private sector to provide water services. Both public and private entities are entitled to get funding from this programme, which comes from FGTS and the FAT[6] (a special fund that finances unemployment benefits and economic development programmes). These companies have to sign a contract that establishes performance targets. Those who manage to achieve the targets on schedule are given loans at reduced interest rates and longer for maturities. Besides the usual water projects in water supply, sewage collection and treatment, institutional development, solid waste and pluvial waters management, the programme also finances the preservation and recovery of water fountains and construction and demolition waste management. The initial amount of financial resources allotted to this programme was R$2.2 billion (approximately US$1.07 billion).

In 2005, the federal government pledged R$700 million (approximately US$342 million) to finance public water projects, and another R$640 million (approximately US$312 million) to private companies for water infrastructure projects. An additional R$800 million (approximately US$390 million) was given in grants to state and municipal governments.

### Policies addressing affordability

The above-mentioned programmes for the water sector present a form of social policy based mainly on favourable loans (investments) to expand and improve the quality of water services, with the intention of benefiting low-income families. Thus, the main concern is to increase access, with affordability being given a much lower priority. Policies that target affordability issues are essentially those based on cross-subsidies, which allow companies to charge 'social tariffs' to low-income families. These are usually expressed in terms of a certain percentage of the full tariff.

Almost all of the water companies, public and private, adopt social tariffs. In the case of state regional companies, their tariff structures generally have to abide by rules specified in state and/or municipal laws, but there are many cases in which they have some leeway in respect of setting tariffs. There is widespread use of increasing block tariffs. For example, residential tariffs follow an increasing block scheme, with higher prices per cubic metre for higher consumption rates. Some companies charge a flat rate up to a certain consumption level, usually around 10 cubic metres. However, some companies (such as SANEPAR, the state water company in the state of Paraná) adopt a two-part tariff, with a fixed rate (independent of consumption level) and a per cubic metre charge.

Most private companies also use social tariffs. Some private companies (like Citágua, in Cachoeiro de Itapemirim, in the state of Espírito Santo) put in place tariff policies designed for low-income families, usually in cooperation with the municipalities. Citágua, for example, gives waivers to low-income families with up to 10 cubic metres of consumption.

## Access to and affordability of water services in Brazil

This section provides some statistics relating to the evolution of the water sector in Brazil. Figure 5.3 shows that access to water services increased significantly in Brazil between 1970 and 2000. As mentioned earlier, heavy public investment was instrumental in improving the coverage. However, the level of coverage in rural areas is still very low. At a national level, household connection rate was 76 per cent in 2000, 90 per cent in urban areas and only 18 per cent in rural areas.[7] Indicators of access to sewage services (including system connections and septic tanks) are even worse: 60 per cent access overall, with 72 per cent for urban and 13 per cent for the rural population.[8]

As mentioned earlier, due to the very high levels of income distribution in Brazil, access to public services is also very uneven. Water supply is no exception to this pattern. Table 5.1 shows the evolution of access to water services by income deciles for the period 1995–2003.

Despite the significant increase in coverage for the lowest deciles over the period, the gap between the poorest and the richest is still very large. In 2003, for instance, the access rate for households in the top 10% income brachet was 31.35 percentage points above that for household in the bottom 10%. Not only is the distribution of access to water by income groups uneven, it is also distributed unevenly by region or locality (urban or rural). Table 5.2 provides us with data which shows how skewed those distributions are.

Coverage rates in rural areas are significantly lower than in urban areas in all geographic regions, but this disparity is more acute in the

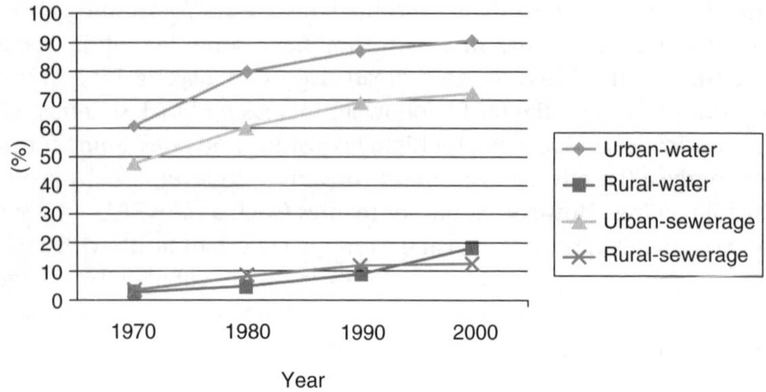


*Figure 5.3* Access to water and sewage services (national averages) – Percentage of households, 1970, 1980, 1990, 2000

*Source*: IBGE – 1970, 1980, 1991 and 2000 demographic censuses.

*Table 5.1* Access to water supply by deciles, 1995–2003 (per cent)

| | *1995* | *1996* | *1997* | *1998* | *1999* | *2000* | *2001* | *2002* | *2003* |
|---|---|---|---|---|---|---|---|---|---|
| *1st decile* | 51.73 | 52.37 | 53.83 | 56.34 | 60.05 | 60.94 | 61.85 | 68.16 | 68.29 |
| *2nd decile* | 54.12 | 54.66 | 56.90 | 59.73 | 62.41 | 69.19 | 71.65 | 73.22 | 75.41 |
| *3rd decile* | 67.26 | 68.15 | 69.45 | 72.81 | 80.13 | 77.94 | 81.33 | 81.98 | 81.15 |
| *4th decile* | 76.47 | 78.22 | 79.42 | 81.95 | 82.68 | 84.70 | 84.07 | 82.26 | 85.63 |
| *5th decile* | 84.52 | 86.89 | 88.57 | 86.66 | 87.76 | 89.19 | 87.68 | 90.26 | 91.02 |
| *6th decile* | 89.89 | 90.02 | 91.26 | 91.65 | 91.71 | 93.05 | 92.46 | 93.26 | 94.18 |
| *7th decile* | 95.12 | 94.29 | 94.19 | 94.61 | 95.73 | 95.51 | 94.91 | 94.25 | 97.26 |
| *8th decile* | 95.37 | 96.44 | 98.21 | 97.72 | 98.08 | 96.97 | 97.45 | 97.84 | 98.26 |
| *9th decile* | 98.52 | 98.79 | 99.11 | 98.97 | 98.74 | 98.08 | 98.63 | 98.74 | 98.90 |
| *10th decile* | 98.79 | 99.12 | 99.79 | 99.53 | 99.90 | 98.90 | 99.02 | 99.64 | 99.64 |

*Note*: Access to water supply is defined as percentage of households with piped water in at least one room of the house.

*Source*: IBGE – PNADs 1995–99 and 2001–03, Demographic Census 2000.

north and northeast, where overall coverage rates are well below those in the midwest, southeast and southern regions. The north and northeast regions of Brazil are much less developed and thus poorer than the other regions. The low water supply access rates only reinforce this disparity. It is also worthwhile drawing a profile of households both with and without access to piped water.[9] This may help policy makers to understand what types of households or regions need more attention. In terms of regional location, we find that a third of households with access to piped water supply are in the southeast region. In addition, around half of the

*Table 5.2* Access to water supply by region and location, 2001–2004 (per cent)

| *Region* | | *2001* | *2002* | *2003* | *2004* |
|---|---|---|---|---|---|
| *North* | Total | — | — | — | 69.54 |
| | Urban | 73.47 | 77.43 | 76.48 | 79.66 |
| | Rural | — | — | — | 39.19 |
| *Northeast* | Total | 67.02 | 69.52 | 71.02 | 72.83 |
| | Urban | 83.99 | 85.91 | 86.80 | 87.73 |
| | Rural | 22.85 | 25.82 | 28.59 | 31.49 |
| *Midwest* | Total | 90.36 | 92.26 | 93.35 | 94.02 |
| | Urban | 93.96 | 95.31 | 96.21 | 96.47 |
| | Rural | 67.17 | 72.03 | 75.56 | 78.69 |
| *Southeast* | Total | 96.83 | 97.32 | 97.60 | 98.11 |
| | Urban | 98.13 | 98.42 | 98.54 | 99.01 |
| | Rural | 81.76 | 83.82 | 85.95 | 86.76 |
| *South* | Total | 96.55 | 97.41 | 97.65 | 97.87 |
| | Urban | 98.28 | 98.78 | 98.64 | 98.74 |
| | Rural | 88.43 | 90.92 | 92.80 | 93.52 |

*Source*: *IBGE* – PNADs 2001–04.

population without access to water are located in the northeast region. This is linked to the fact that the Planasa system placed more emphasis on projects that could generate reasonable rates of return, and these were usually associated with more developed regions. We find that the profile of households and individuals without access to the piped water system are those usually associated with low-income families. Therefore, an increase in coverage of water services should primarily benefit poorer families.

Affordability of water services in Brazil is another important issue. The first indicator we could consider is the percentage of household income spent on water and sewage payments. Figure 5.4 shows the average percentage of household income spent on water and sewage bills by income groups, where these groups are defined in terms of multiples of the minimum salary as of 15 January 2003.[10]

Figure 5.4 is striking evidence of how water and sewage bills are much more burdensome for low-income families than high-income families. For instance, whereas families with incomes no greater than two minimum salaries (MS) spend 1.46 per cent of their monthly budget on water and sewage payments, families in the top tier – that is, those who earn more than 30 MS – spend only 0.29 per cent of their monthly budget on those services (a differences of over five times).

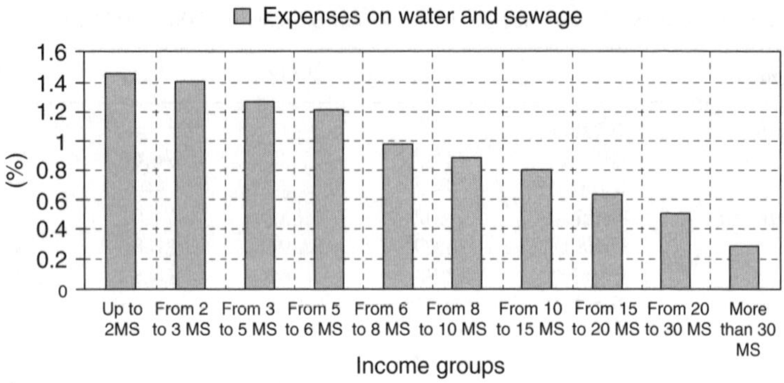


*Figure 5.4* Affordability by income groups
*Source*: IBGE – 2002–03 Survey of Household Budgets (POF).

In order to increase coverage and additional investment, the government has been encouraging PSP in the water since the mid-1990s. What has been the impact of such policy reform, especially on the poor? The next section tries to answer this question by considering the impact of PSP on access and affordability.

## The impact of private provision on the access to water services

Using data from the National Sanitation Information System (SNIS)[11] for 2001–2004, we tried to get a clearer picture of the extent of PSP in the water sector. We present some data which illustrate the evolution of access for four different types of companies: direct public administration, autarky, privately-owned or managed companies and publicly-owned or managed companies.[12] We also analyse the access rate by different categories of operators: local, microregional or regional (Table 5.3).[13]

When considering the overall access rates, data reveal that in 2002–03 the privately owned or managed companies were located in areas with higher coverage rates. In 2004, there is a convergence of access rates in all types of companies around 80 per cent (except for autarky types at regional level, of which there is only one company, located in the northern state of Acre, a poor and sparsely populated state). When we take into account the size of the companies, we notice that those results come mainly from the performance of regional private companies, whose access rates are superior to autarky and publicly-owned or managed companies. Local publicly-owned or managed companies and micro-regional autarkies do better than their private counterparts in that respect.

*Table 5.3* Access to water supply by type and size of operator (percentage)

| | *2001* | *2002* | *2003* | *2004* |
|---|---|---|---|---|
| *Direct public administration* | 72.4143 | 76.9811 | 79.1727 | 83.6724 |
| Local | 72.4143 | 76.9811 | 79.1727 | 83.6724 |
| Microregional | — | — | — | — |
| Regional | — | — | — | — |
| *Autarky* | 83.2240 | 83.3201 | 84.2267 | 82.3152 |
| Local | 83.5663 | 83.6728 | 84.7061 | 82.6169 |
| Microregional | 82.1144 | 84.1454 | 78.5357 | 80.0057 |
| Regional | 36.4918 | 26.0451 | 26.8835 | 29.1208 |
| *Privately-owned company or public company with private management* | 78.4824 | 84.9842 | 88.2946 | 81.4891 |
| Local | 78.0273 | 86.0125 | 90.4376 | 81.5314 |
| Microregional | 79.5160 | 81.2885 | 80.3788 | 79.6817 |
| Regional | 80.8620 | 80.9683 | 85.1671 | 83.5037 |
| *Publicly-owned company or public company with public management* | 75.5677 | 78.6962 | 80.9021 | 80.9004 |
| Local | 95.4283 | 97.4501 | 98.9350 | 98.3338 |
| Microregional | — | — | — | — |
| Regional | 68.6596 | 71.0241 | 71.8857 | 72.1837 |

*Source*: National Sanitation Information System.

We also analysed the efficiency of private and public entities. We look at two indicators: a productivity index, defined as the number of employees per thousand water connections; and an index of losses in distribution (Table 5.4).

The productivity, as measured by the number of employees per thousand water connections, seems to be higher in privately-owned or managed companies than in their state-owned or managed counterparts in all size categories. This may be construed as an indication that private companies are more efficient in terms of using labour.

Distribution losses (due to technical problems, such as leakages) are also lower in privately-owned or managed companies than in public (state)-owned or managed companies, at all size levels (Table 5.5). However, direct public administration and autarkies do better than private enterprises when average figures (over local, microregional and regional numbers) are considered.

*Table 5.4* Productivity index (defined as the number of employees per thousand water connections) by type and size of operator

| | *2001* | *2002* | *2003* | *2004* |
|---|---|---|---|---|
| *Direct public administration* | 4.7742 | 4.8514 | 5.2623 | 7.8864 |
| Local | 4.7742 | 4.8514 | 5.2623 | 7.8864 |
| Microregional | — | — | — | — |
| Regional | — | — | — | — |
| *Autarky* | 5.6661 | 5.6753 | 5.7957 | 5.7753 |
| Local | 5.5528 | 5.5950 | 5.7414 | 5.7264 |
| Microregional | 6.5836 | 5.6416 | 5.2774 | 5.3406 |
| Regional | 19.7956 | 18.1661 | 18.1562 | 17.6457 |
| *Privately-owned company or public company with private management* | 4.2171 | 3.9062 | 3.9879 | 3.9161 |
| Local | 4.2573 | 3.8862 | 4.0055 | 3.8642 |
| Microregional | 4.3998 | 3.9577 | 3.8824 | 4.4958 |
| Regional | 3.7734 | 4.0043 | 4.0233 | 3.9046 |
| *Publicly-owned company or public company with public management* | 4.8325 | 4.7369 | 4.8889 | 4.3840 |
| Local | 6.8786 | 6.7092 | 7.1408 | 5.9078 |
| Microregional | — | — | — | — |
| Regional | 4.1208 | 3.9300 | 3.7629 | 3.6221 |

*Source*: National Sanitation Information System.

The final aspect of public versus private provision considered here is investment (Table 5.6). Investments by privately-owned or managed firms are consistently higher than those by state-owned or managed companies for local and regional sizes (there are no microregional state-owned or managed companies). There is one exception, however. In 2004 local state companies invested more than local private companies. In this instance, a comparison with investment levels of direct public administration and autarkic companies is not very informative, for these two types of companies are in general significantly smaller than privately-owned or managed and state-owned or managed companies.

The data presented above suggest that privately owned or managed companies tend to have a higher level of productivity (as measured by the number of employees per thousand water connections) than other types of firms. It is well known that private firms are particularly concerned

*Table 5.5* Losses in distribution by type and size of operator (percentage)

| | *2001* | *2002* | *2003* | *2004* |
|---|---|---|---|---|
| *Direct public administration* | 35.46 | 33.22 | 31.11 | 29.40 |
| Local | 35.46 | 33.22 | 31.11 | 29.40 |
| Microregional | — | — | — | — |
| Regional | — | — | — | — |
| *Autarky* | 35.03 | 33.02 | 33.08 | 32.21 |
| Local | 35.03 | 32.71 | 32.94 | 32.05 |
| Microregional | 18.38 | 34.33 | 29.71 | 30.49 |
| Regional | 67.52 | 69.00 | 67.96 | 67.36 |
| *Privately-owned company or public company with private management* | 39.46 | 44.05 | 38.67 | 34.61 |
| Local | 38.94 | 43.92 | 38.97 | 33.23 |
| Microregional | 44.65 | 64.29 | 43.20 | 55.55 |
| Regional | 36.46 | 34.70 | 32.66 | 32.34 |
| *Publicly-owned company or public company with public management* | 46.71 | 45.67 | 45.38 | 46.59 |
| Local | 43.43 | 38.79 | 38.13 | 41.17 |
| Microregional | — | — | — | — |
| Regional | 47.75 | 48.48 | 48.67 | 49.30 |

*Source*: National Sanitation Information System.

about productivity and therefore it is natural that they score high on this indicator. Moreover, they have lower distribution losses than state-owned or managed companies, but one that is higher than direct public administration or autarkic companies. In general, private firms invest more than state companies, but local state companies caught up with their private counterparts in that respect in 2004. Finally, we found that private firms are located predominately in areas with higher access rates.

## The effect of private provision on the affordability of water services

As mentioned earlier, the affordability of water services is a major issue in Brazil. What is the impact of PSP on the affordability of water services? Data reveal that the tariffs charged by private entities are higher than those charged by public entities, regardless of the size of the company (local, microregional or regional) (Table 5.7). However, in recent years the average tariffs of publicly owned or managed companies

*Table 5.6* Investments by type and size of operator (reais)

| | *2001* | *2002* | *2003* | *2004* |
|---|---|---|---|---|
| *Direct public administration* | 136,453 | 143,025 | 103,051 | 111,429 |
| Local | 136,453 | 143,025 | 103,051 | 111,429 |
| Microregional | — | — | — | — |
| Regional | — | — | — | — |
| *Autarky* | 532,386 | 557,997 | 547,127 | 457,646 |
| Local | 513,055 | 521,469 | 548,444 | 43,498 |
| Microregional | 405,258 | 602,675 | 608,623 | 541,249 |
| Regional | 3,454,310 | 5,785,507 | 5,174 | 4,792,125 |
| *Privately-owned company or public company with private management* | 8,480,585 | 9,251,176 | 9,686,444 | 5,560,121 |
| Local | 3,041,880 | 3,725,373 | 2,876,373 | 1,516,336 |
| Microregional | 4,537,491 | 4,189,317 | 4,408,821 | 3,548,445 |
| Regional | 50,494,616 | 52,993,655 | 65,273,375 | 69,234,409 |
| *Publicly-owned company or public company with public management* | 23,075,694 | 25,684,752 | 17,500,183 | 25,234,027 |
| Local | 1,950,979 | 1,587,031 | 2,007,810 | 2,431,745 |
| Microregional | — | — | — | — |
| Regional | 30,757,408 | 35,542,911 | 25,246,369 | 37,178,080 |

*Source*: National Sanitation Information System.

have increased, approaching those of the private sector. On average, direct public administration has the lowest tariffs.

That private firms tend to have higher tariffs than state companies is to be expected. Perhaps state companies' social equity concerns can explain this finding. In addition, it is not unusual for state companies to be controlled by local politicians, whose principal concern is with their fate in the coming elections. That might make it harder for state companies to increase tariffs.

## Conclusion

Despite the heavy public investment programmes undertaken by the government from the 1970s onwards to increase access to water, the provision of water services in Brazil is still very deficient. As was shown in this chapter, lack of access is predominantly a rural phenomenon

*Table 5.7* Tariffs by type and size of operator (reais per cubic metre)

| | *2001* | *2002* | *2003* | *2004* |
|---|---|---|---|---|
| *Direct public administration* | 0.6316 | 0.5648 | 0.6884 | 0.6682 |
| Local | 0.6316 | 0.5648 | 0.6884 | 0.6682 |
| Microregional | — | — | — | — |
| Regional | — | — | — | — |
| *Autarky* | 0.7033 | 0.7613 | 0.8579 | 0.8968 |
| Local | 0.7025 | 0.7529 | 0.8529 | 0.8890 |
| Microregional | 0.6206 | 0.9941 | 0.9989 | 1.2714 |
| Regional | 0.9597 | 1.0358 | 0.9922 | 0.9406 |
| *Privately-owned company or public company with private management* | 1.0511 | 1.2867 | 1.3580 | 1.3660 |
| Local | 1.0027 | 1.2573 | 1.3527 | 1.3392 |
| Microregional | 1.2546 | 1.5426 | 1.3049 | 1.3641 |
| Regional | 1.3213 | 1.3651 | 1.4725 | 1.7715 |
| *Publicly-owned company or public company with public management* | 1.0397 | 1.1582 | 1.3087 | 1.4641 |
| Local | 0.9030 | 0.9378 | 1.0687 | 1.1797 |
| Microregional | — | — | — | — |
| Regional | 1.0872 | 1.2484 | 1.4178 | 1.6063 |

*Source*: National Sanitation Information System.

(especially in the poorest regions of the country), although poor households in urban areas are still not connected. We also demonstrated that the poor bear a relatively greater burden from water and sewage bills. In other words, the poorer households are having difficulties accessing and paying for water.

There have been some improvements, especially in providing incentives for increasing investment and introducing social policies to benefit the poorest households. These policies have been structured mainly in the form of programmes managed by different ministries. The main objective of most of these projects has been to increase the production capacity and the coverage of water supply, especially to low-income families, while others were tailored to increase coverage and improve the quality of service in rural areas. There has been some relative success since coverage rates for the lowest three deciles (the poorest households) have been increasing. This could be an indication that the poor have been benefiting from social policies. In spite of the relative success of social policies in reducing inequality, the distribution of access across income deciles in Brazil continues to be very uneven.

We have argued that these social policies, which principally encourage investments through loans, have focused essentially on increasing coverage but have tended to neglect the affordability issue. Policies that target affordability issues are based essentially on cross-subsidies and increasing block tariffs, which allow companies to charge 'social tariffs' to low-income families.

There is no federal regulatory agency in charge of tariff setting or other regulatory functions in the water sector. In addition, the few state regulatory agencies that have been established are not yet effective and small municipalities' administrations lack the knowledge, staff and capacity to regulate effectively. Tariff-setting rules are, by and large, the result of negotiations between the companies and the state or municipal administrations.

One option to solve the problem of access and affordability is to rely on public investments and state-owned companies. Although this model has served the sector well in the past, it now seems to have reached its limit. Restrictions imposed on public investment by a macroeconomic policy with strict targets combined with constraints on state-owned companies' ability to increase debt have sharply decreased the level of investment in the water sector. As a result, many levels of government have been resorting to PSP. Despite the limited experience of PSP in the country, we were able to show that the private sector is usually in charge of service provision in areas that have high coverage rates. We also showed that private companies are usually able to achieve higher levels of productivity and efficiency, as well as lower losses. In terms of the levels of investment, we found that in general (if microregional private companies are excluded from the comparison) they are higher for private companies. Finally, private firms generally charge higher tariffs.

We argued that the impact of PSP would have been greater if there were better social policies that placed an emphasis on the design of tariffs, so that low-income families were not affected adversely. Universal service obligations, currently absent from most concession contracts, could be negotiated with or even imposed on private operators.

## Notes

1. Full concessions comprise water and sewerage services whereas partial concessions comprise only water services.

2. In Portuguese, *Fundo de Garantia por Tempo de Serviço.*
3. Most governmental programmes use the minimum salary as the unit of measurement of income in order to define the target population. The last change in the value of the minimum salary in Brazil occurred on 1 April 2007, when it became R$380. At the then current exchange rate, 12 minimum salaries corresponded to approximately US$2,200.
4. The exchange rate, on 2 April 2007, was 2.047 reais per US$. Unless otherwise stated, all dollar values in the text were calculated using this exchange rate.
5. This is a new concept concocted by the government to convey the message that water and sewage services cannot be thought of dissociated from their environmental impacts.
6. Portuguese, *Fundo de Amparo ao Trabalhador.*
7. These are all national figures.
8. Since our main concern in this chapter is with water services, sewage numbers are only mentioned here in this broad picture of the evolution of access to sanitation services in Brazil.
9. The discussion that follows is based primarily on a monograph by Marcelo Quintão (2006) entitled *Setor de Saneamento Básico no Brasil: Características do Setor, Perfil de Acesso do Usuário e Participação da Iniciativa Privada.* The monograph was written under the supervision of this chapter's author.
10. The minimum salary was R$200, then approximately US$58 at the average exchange rate at the time, and approximately US$88 at the exchange rate in November 2005.
11. Maintained by the Programme for the Modernization of the Sanitation Sector (PMSS) of the Brazilian Ministry of Cities.
12. Direct public administration means a department of the local or state administration. An autarky is an autonomous entity under federal, state or local government control. A privately-owned or managed company is a company whose capital is predominantly private or which is managed by someone appointed by the private partners or shareholders. Finally, a publicly-owned or managed company is a state-owned company or a company managed exclusively by state appointees
13. Local operators are those that provide water service only to the municipality where they are located. Microregional operators are those which provide services to more that one municipality, normally in small numbers and adjacent to each other, including intermunicipal consortia. Regional providers are those that serve several municipalities, including the CESBs (state companies).

## References

Estache, Antonio, Andrés Gómez-Lobo and Danny Leipziger (2001) 'Utilities Privatization and the Poor: Lessons and Evidence from Latin America', *World Development* 29(7), 1179–98.

Fujiwara, Thomas (2004) *A Privatização Beneficia os Pobres? Os Efeitos da Desestatização do Saneamento Básico na Mortalidade Infantil.* Paper presented at the 33rd Annual Meeting of the Brazilian Association of Post-Graduate Centers in Economics, Natal, 6–9 December (Rio de Janeiro: ANPEC).

Galiani, Sebastian, Paul Gertler and Ernesto Schargrodsky (2005) 'Water for Life: the Impact of the Privatization of Water Services on Child Mortality', *The Journal of Political Economy* 113(1), 83–120.

Mello, Marina F. (2001) *Privatização do Setor de Saneamento no Brasil: Quatro Experiências e muitas Lições*. Discussion Paper No. 447, Economics Department (Rio de Janeiro: PUC-Rio).

Noll, Roger G., Mary Shirley and Simon Cowan (2000) 'Reforming Urban Water Systems in Developing Countries', in Anne O. Krueger (ed.), *Economic Policy Reform: The Second Stage* (Chicago, IL: University of Chicago Press).

Owen, D.L. (2006) *Pinsent Masons Water Yearbook, 2006–2007* (London: Masons Solicitors).

Parlatore, Antônio C. (2000) 'A privatização do setor de saneamento no Brasil', in Armando C. Pinheiro and Kiichiro Fukasaku (eds), *A Privatização no Brasil: O Caso dos Serviços de Utilidade Pública* (Rio de Janeiro: BNDES).

Rezende, F.C. (1996) 'Políticas públicas e saneamento básico: A compesa entre o estado e o mercado', *Revista de Administração Pública* 30(4), 87–107.

Seroa da Motta, R. (2004) *Questões Regulatórias do Setor de Saneamento no Brasil*. Technical Note No. 5 (Rio de Janeiro: IPEA).

Seroa da Motta, R. and Ajax R.B. Moreira (2004) *Efficiency and Regulation in the Sanitation Sector in Brazil*. Discussion Paper No. 1059 (Rio de Janeiro: IPEA).

Shleifer, Andrei (1998) 'State versus Private Ownership', *Journal of Economic Perspectives* 12(4), 133–50.

Turolla, Frederico A. (2002) *Política de Saneamento Básico: Avanços Recentes e Opções Futuras de Políticas Públicas*. Discussion Paper No. 922 (Rio de Janeiro: IPEA).

United Nations Commission for Latin America and the Caribbean (2006) *Social Panorama of Latin America 2006* (Santiago, Chile: ECLAC).

Wooldridge, Jeffrey M. (2002) *Econometric Analysis of Cross Section and Panel Data* (Cambridge, MA: The MIT Press).

# 6
# Malaysia

*Cassey Lee*

## Introduction

Infrastructure development has been an important component of Malaysia's economic development strategy since the country achieved independence in 1957. Significant amounts of investment were made in the infrastructure sector to enhance and maintain the country's export competitiveness. These investments have also contributed to the eradication of poverty and have raised the standards of living throughout the country. However, despite the progress made in these areas, levels of infrastructure development across and in the different sectors have been distinctly uneven.

In the water sector, the more developed states have achieved almost universal access while others continue to struggle with providing access to treated water supply, particularly in rural areas. The inability to recover revenue from water produced (non-revenue water) continues to be a serious problem in the sector. Underinvestment in the sector has also resulted in the deterioration of the water distribution systems.

In Malaysia, water is constitutionally under the responsibility of the state and some states have opted to privatize the provision of water supply. However, there is currently no consensus about whether or not privatization is the solution to water problems in Malaysia. Implicitly, some states continue to support privatization, but others have no plans to privatize their water sector. Many non-governmental organizations (NGOs) continue to vehemently oppose privatization in general – and water in particular. Surprisingly, despite the significant amount of interest generated by the debate on the efficacy of privatization, to our knowledge there have been no empirical studies on the issue in Malaysia.

This chapter attempts to shed some light on the impact of privatization on the Malaysian water sector by employing a quantitative empirical analysis. Malaysia is a useful country on which to base a study of the impact of privatization in the water sector since the country has a variety of forms of institutions in its water sector – full privatization, partial privatization and public ownership. The country is also a developing economy, with a significant rural population where access to supply water continues to be a serious problem. Malaysia also reflects the policy reform issues confronting the Asia region. Finally, this is the first study of the Malaysian water sector using household expenditure data.

The outline of the rest of the chapter is as follows. The next section gives a brief background of the water sector in Malaysia. This is followed by a discussion of water institutions in Malaysia. Then we examine social and economic regulation in the sector, and follow this with a discussion of water tariffs. Issues of equity, access, and affordability are examined in the following section using household expenditure data.

## The water sector in Malaysia

### The role of the water sector in development

Infrastructure development has made significant contributions to Malaysia's economic growth and development since the country's independence in 1957.[1] Malaysia's success in transforming its economy from one predominantly dependent on primary commodity exports in the 1950s and 1960s (for example, rubber and tin) to an economy based on manufacturing activities is due partly to the government's emphasis on investments in infrastructure development. Foreign direct investment (FDI) has played a significant role in the development of the manufacturing sector in Malaysia. The availability of efficient infrastructure, among other things, has been instrumental in attracting FDI in the manufacturing sector.

Infrastructure development has also made important contributions to socioeconomic development in Malaysia. Following the racial riots in Malaysia in 1969, the Malaysian government began to place an increasing emphasis on solving two problems that were perceived to be the main causes of social instability in the country – namely, poverty and unequal wealth distribution. Thus, the Malaysian government's development policy since the early 1970s has also focused on both poverty eradication and wealth redistribution (between the three main races of the country). Both the number of poor households and the incidence of poverty in Malaysia have declined substantially in the past 30 years (see Table 6.1).

*Table 6.1* Poverty and income distribution in Malaysia, 1970–2004

| | *1970* | *1980* | *1990* | *2004* |
|---|---|---|---|---|
| *No. of poor households* | | | | |
| Rural | 1,203,400 | 568,500 | 530,300 | 219,700 |
| Urban | 402,600 | 97,600 | 89,100 | 91,600 |
| Total | 1,606,000 | 666,100 | 619,400 | 311,300 |
| *Incidence of poverty (%)* | | | | |
| Rural | 58.7 | 47.8 | 21.8 | 11.9 |
| Urban | 21.3 | 17.9 | 7.5 | 2.5 |
| Total | 49.3 | 39.6 | 17.1 | 5.7 |
| *Mean monthly household income (RM, at current prices)*[1] | *1970* | *1979* | *1995* | *2004* |
| Bumiputra | N/A | 492 | 1,604 | 2,711 |
| Chinese | N/A | 938 | 2,890 | 4,437 |
| Indian | N/A | 756 | 2,140 | 3,456 |
| All ethnic groups | N/A | 693 | 2,020 | 3,249 |
| Gini coefficient | N/A | 0.51 | 0.46 | 0.46 |

*Sources*: 1970 poverty figures are from the Fifth Malaysia Plan (p. 86); 1980 poverty figures are from the Fourth Malaysia Plan (p. 34); 1979 mean household income figures are from Bruton (1992: 319); 1990 poverty figures are from the Sixth Malaysia Plan, p. 32; 1995 mean household income figures are from the Eighth Malaysia Plan, p. 61; 2004 figures are from the Ninth Malaysia Plan, p. 330 and p. 333.
*Note*: [1]Exchange rate of RM3.70 = US$1. N/A = not available.

The achievements in wealth redistribution remain a contentious issue, even though the mean household income levels in all ethnic groups have increased significantly during the same period (Table 6.1). The Gini coefficient, which measures income inequality, is relatively high (0.46) and has not declined.

One important aspect of the poverty eradication programme in Malaysia is the provision of adequate infrastructure services (such as water and electricity), especially in rural areas. This emphasis can be seen from the Federal Government's development expenditures in these sectors (Table 6.2). In the Eighth Malaysia Plan, the Federal Government's development expenditure for the infrastructure sector amounted to about RM39.7 billion (or US$10.7 billion).[2] Of this amount, 12.1 per cent were allocated to water supply. These funds were used primarily for capital expenditures such as the construction of dams, new treatment plants, the rehabilitation and upgrading of treatment plants and distribution systems.

The allocation for the rural water supply programme in Malaysia has increased during the period 1976–90 (Table 6.3). For the more remote

*Table 6.2* Infrastructure development expenditures, 1996–2005 (RM million, current prices)

| *Sector* | *7th Malaysia Plan, 1996–2000* | *8th Malaysia Plan, 2001–2005** |
|---|---|---|
| Water supply | 2,382.7 | 4,810.0 |
| Sewerage | 665.3 | 1,666.0 |
| Energy | 2,543.6 | 2,288.8 |
| Transport | 20,484.2 | 30,941.8 |
| Total | 26,075.80 | 39,706.60 |

*Source*: Eighth Malaysia Plan.
*Note*: *Allocation.

*Table 6.3* Rural Water Supply Programme, 1971–2005

| *Development Plan* | *Allocation (RM million)* | *Beneficiaries (person)* |
|---|---|---|
| Second Malaysia Plan (1971–75) | 5 | N/A |
| Third Malaysia Plan (1976–80) | 147 | 300,000 |
| Fourth Malaysia Plan (1981–85) | 350 | 1,800,000 |
| Fifth Malaysia Plan (1986–90) | 1,430 | 2,022,600 |
| Sixth Malaysia Plan (1991–95) | N/A | 1,500,000 |
| Seventh Malaysia Plan (1996–00) | 12 | 53,000 |
| Eighth Malaysia Plan (2001–05)* | 734 | 354,000 |

*Source*: Actual expenditures*, Third Malaysia Plan, pp. 377, 379 and 383, Fourth Malaysia Plan, p. 337, 339 and 342, Fifth Malaysia Plan, p. 471 and 476, Sixth Malaysia Plan, p. 340. Mid-Term Review of the Eighth Malaysia Plan, p. 258, Ninth Malaysia Plan, p. 380.

rural areas (especially in Sabah and Sarawak), alternative water supply systems such as gravity flow, tube well and rainwater harvesting were also implemented. One such project under the Eighth Malaysia Plan is the Alternative System of the Rural Water Supply Programme, which benefited 43,000 people in Sabah and 10,000 people in Sarawak.[3]

**Water resources**

Although Malaysia has abundant water resources, they are not distributed equally across the different states in the country. Several interstate water transfer projects and agreements between the different states have been implemented to deal with the unequal distribution of water resources. Direct extraction from rivers is the most important source of raw water – accounting for two-thirds of raw water supply in the country

*Table 6.4* Raw water resources in Malaysia, 2003 (cubic metres/year)

| *State* | *Direct extraction from river* | *Storage dam* | *Groundwater* | *Total* |
|---|---|---|---|---|
| Kedah | 335,531,444 | 1,766,168 | 0 | 357,297,612 |
| Sarawak* | 58,035,000 | 0 | 0 | 58,035,000 |
| Labuan | 9,938,360 | 2,975,940 | 0 | 12,914,300 |
| Perlis | 16,097,000 | 15,175,000 | 2,493,000 | 33,765,000 |
| Pahang | 246,827,600 | 0 | 0 | 246,827,600 |
| N.Sembilan | 162,716,598 | 80,134,090 | 331,785 | 243,182,473 |
| Sabah | 196,094,090 | 72,381,086 | 12,064,928 | 280,540,104 |
| Perak | 343,877,960 | 0 | 0 | 343,877,960 |
| Melaka | 143,120,024 | 54,928,877 | 0 | 198,048,901 |
| Kuching** | 108,040,941 | 0 | 0 | 108,040,941 |
| Sibu** | 33,827,631 | 0 | 0 | 33,827,631 |
| Pulau Pinang | 278,526,228 | 29,337,081 | 0 | 307,863,309 |
| Terengganu | 85,075,726 | 55,960,145 | 79,012 | 141,114,883 |
| Selangor*** | 909,768,401 | 939,680,294 | 0 | 1,849,448,695 |
| Johor | 167,141,518 | 256,073,108 | 0 | 423,214,626 |
| Kelantan | 39,364,288 | 1,742,340 | 42,165,524 | 83,272,152 |
| LAKU** | 32,500,699 | 29,751,900 | 1,678,015 | 63,930,614 |
| Total | 3,186,483,508 | 1,539,906,029 | 58,812,264 | 4,785,201,801 |

*Source*: MWA (2005).
*Note*: *Excluding the divisions of Kuching, Sibu, and LAKU.
**Kuching and Sibu are divisions within the state of Sarawak.
***Includes Kuala Lumpur and Putrajaya.

(Table 6.4). Second in importance are storage dams. Groundwater is an important source of raw water in some of the less developed states such as Sabah and Kelantan.

### Design capacity and production

Water capacity and production in Malaysia has increased rapidly as a result of the significant amount of public expenditure in the water sector. The water supply design capacity and production in Malaysia expanded at a compounded average growth rate of 7.8 per cent and 7.6 per cent, respectively, between 1981 and 2003. By 2003, the water supply design capacity and production had reached 13,343 mld and 11,054 mld, respectively.

### Water coverage

The water supply coverage in rural and urban areas in the various states has also improved significantly in most states since 1980 (Table 6.5).

*Table 6.5* Urban and rural water supply coverage, 1980–2003 (percentage of population)

| *State* | 1980 | | *1985* | | *1990* | | *1995* | | *2000* | | *2003* | |
|---|---|---|---|---|---|---|---|---|---|---|---|---|
| | *Urban* | *Rural* | *Urban* | *Rural* | *Urban* | *Rural* | *Urban* | *Rural* | *Urban* | *Rural* | *Urban* | *Rural* |
| Johor | 87 | 28 | 92 | 61 | 96 | 67 | 99 | 96 | 100 | 98 | 100 | 99 |
| Kedah | 90 | 52 | 95 | 58 | 98 | 69 | 100 | 89 | 100 | 97 | 100 | 99 |
| Kelantan | 58 | 17 | 65 | 30 | 70 | 40 | 85 | 45 | 63 | 48 | 72 | 57 |
| Melaka | 98 | 70 | 100 | 82 | 100 | 98 | 99 | 97 | 100 | 99 | 100 | 99 |
| Negeri Sembilan | 87 | 66 | 89 | 75 | 96 | 89 | 98 | 95 | 100 | 99 | 100 | 99 |
| Pahang | 92 | 47 | 95 | 65 | 98 | 70 | 98 | 86 | 98 | 89 | 98 | 89 |
| Perak | 96 | 55 | 98 | 75 | 99 | 77 | 98 | 84 | 100 | 99 | 100 | 99 |
| Perlis | 90 | 45 | 93 | 50 | 97 | 75 | 99 | 89 | 100 | 97 | 100 | 99 |
| Pulau Pinang | 97 | 78 | 98 | 85 | 99 | 96 | 98 | 98 | 100 | 99 | 100 | 99 |
| Sabah | 99 | 18 | 100 | 38 | 100 | 52 | 87 | 42 | 89 | 60 | 90 | 59 |
| Sarawak | 87 | 20 | 95 | 33 | 98 | 47 | 93 | 80 | 100 | 92 | 100 | 92 |
| Selangor | 90 | 65 | 95 | 73 | 90 | 85 | 100 | 92 | 100 | 98 | 100 | 99 |
| Terengganu | 75 | 25 | 85 | 40 | 100 | 54 | 90 | 77 | 84 | 78 | 97 | 79 |
| Kuala Lumpur | | | | | 100 | — | | | | | | |
| Labuan | | | | | — | — | | | 100 | 100 | 100 | 100 |
| Malaysia | | | | | 96 | 67 | 96 | 82 | 97 | 85 | 98 | 86 |

*Sources*: 1980 and 1985: Fifth Malaysia Plan, p. 472. Figures for Sabah includes Labuan FT. Figures for Selangor include Kuala Lumpur. 1990: Seventh Malaysia Plan, p. 361. Figures for Sabah includes Labuan FT. 1995: Eighth Malaysia Plan, p. 284. Figures for Sabah includes Labuan FT. Figures for Selangor include Kuala Lumpur and Putrajaya FT. 2000: Mid-Term Review of Eighth Malaysia Plan, p. 257. Figures for Selangor includes Kuala Lampur and Putrajaya FT. 2003: Malaysia Water Association (2005).

*Table 6.6* Water consumption in Malaysia, 2003

| | *Population served* | *Domestic water consumption ($m^3$)* | *Non-domestic water consumption ($m^3$)* | *Total water consumption ($m^3$)* | *Per capita domestic water consumption (litre per day)* |
|---|---|---|---|---|---|
| Johor | 2,931,650 | 204,471,885 | 89,771,186 | 294,243,071 | 191 |
| Kedah | 1,668,044 | 141,613,051 | 49,451,417 | 191,064,468 | 232 |
| Kelantan | 865,523 | 34,343,485 | 12,798,236 | 47,141,721 | 109 |
| Melaka | 681,756 | 55,925,509 | 52,333,426 | 108,258,935 | 225 |
| Negeri Sembilan | 909,025 | 62,279,282 | 44,666,278 | 106,945,560 | 202 |
| Pahang | 1,298,456 | 77,020,703 | 47,749,296 | 124,769,999 | 162 |
| Perak | 2,105,966 | 164,205,440 | 54,547,917 | 218,753,357 | 213 |
| Perlis | 216,454 | 17,023,079 | 2,689,725 | 19,712,804 | 215 |
| Pulau Pinang | 1,414,080 | 137,654,109 | 85,735,510 | 223,389,619 | 266 |
| Sabah | 2,027,468 | 57,007,465 | 35,452,649 | 92,460,114 | 77 |
| Sarawak | 2,194,919 | 116,151,542 | 763,421,162 | 879,572,704 | 145 |
| Selangor | 6,748,040 | 478,995,217 | 245,490,214 | 724,485,431 | 194 |
| Terengganu | 864,385 | 56,981,602 | 42,962,716 | 99,944,318 | 180 |
| Labuan | 80,000 | 5,902,324 | 3,397,688 | 9,300,012 | 202 |
| Malaysia | 24,005,766 | 1,609,574,693 | 843,388,420 | 2,452,963,113 | 194 |

Universal access has almost been achieved in most urban and rural areas in the various states in Malaysia. However, there are a few states where the coverage of water supply is low, particularly in rural areas. The three states with the lowest coverage of water supply in rural areas are Kelantan (57 per cent), Sabah (59 per cent) and Terengganu (79 per cent). These are states with relatively high levels of poverty and a larger share of the population living in rural areas. It is likely that these states may not have the financial capacity to improve water supply coverage.

## Water consumption

The distribution of population across the different states of Malaysia is fairly uneven. A significant proportion of the population is concentrated in the more developed states (such as Kuala Lumpur, Johor, Pulau Pinang and Selangor) or in the large states (such as Sabah and Sarawak) (Table 6.6). Total water consumption is highest in the states of Sarawak, Selangor (including Kuala Lumpur), Pulau Pinang and Perak. By contrast, smaller states (such as Perlis) and less developed states (such as Kelantan and Sabah) have relatively low levels of total water consumption. This is likely to be partly due to a lack to access to treated water supply. Domestic per capita water consumption does not seem to be correlated with per capita GDP for the various states.[4]

## Water institutions in Malaysia

### Public and private participation

Under Malaysia's Federal Constitution, water resources fall under the jurisdiction of the respective states. In the past, treatment and distribution of water was undertaken exclusively by state water agencies. These may differ from state to state and can be either State Public Works Departments (PWD), State Water Supply Departments (WSD), or State Water Supply Boards (WSB).

Since the early 1990s, many states have opted to establish water supply companies via corporatization (via establishment of limited liability firms that are wholly owned by the state). In a few cases, these companies were privatized via partial or full divestiture of equity in these companies. Table 6.7 summarizes the current situation of water institutions in Malaysia.

Some states have fully privatized the provision of water services. These include the more developed states (in terms of GDP per capita), such as Selangor, Pulau Pinang and Johor. In most cases, the state government continues to hold equity in the privatized water entities. A few states (Labuan, Negeri Sembilan and Sabah) have chosen a dual structure water system – whereby distribution is undertaken by state agencies and water treatment is privatized via concessions. Some of the smaller states (Melaka and Perlis) and less-developed states (Kedah, Sarawak and Pahang) have generally chosen to maintain a public water provision system. In 2003 The four states where water services are fully privatized (namely, Kelantan, Selangor, Pulau Pinang and Johor) accounted for 49 per cent of total water production and 46.2 per cent of total population served. It is estimated that 64 per cent of the total population is served by the private sector.

### Financial performance in the water sector

In 2003, the Malaysian water sector experienced a revenue–cost deficit of about RM245.5 million (or about 9.1 per cent of costs – defined as operating and maintenance costs).[5] About half of the states in Malaysia are currently experiencing a financial deficit in their water operations (see Table 6.8). Of these, states with large deficits include Selangor (–RM449.1 million) and Sabah (–RM125.0 million).[6] Interestingly, the unit revenue exceeds the unit cost in all the states experiencing financial deficits in water operations, with the exception of Labuan.[7] Of the four states where water is fully privatized – namely, Selangor, Pulau Pinang, Johor and Kelantan – only one state (Selangor) suffered losses in 2005. However,

*Table 6.7* Water supply institutions in Malaysia, 2005

| | |
|---|---|
| *Public Works Dept* | |
| Kedah | (1) Production and distribution by PWD<br>(2) Privatized production and distribution<br>(3) Privatization of 5 treatment plants |
| Sarawak | (1) Production and distribution by PWD<br>(2) Miri, Bintulu and Limbang (LAKU) – served by a state-owned corporatized body |
| Labuan | (1) Distribution by PWD<br>(2) Management contract of production |
| Perlis | Production and distribution by PWD |
| *Water Supply Dept* | |
| Pahang | Production and distribution by WSD |
| Negeri Sembilan | (1) Distribution by WSD<br>(2) Privatization of two water treatment plants |
| Sabah | (1) Distribution by WSD<br>(2) Privatization of three water treatment plants |
| *Water Supply Board* | |
| Perak | (1) Distribution by WSB<br>(2) Privatization of three water treatment plants |
| Melaka | Production and distribution by WSB |
| *Water Supply Company* | |
| Pulau Pinang | Privatized in 2000:<br>Production and distribution by PBA Holdings Berhad (state government share 55%) |
| Terengganu | Corporatized in 1999:<br>Production and distribution by Syarikat Air Terengganu Sdn Bhd (state government share 100%) |
| Selangor | Privatized in 2002:<br>(1) Monopoly distribution by Perbadanan Urus Air Selangor (state goverment share 30%)<br>(2) seven water treatment plants (four existing, three BOT) operated by 5 firms |
| Johor | Privatized in 2001:<br>Production and distribution by SAJ Holdings Sdn Bhd (state government share 0%) |
| Kelantan | Privatized in 1996:<br>Production and distribution by Air Kelantan Sdn Bhd (state government share 70%) |

*Source*: MWA (2004).

*Table 6.8* Financial performance of water operations in Malaysia, 2003

| *State* | *Cost* | *Revenue* | *Revenue Cost gap* | *% Deficit* | *Unit cost* | *Unit revenue* |
|---|---|---|---|---|---|---|
| Kedah | 117,110,842 | 148,520,086 | 31,409,244 | | 0.37 | 0.81 |
| Sarawak | 26,209,664 | 22,001,870 | −4,207,794 | 16.1 | 0.48 | 0.51 |
| Labuan | 16,555,975 | 9,640,336 | −6,915,639 | 41.8 | 1.35 | 0.98 |
| Perlis | 13,748,304 | 12,849,629 | −898,675 | 6.5 | 0.43 | 0.67 |
| Pahang | 109,257,244 | 98,722,938 | −10,534,306 | 9.6 | 0.47 | 0.83 |
| Negeri Sembilan | 72,752,318 | 99,561,120 | 26,808,802 | | 0.32 | 0.95 |
| Sabah | 200,872,317 | 75,850,000 | −125,022,317 | 62.2 | 0.80 | 1.15 |
| Perak | 166,221,930 | 201,056,555 | 34,834,625 | | 0.55 | 0.95 |
| Melaka | 77,837,946 | 105,486,723 | 27,648,777 | | 0.62 | 1.20 |
| Kuching | 55,743,344 | 62,795,270 | 7,051,926 | | 0.54 | 0.91 |
| Sibu | 21,247,969 | 19,508,893 | −1,739,076 | 8.2 | 0.76 | 0.98 |
| P. Pinang | 107,501,332 | 167,950,719 | 60,449,387 | | 0.38 | 0.75 |
| Terengganu | 45,619,654 | 80,750,864 | 35,131,210 | | 0.34 | 0.89 |
| Selangor | 1,310,523,468 | 861,421,335 | −449,102,133 | 34.3 | 1.07 | 1.28 |
| Johor | 270,722,202 | 382,373,342 | 111,651,140 | | 0.59 | 1.23 |
| Kelantan | 34,183,814 | 45,704,857 | 11,521,043 | | 0.43 | 1.05 |
| LAKU | 40,283,687 | 46,679,330 | 6,395,643 | | 0.68 | 0.96 |
| *National average* | 2,686,392,010 | 2,440,873,867 | −245,518,143 | 9.1 | 0.69 | 1.05 |

*Source*: MWA (2005).

ownership status in the water sector (private/public) is not a significant explanatory variable for profitability.[8]

A major reason for these financial deficits is the loss of revenues from non-revenue waters (NRW), that is water that is produced but not billed to consumers due to leakages, under-meter registration, and pilferage. NRW is measured by the difference between the quantity of water that leaves the treatment plants and the quantity billed to users based on metered consumption. The average percentage of NRW in Malaysia is very high, at 40.6 per cent in 2003. In general, the worldwide figure for leakages is around 33 per cent. This problem is more serious in some states than in others (Table 6.9). The states with the highest levels of NRW include: Sabah (73.9 per cent); Negeri Sembilan (53.8 per cent); Kelantan (44.9 per cent); and Selangor (44.7 per cent).

Those states that have involved the private sector seem to have lower levels of NRW and most of them have levels that are lower than the national average NRW of 40.6 per cent. This may be an indicator of the relative efficiency of the private sector. The main causes of water losses are leakages (16–30 per cent), meter under registration (3–7 per cent) and pilferages (1–8 per cent).[9]

*Table 6.9* Non-revenue water, 2003

| *State* | *Metred consumption* | *Non-revenue water* | *Production* | *% NRW* |
|---|---|---|---|---|
| Kedah | 183,189,082 | 132,097,188 | 315,286,270 | 41.9 |
| Sarawak* | 43,151,590 | 11,598,410 | 54,750,000 | 21.2 |
| Labuan | 9,860,698 | 2,410,967 | 12,271,665 | 19.6 |
| Perlis | 19,162,722 | 12,809,453 | 31,972,175 | 40.1 |
| Pahang | 119,213,467 | 111,355,573 | 230,569,040 | 48.3 |
| Negeri Sembilan | 104,690,218 | 121,830,972 | 226,521,190 | 53.8 |
| Sabah | 65,913,151 | 186,236,149 | 252,149,300 | 73.9 |
| Perak | 211,553,576 | 91,407,374 | 302,960,950 | 30.2 |
| Melaka | 87,756,775 | 38,405,110 | 126,161,885 | 30.4 |
| Kuching** | 69,032,641 | 33,807,204 | 102,839,845 | 32.9 |
| Sibu** | 19,850,605 | 8,068,610 | 27,919,215 | 28.9 |
| Pulau Pinang | 224,632,200 | 55,528,660 | 280,160,860 | 19.8 |
| Terengganu | 90,794,768 | 43,916,877 | 134,711,645 | 32.6 |
| Selangor*** | 674,900,649 | 545,898,791 | 1,220,799,440 | 44.7 |
| Johor | 309,702,905 | 150,182,495 | 459,885,400 | 32.7 |
| Kelantan | 43,444,811 | 35,448,479 | 78,893,290 | 44.9 |
| LAKU** | 48,495,573 | 10,663,627 | 59,159,200 | 18.0 |
| Total | 2,325,345,431 | 1,591,665,939 | 3,917,011,370 | 40.6 |

*Note*: *Excluding the province of Kuching, Sibu and LAKU;
**Province within Sarawak;
***Includes Kuala Lumpur and Putrajaya.
*Source*: MWA (2004).

In Table 6.10, we compute the level of losses in revenues from NRW and compare them with the financial deficits from each state's water operations. Clearly, the financial deficits in state water operations can be reduced if the level of NRW is lower. For some states, the magnitude of reduction in NRW is small to achieve a breakeven point – for example, Perlis (10 per cent) and Pahang (11 per cent). Others require more substantial reduction in NRW to achieve breakeven – for example, Sabah (58 per cent), Selangor (64 per cent) and Sarawak (71 per cent).

It may be that part of the financial deficit experienced by state water operations is due to the subsidy on residential water consumption. Generally, water subsidies are available only for residential water consumption (see Table 6.11). These subsidies usually apply only for the first block of consumption (around 10–20 cubic metres). These subsidies range from 7 per cent (in Perlis) to as high as 49 per cent (in Johor). With the exception of the island of Labuan, there is no subsidy for industrial water consumption.

*Table 6.10* Reducing financial deficits via NRW reduction in water operations in Malaysia, 2003 (RM)

| *State* | *Revenue–Cost gap* | *NRW losses* | *Augmented R-C gap* | *% reduction in NRW for breakeven* |
|---|---|---|---|---|
| Kedah | 31,409,244 | 107,097,462 | 138,506,706 | |
| Sarawak | −4,207,794 | 5,913,727 | 1,705,933 | 71 |
| Labuan | −6,915,639 | 2,357,088 | −4,558,551 | |
| Perlis | −898,675 | 8,589,423 | 7,690,748 | 10 |
| Pahang | −10,534,306 | 92,215,667 | 81,681,361 | 11 |
| Negeri Sembilan | 26,808,802 | 115,862,095 | 142,670,897 | |
| Sabah | −125,022,317 | 214,312,496 | 89,290,179 | 58 |
| Perak | 34,834,625 | 86,871,856 | 121,706,481 | |
| Melaka | 27,648,777 | 46,164,290 | 73,813,067 | |
| Kuching | 7,051,926 | 30,752,590 | 37,804,516 | |
| Sibu | −1,739,076 | 7,929,715 | 6,190,639 | 22 |
| Pulau Pinang | 60,449,387 | 41,517,104 | 101,966,491 | |
| Terengganu | 35,131,210 | 39,058,702 | 74,189,912 | |
| Selangor | −449,102,133 | 696,767,541 | 247,665,408 | 64 |
| Johor | 111,651,140 | 185,422,163 | 297,073,303 | |
| Kelantan | 11,521,043 | 37,292,547 | 48,813,590 | |
| LAKU | 6,395,643 | 10,264,256 | 16,659,899 | |
| | −245,518,143 | 1,670,743,514 | 1,425,225,371 | |

*Source*: MWA (2005).

## Private water companies

The four major private participants in the water sector are:

- Taliworks Corp. Berhad – which operates in Langkawi (since 1995), Selangor (1991–2001) and Negeri Sembilan
- Puncak Niaga Berhad – which operates in Selangor (since 1998)
- PBA Holdings Berhad – which operates in Penang (since 2000)
- Ranhill Utilities Berhad[10] – which operates in Johor (since 1992)

Recent financial indicators show that the revenues of these companies have been rising during the period 2000–04 (Table 6.12). The profitability of the companies and earning per share has generally declined, especially since 2002/03.

As the case of Kelantan illustrates, water privatization in Malaysia has not always been successful. The water supply operations in Kelantan was privatized in 1995 with the establishment of Kelantan Waters Sdn

*Table 6.11* Residential and industrial water tariffs and subsidies, 2003

| *State* | *Unit cost (a)* | *Residential* | | | *Industrial* | |
|---|---|---|---|---|---|---|
| | | *1st/2nd block ($m^3$) (b)* | *Rate ($RM/m^3$) (c)* | *Subsidy* (d) = [(a)–(c)]/(a) (per cent)* | *1st/2nd block ($m^3$)* | *Rate ($RM/m^3$)* |
| Kedah | 0.37 | 20 | 0.40 | −8.1 | 10,000 | 1.20 |
| Sarawak | 0.48 | 15 | 0.44 | 8.3 | 25 | 0.97 |
| Labuan | 1.35 | Flat | 0.90 | 33.3 | Flat | 0.90 |
| Perlis | 0.43 | 15 | 0.40 | 7.0 | Flat | 1.10 |
| Pahang | 0.47 | 18 | 0.37 | 21.3 | 227 | 0.92 |
| Negeri Sembilan | 0.32 | 20 | 0.55 | −71.9 | 35 | 1.50 |
| Sabah | 0.80 | Flat | 0.90 | −12.5 | Flat | 0.90 |
| Perak | 0.55 | 10 | 0.30 | 45.5 | 10 | 1.20 |
| Melaka | 0.62 | 15 | 0.45 | 27.4 | Flat | 1.40 |
| Kuching | 0.54 | 15 | 0.48 | 11.1 | 25 | 0.97 |
| Sibu | 0.76 | 15 | 0.48 | 36.8 | 25 | 0.97 |
| Pulau Pinang | 0.38 | 20 | 0.22 | 42.1 | 20 | 0.52 |
| Terengganu | 0.34 | 20 | 0.42 | −23.5 | Flat | 1.15 |
| Selangor | 1.07 | 20 | 0.57 | 46.7 | 35 | 1.80 |
| Johor | 0.59 | 15 | 0.30 | 49.2 | 20 | 1.68 |
| Kelantan | 0.43 | 20 | 0.25 | 41.9 | Flat | 1.25 |
| | | 21–40 | 0.40 | 7.0 | | |

*Note*: *Positive sign indicates subsidy, negative sign indicates non-subsidy.

Bhd – a 70:30 joint venture between Thames Water and Yayasan Kelantan Darulnaim. The joint venture was granted a 25-year concession contract worth RM1 billion.[11] By 1998, Kelantan Waters had accumulated debts in excess of RM100 million and had to be rescued by the federal government via a RM600 million soft loan. In the following year, the Kelantan state government acquired Thames Water's 70 per cent stake in Kelantan Waters for RM50 million.[12]

## Social and economic regulation in the water sector

The regulatory structure in the water sector in Malaysia is complex due to the coexistence of a variety of state-level and federal-level water supply institutions. There are both state-level and federal-level regulators in Malaysia (Table 6.13). The type of state-level regulatory agency depends upon the institutional status of the water service provider within each state. Self-regulation is practised in states where water is supplied by government agencies, such as the public works department and the water

*Table 6.12* Financial performance of private water companies, 2000–2004

| | *2000* | *2001* | *2002* | *2003* | *2004* |
|---|---|---|---|---|---|
| 1. Taliworks Corp. Berhad | | | | | |
| Revenue (RM million) | 116.6 | 117.5 | 126.9 | 134.8 | 171.5 |
| Profit before tax (RM million) | 33.3 | 38.5 | 53.4 | 52.4 | 39.4 |
| Earnings per share | 0.212 | 0.228 | 0.222 | 0.208 | 0.158 |
| 2. Puncak Niaga Berhad | | | | | |
| Revenue (RM million) | 350.6 | 552.3 | 565.1 | 578.3 | 566.8 |
| Profit after tax (RM million) | 91.2 | 124.5 | 127.1 | 129.6 | 46.4 |
| Earnings per share | 0.218 | 0.285 | 0.290 | 0.293 | 0.102 |
| 3. PBA Holdings Berhad | | | | | |
| Revenue (RM million) | — | 122.7 | 150.9 | 150.0 | 153.7 |
| Profit before tax (RM million) | — | 50.4 | 61.6 | 51.1 | 49.6 |
| Earnings per share | — | 0.181 | 0.159 | 0.123 | 0.120 |
| 4. Ranhill Berhad | | | | | |
| Revenue (RM million) | 63.0 | 424.9 | 620.8 | 770.6 | 792.9 |
| Profit before tax (RM million) | 13.5 | 9.7 | 82.9 | 81.8 | 75.6 |
| Earnings per share | 0.110 | 0.329 | 0.466 | 0.470 | 0.409 |

*Source*: Compiled from annual reports, various years.

*Table 6.13* Regulatory structure in the Malaysian water sector

| | *Types of Water Supply Institutions* | | | | |
|---|---|---|---|---|---|
| | *Public Works Department* | *Water Supply Department* | *Water Supply Board* | *Corporatized company* | *Privatized company* |
| States/district | Kedah<br>Perlis<br>Labuan<br>Sarawak* | Pahang<br>Negeri Sembilan<br>Sabah | Melaka<br>Perak<br>Kuching and Sibu | Terengganu<br>LAKU | Penang<br>Johor<br>Selangor<br>Kelantan |
| Status | Federal government | State government | Statutory body | Corporatized state-owned | Private company |
| State-level regulator | State Public Works Dept | State Water Supply Dept | State Water Supply Board | State Water Department/ Board | State Water Department/ Board |
| Federal-level regulator | Water Unit, Ministry of Energy, Water and Communication<br>Environmental Health Engineering Section, Ministry of Health<br>Department of Drainage and Irrigation, Ministry of Natural Resources and Environment | | | | |

*Note*: *Except for Kuching and Sibu.

supply department. For corporatized bodies and privatized companies, new state regulatory agencies are created. Generally, state-level regulatory agencies undertake economic regulation such as setting tariff levels. On the other hand, federal-level regulatory agencies undertake technical regulation and the coordination of matters involving: (a) several states (such as inter-state water transfers) and, (b) funding from the Federal government.

In recent years, regulation of the sector at the federal level has undergone some significant changes. On 27 March 2004, the federal-level regulatory function was transferred from the Water Supply Branch under the Ministry of Works to the Water Unit under the Ministry of Energy, Water and Communication. The functions of the Water Unit include:

- To plan, impart technical advice and coordinate projects which are related to the development of water resources.
- To investigate, design and prepare tender documents for water supply projects which are funded by the federal government (through grants or loans).
- To provide water quality control (raw and processed), control of water loss, safety of dams, coordination of fluoridization programme, water supply material and information management.

Other federal-level agencies are also involved in regulatory matters in the sector. The Environmental Health Engineering Section, under the control of the Ministry of Health, monitors the quality of drinking water supplies in the country. The Department of Drainage and Irrigation, under the Ministry of Natural Resources and Environment, undertakes river basin management, including the monitoring of pollution levels in rivers. The National Water Resource Council (NWRC) is a council comprising of representatives from federal and state governments that is in charge of formulating national-level policies.

Both state and federal agencies address the issue of access to treated water supply. State regulatory agencies plan and propose water projects to the federal government that can be funded by the latter. This can take the form of soft loans to state governments for public water supply infrastructure or grants for rural water supply development. At the federal level, projects to improve access to water supply in rural areas are undertaken by the Ministry of Regional and Rural Development. As discussed earlier, the federal government has allocated a large amount of resources to improving access to water supply in the rural areas. It is estimated that the government has provided RM8.3 billion loan to state governments for the water supply sector.[13]

There are currently no universal service provisions (USP) in the privatization agreements in the water sector. This is probably due to the fact that activities related to USP are carried out by the federal government via the Ministry of Regional and Rural Development. However, private water companies have been encouraged to improve access to treated water supply in their efforts to expand their markets.

## Recent regulatory reforms

On 18 January 2005, the Malaysian Parliament amended the Constitution to affect the transfer of the jurisdiction of water supply management from the respective states to the federal government. With this change, the federal government now has full control over water supply management in the country.[14]

In May 2006, the government enacted two pieces of legislation that further transformed the industry – namely the Water Services Industry Bill 2006 (WSI) and the National Water Service Commission Bill 2006 (SPAN, the Malay acronym for Suruhanjaya Perkhidmatan Air Negara). Both pieces of legislation contained provisions for the establishment of a government-owned agency, tentatively named the Water Asset Management Company (WAMCo) and an industry regulator, namely the National Water Service Commission.

These reforms are expected to overcome some of the perceived shortcomings and weaknesses of the existing water institutions in Malaysia, namely:[15]

- Lack of coordination among various stakeholders leading to the awarding of ad hoc contracts;
- Ineffective regulatory structure and poor enforcement;
- Capital expenditure constraints; and
- Varied success of privatization of water supply projects.

In the past, regulation was agreed within the terms of the individual contracts. In some cases, there were inputs from the government regarding both health and environmental matters.

The problem of capital expenditure constraints is attributed to the inability of the existing operators to obtain sufficient revenues to cover capital expenditures (investment). This, in turn, is due to water tariffs being currently set at less than full-cost recovery levels.

## Water tariffs in Malaysia

### Water tariffs structure

The general principles underlying the present water tariffs in Malaysia include the following:[16]

- a higher rate for higher consumption to discourage wastage;
- cross-subsidy for domestic consumers by industrial consumers;
- a very low 'lifeline' rate to meet the 'ability to pay' criterion of the lower-income group to cover basic everyday needs for domestic purposes.

The incentives for the efficient use of water are applied through the use of volumetric charges (based on measured water use) under an increasing block structure (where block price rises with consumption). This approach is used for the water tariffs for residential homes (with the exception of Sabah, which uses a flat rate). There are significant differences in the structure of residential water tariffs between the different states. Most states have a three-tiered structure, while one state (Sabah) has a flat rate. Similarly, many states use an increasing block tariff structure for industrial and commercial water tariffs. However, such block structures are not very steep – that is, the block increments are relatively small. There are also a number of states (Melaka, Terengganu, Perlis, Kelantan and Sabah) that use flat rate tariffs for industrial and commercial users. Overall, in almost all states (with the exception of Sabah), residential water users are subsidized by industrial/commercial water users. This is illustrated by Table 6.14, which summarizes the average tariff rates in various states.[17] The industry–domestic tariff ratio ranges from 1.7 to 3.0.

The link between the incidence of poverty and domestic water rates is a weak one (Figure 6.1). Some of the states with high incidences of poverty have relatively low or moderate levels of tariff (for example, Kelantan and Kedah). However, there are also states with very low poverty levels where domestic water tariffs are very low (for example, Pulau Pinang).

### Tariff revision

As the provision of water is the responsibility of the state, revisions of water tariffs are approved at the state level. However, cabinet approval is required for cases where the privatization agreement provides for federal-level approval – for example, the privatization of the water utility in the state of Selangor (Perbadanan Urus Air Selangor, or PUAS). There are no

*Table 6.14* Average domestic and industry water rates, 2004 (RM/cubic metre)

| *State/area* | *Domestic rate* | *Industry rate* | *Ratio: industry/domestic* |
|---|---|---|---|
| Kelantan | 0.31 | 0.70 | 2.26 |
| Pulau Pinang | 0.31 | 0.94 | 3.03 |
| Terengganu | 0.52 | 1.15 | 2.21 |
| Kedah | 0.53 | 1.20 | 2.26 |
| Sarawak | 0.56 | 1.19 | 2.13 |
| Perlis | 0.57 | 1.30 | 2.28 |
| Pahang | 0.57 | 1.40 | 2.46 |
| Melaka | 0.59 | 1.40 | 2.37 |
| Bintulu | 0.61 | 1.21 | 1.98 |
| Kuching | 0.62 | 1.06 | 1.71 |
| Sibu | 0.62 | 1.06 | 1.71 |
| Sri Aman | 0.62 | 1.06 | 1.71 |
| Limbang | 0.62 | 1.06 | 1.71 |
| Sarikei | 0.62 | 1.06 | 1.71 |
| Kapit | 0.62 | 1.06 | 1.71 |
| Perak | 0.67 | 1.45 | 2.16 |
| Negeri Sembilan | 0.68 | 1.59 | 2.34 |
| Selangor | 0.72 | 1.91 | 2.65 |
| Labuan | 0.90 | 0.90 | 1.00 |
| Sabah | 0.90 | 0.90 | 1.00 |
| Johor | 0.90 | 2.93 | 3.26 |

*Source*: MWA (2004).

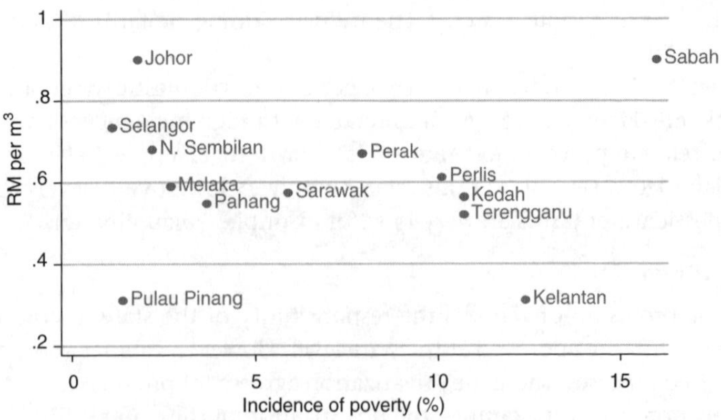


*Figure 6.1* Domestic water tariff and incidence of poverty, 2002

*Table 6.15* History of tariff revisions in the water sector

| | *1950s* | *1960s* | *1970s* | *1980s* | *1990s* | *2000–* |
|---|---|---|---|---|---|---|
| Johor | | 1968 | 1977 | 1983,1986 | 1991 | 2001, 2003 |
| Kedah | | | | 1980, 1983 | 1993 | |
| Kelantan | | 1968 | | 1983 | | 2001 |
| Melaka | | 1965 | 1976 | 1983 | 1992 | 2005 |
| Negeri Sembilan | | | 1973 | 1981,1984 | 1993 | 2002 |
| Pahang | 1958 | | | 1983 | | |
| Perak | | 1966 | | 1982, 1985 | 1991 | |
| Perlis | | 1960 | | 1984 | 1993, 1996 | |
| Pulan Pinang | | | | 1981, 1983, 1985 | 1993 | 2001 |
| Sabah | | | 1975 | 1982 | | |
| Sibu | | | | 1982 | 1992 | |
| Kuching | | | | 1982 | 1992 | |
| Sarawak | | | | 1982, 1984 | 1992 | |
| Selangor | | | 1976 | 1984, 1989 | 1991 | 2001 |
| Terengganu | | 1960, 1969 | 1975 | 1982, 1984 | 1997 | |
| Labuan | | | 1975 | 1982 | | |

*Source*: MWA (various reports, various years).

*Table 6.16* Corporatization, privatization and tariff revision in the water sector

| | *Year of corporatization* | *Year of privatization (distribution)* | *Year of most recent tariff revisions* |
|---|---|---|---|
| Johor | 1999 | 1999 | 1991, 2001, 2003 |
| Kelantan | 1994 | 1994 | 1983, 2001 |
| Pulau Pinang | 1999 | 2000 | 1993, 2001 |
| Selangor | 2002 | 2005 | 1991, 2001 |
| Terengganu | 1999 | — | 1984, 1997 |
| Labuan | 1987 | 1987 | 1975, 1982 |

formal schedules for tariff revisions in the water sector in Malaysia. As a result, there have been significant variations in the frequency of tariff revisions across the different states in Malaysia. In some states, such as Pahang and Sabah, tariffs have been revised only twice since the 1960s (Table 6.15).

In other states, such as Johor and Pulau Pinang, water tariffs have been revised five times since the 1980s. There appears to be some relationship between tariff revision and privatization. Five of the six states that have revised their water tariff since 2000 are states where water distribution has been corporatized or privatized (Table 6.16).

## Affordability: lifeline consumption

The 'lifeline' rate to meet the 'ability to pay' criterion of the lower-income group can be measured by the minimum charges that are imposed for residential water consumption. These range typically from RM2.50 to RM5.00 per month. There are two ways of looking at this. We can evaluate this minimum charge in comparison with the poverty income line. The minimum payment of RM2.50–RM3.00 amounts to about 0.83 per cent–1.00 per cent of the official hardcore poverty income line of RM300 per month.

Alternatively, we can examine whether or not the consumption level associated with the lifeline minimum rate is adequate (using the World Health Organization/WHO benchmark). To obtain this minimum level of consumption, we divide the minimum charge by the first block tariff rate. This computed level of consumption can be used as a proxy of the minimum level of consumption affordable by lowest income households. The WHO (2005) standards for water consumption are as follows:[18]

- Short-term survival: 20 litres per person per day (0.02 cubic metre per person per day). Assuming an average household size of 4.4 persons (DOS 2000), this translates into 2.6 cubic metres per household per month).
- Medium-term maintaining: 70 litres per person per day (0.07 cubic metre per person per day or 9.2 cubic metres per household per month).

Based on a comparison between the computed consumption (associated with the minimum charges and minimum tariff rates) and the WHO standards, we estimated that water consumption exceeds the medium-term 'lifeline' level (corresponding to 9.2 cubic metres per household per month) in only six out of the 13 states surveyed (Figure 6.2). Interestingly, three of these six states (Johor, Kelantan, Pulau Pinang) have privatized their water sector fully. The above analysis indicates that the prevailing lifeline tariff rates in some states are sufficiently high.[19]

## Towards full-cost recovery and the elimination of subsidies

Following the passage of the Water Services Industry Bill 2006, all state water departments will now be corporatized and regulated by the water commission, Suruhanjaya Perkhidmatan Air Negara (SPAN). Another agency, namely WAMCo, was established to overcome this problem by

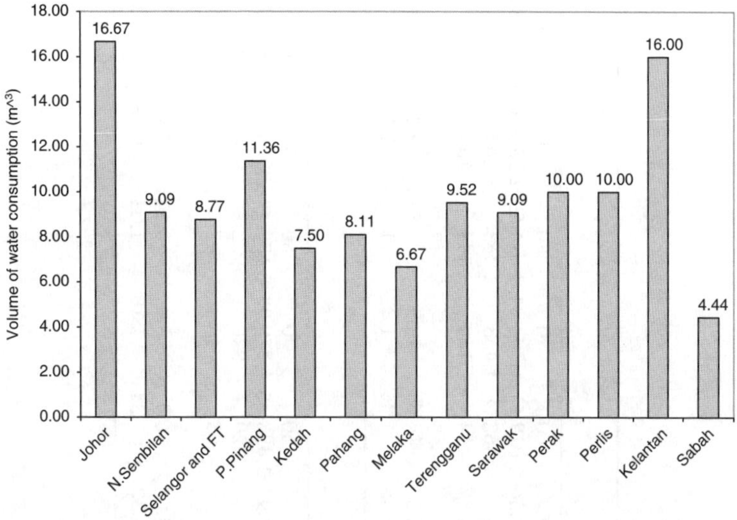


*Figure 6.2* Level of residential water consumption associated with minimum charge

providing financing to upgrade the water supply infrastructure in the country. It is estimated that between 2005 and 2010 Malaysia needs to spend RM50 billion (US$3.2 billion) to upgrade water and sewage services. The Minister of Energy, Water and Communications envisaged WAMCo as a temporary entity that would be 'relevant until the water services industry reached a full cost recovery level'.[20] This implies a gradual reduction of water subsidies in Malaysia in future. There has been some public concern about affordability under the proposed changes, particularly the possibility of future tariff increase. Some argue that the quality of treated water ought to be improved before there is any increase in the water tariff. NGOs argue for a re-examination of water privatization. The media also continue to occasionally highlight the lack of access to treated water, particularly in the rural areas.

## Evidence from household expenditure data

### Data source

The two sets of household expenditure data used in this section are:

- the 1993/1994 Household Expenditure Survey (HES94); and
- the 1998/1999 Household Expenditure Survey (HES99).

*Table 6.17* Access and mean expenditure on water, 1993/94 and 1998/99

| | *Percentile total household expenditure* | | | | | | | | | |
|---|---|---|---|---|---|---|---|---|---|---|
| HES94 | 10 | 20 | 30 | 40 | 50 | 60 | 70 | 80 | 90 | 100 |
| Percentile total expenditure (RM) | 365.20 | 510.55 | 634.54 | 770.22 | 907.56 | 1,079.51 | 1,303.04 | 1,624.59 | 2,256.16 | 18,569.86 |
| Number of households | 1,464 | 1,463 | 1,463 | 1,463 | 1,464 | 1,462 | 1,463 | 1,463 | 1,463 | 1,463 |
| Number of households without access | 627 | 461 | 355 | 301 | 241 | 214 | 160 | 144 | 135 | 75 |
| % households without access | 42.8 | 31.5 | 24.3 | 20.6 | 16.5 | 14.6 | 10.9 | 9.8 | 9.2 | 5.1 |
| Mean % expenditure on water | 1.29 | 1.38 | 1.47 | 1.42 | 1.45 | 1.36 | 1.32 | 1.2 | 1.11 | 0.79 |

| | *Percentile total household expenditure* | | | | | | | | | |
|---|---|---|---|---|---|---|---|---|---|---|
| HES99 | 10 | 20 | 30 | 40 | 50 | 60 | 70 | 80 | 90 | 100 |
| Percentile total expenditure (RM) | 549.76 | 729.59 | 903.79 | 1,078.46 | 1,278.94 | 1,493.35 | 1,770.93 | 2,179.47 | 2,978.78 | 42,875.47 |
| Number of households | 920 | 920 | 921 | 919 | 919 | 920 | 920 | 922 | 918 | 919 |
| Number of households without access | 245 | 150 | 127 | 86 | 83 | 63 | 46 | 47 | 38 | 29 |
| % households without access | 26.6 | 16.3 | 13.8 | 9.4 | 9.0 | 6.8 | 5.0 | 5.1 | 4.1 | 3.2 |
| Mean % expenditure on water | 1.45 | 1.53 | 1.44 | 1.36 | 1.32 | 1.34 | 1.18 | 1.04 | 0.98 | 0.68 |

*Note*: All expenditures are reported in current prices.

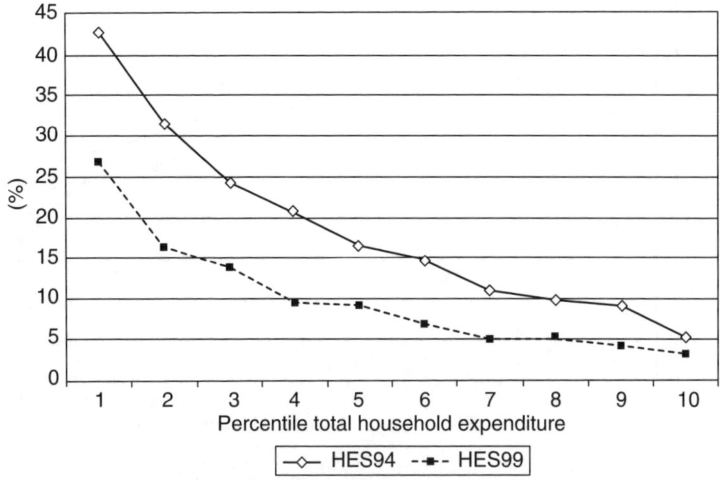


*Figure 6.3* Percentage of households with access to water, 1993/1994 and 1998/1999

Both of these datasets were obtained from the Department of Statistics, Malaysia. The HES94 dataset contains 14,631 observations while the HES99 contains 9,198 observations. Unfortunately, neither survey collects information relating to income. Total expenditure is used as a basis for constructing percentile tables. The distribution of respondents by state for both surveys is very similar. The largest share of total number of respondents came from the states of Selangor, Sabah, Sarawak, Perak and Kuala Lumpur.

## Equity

A household with no access to water supply is defined as one with zero expenditure on water. As expected, the percentage of households with no access to water supply declines with higher levels of total expenditures (Table 6.17 and Figure 6.3).

This is observed in both the HES94 and HES99 data. The percentage of households without access to water seems to have declined across all total expenditure percentiles. This indicates an improvement in access to water supply across all income percentiles from 1993/94 to 1998/99. This may be due to the higher levels of average income in 1998/99 compared to 1993/94 (see Table 6.17).

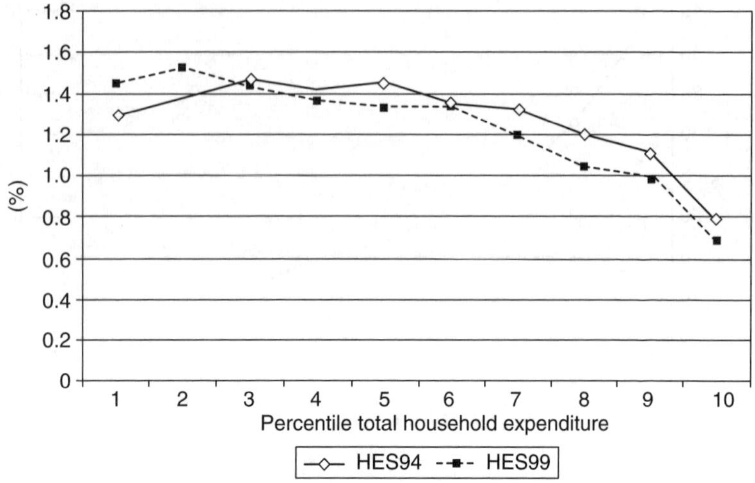


*Figure 6.4* Percentage of expenditure on water, 1993/94 and 1998/99

A comparison between the mean expenditure on water by total household expenditure percentiles indicates the following (Table 6.17 and Figure 6.4):

- The percentage of expenditure on water has increased for households in the lowest 20 percentiles of total expenditures between 1993/94 and 1998/99 (and decreased or remained stable for other percentiles).
- The percentage of expenditure on water has decreased for households in the 30 percentiles and above of total expenditures between 1993/94 and 1998/99.

These findings seem to indicate that water affordability for those households with lower incomes (proxied by total expenditure) has worsened over the period from 1993/94 to 1998/99. In contrast, water affordability for the households with higher incomes has improved during the same period.

## Access

As discussed earlier, access to water supply is defined in terms of expenditure on water – household with no access to water supply is defined as one with zero expenditure on water.

When analysing the data using various econometric models (Lee 2007), we find the following:

- Larger households are more likely than smaller households to have no access to water supply. It is possible that rural households tend to be larger than urban households and larger households tend to be poorer than smaller households.
- Urban households are more likely to have access to water supply than to rural households. This result is consistent with the higher water coverage ratio observed in urban areas compared to rural areas.
- Households with higher total expenditure are more likely to have access to water supply. If total expenditure is used as a proxy for income, households with higher incomes tend to have greater access to water supply.
- Households in states where water distribution is undertaken by state-owned companies are more likely to have access to water than households in states where water distribution is undertaken by private companies. Privatization does not seem to improve access to water.

**Affordability**

Using various econometric models (Lee 2007), we investigated the relationship between the affordability of water supply and other variables. Affordability in the above specification is couched in terms of the notion of 'expenditure water poor'. A threshold of 5 per cent is adopted for this study. Generally, it is accepted that water bills should be around 3–5 per cent of household expenditure. We took the higher threshold.

The results imply that:

- Larger households are more likely to be 'expenditure water poor' than smaller households. This implies that larger households tend to spend a larger proportion of their total expenditure on purchasing water.
- Interestingly, urban households are more likely to be more 'expenditure water poor' compared to rural households. It is possible that urban households have less alternative sources of water compared to their rural counterparts – thus resulting in greater proportion of total expenditure spent on water.
- Households with higher total expenditures (a proxy for income) are less likely to be 'expenditure water poor'. This implies that households with higher income spend a smaller proportion of their income on purchasing water.

- Households in states where water distribution is undertaken by private companies are less likely to become 'expenditure' water poor compared to households in states where water distribution is undertaken by state-owned companies. One possibility is that water tariffs in states with private water distribution companies are lower than water tariffs in states with state-owned water distribution companies. The water tariffs cannot be included as a variable in the models due to lack of data for the period before 2001.

In terms of differences in tariff levels between the private and public sectors, we find that:

- the range of tariff levels for states with private water distribution companies is wider than those with state-owned ones;
- the median tariff level in the former appears to be lower than in the latter.

Our analysis with 2003 data shows that the tariff is kept reasonably low in privatized states. This is linked to the fact that PSP and its varieties are still very sensitive issues. This makes it difficult to increase prices to cost-recovery levels. This has been demonstrated by some political fallout over revising sewerage tariffs after privatization.

Finally, if lower threshold levels for 'expenditure water poor' are used (that is 3–4 per cent), the sign of the coefficient for total expenditures become positive. This implies that adopting a threshold level that is too low result in a definition of 'expenditure poverty' that is not very useful empirically.

These results show that the Malaysian government has been concerned only to ensure the provision of a supply of cheap water to its citizens. In this process, it neglected the need for increasing investments (or efficiency) to expand coverage and renew the water infrastructure. As a result, on the one hand there is increasing pressure to privatize water services in order to recover increased costs, while on the other there is a growing NGO pressure against privatization.

## Conclusion

The development of the water sector is crucial in order to improve and maintain Malaysia's competitiveness as well as to eradicate poverty and improve the quality of life of its citizens. Water coverage is uneven across the different states. The more developed states have almost achieved universal water coverage while less developed states continue to improve water access, particularly in rural areas. Recently, underinvestment in the water distribution systems has also resulted in very serious non-revenue water problems in some states. As a result, about half of the states in Malaysia are currently experiencing a financial deficit in their water operations. Many of the larger and more developed states have opted to privatize the provision of water services in an attempt to solve problems in their water sector.

For consumers, the prevailing 'lifeline' tariff rates (based on WHO's minimum water consumption benchmark) in some of the states are relatively high. Access to treated water has improved in all income categories (proxied by total expenditure) between 1993/94 and 1998/99. However, water affordability for the households with lower incomes has worsened during the same period. Our analysis indicates that privatization does not seem to have improved access to water. This is due partly to the fact that there is a huge problem of cost recovery, which hinders investments. Consequently, we also find that due to very strict rules for increasing tariffs, the poor are safe from price hikes. What this study shows is that in order to expand coverage, renew infrastructure and cushion citizens from abusive tariff increases, the government should be able to strike a balance between encouraging investment (or improving efficiency) and at the same time having appropriate social policies. In the case of Malaysia, a greater emphasis is placed on social policies without consideration of the broader issues of expanding coverage and investment.

At present, the federal government is planning to reform the sector further in order to solve existing problems – particularly the non-revenue problem. More specifically, it proposes placing water supply management under the jurisdiction of the federal government and creating a national water asset company to undertake long-term investments in the sector. While this study indicates this to be in the right direction, it also suggests that the government needs to examine more carefully issues of equity, access and affordability in the context of the different institutional options for the provision of water services.

## Notes

1. See Naidu and Lee (1997) for further discussions.
2. Based on the exchange rate of RM3.70 = US$1.
3. Mid-Term Review of the Eighth Malaysia Plan, pp. 258–9.
4. A simple OLS regression using domestic per capita water consumption as the dependent variable and per capita GDP as the independent variable indicates

that the positive relationship between the two variables is not statistically significant.

5. Exchange rate of RM3.70 = US$1.
6. Exchange rate of RM3.70 = US$1.
7. Unit cost is derived by dividing total operating and maintenance costs by total production while unit revenue is derived by dividing total revenue by total metred water sold.
8. This is based on results from panel regression models (random-effects models and fixed-effects models) involving profitability as the dependent variable and a dummy ownership status as the independent variable.
9. See MWA (2004: 14).
10. Ranhill Utilities has a fairly diversified business portfolio – it owns 70 per cent of Ranhill Utilities Berhad which is involved in the water sector.
11. Exchange rate of RM3.70 = US$1.
12. See Hall *et al.* (2005).
13. See Raja Dato' Zaharaton (2005). Exchange rate of RM3.70 = US$1.
14. Under the proposal, rights over water resources remain with each state.
15. See Lim (2004).
16. MWA (2003: 45).
17. The average tariff rates are computed using total water revenue divided by consumption volumes for the different categories.
18. Short-term survival includes drinking and cooking. Medium-term maintenance include drinking, cooking, personal washing, washing clothes, cleaning home, growing food (for domestic consumption) and waste disposal.
19. Unfortunately, there are no published state-level data on the number of households paying the minimum charge.
20. *Ministry Needs Over USD500 Million to Get WAHCO Going*, Bernama Report, 31 March 2005.

## References


Asian Development Bank (2001) *Project Completion Report on the Rehabilitation and Upgrading of Water Supply Systems Sector Project in Malaysia*, December (Manila: ADB).

Bennett, M., D. Cooke and C. Waddams Price (2002) 'Left out in the Cold? New Energy Tariffs, Low-income Households and the Fuel Poor', *Fiscal Studies* 23(2), 167–94.

Brutton, Henry J. (1992) *The Political Economy of Poverty, Equity and Growth: Sri Lanka and Malaysia* (New York: Oxford University Press).

Department of Statistics (2000) *Report on Household Expenditure Survey Malaysia 1998/99* (Putrajaya, Malaysia: Department of Statistics).

Hall, David, Violeta Corral, Emanuele Lobina and Robin de la Motte (2005) *Water Privatisation and Restructuring in Asia-Pacific*, report commissioned by Public Services International (PSI), Business School, University of Greenwich, United Kingdom. Web publication at http://www.psiru.org/reports/2004-12-W-Asia.doc (accessed 29 October 2007).

Lee, C. (2007) *Social Policies and Private Sector Participation in Water Supply: The Case of Malaysia. Programme on Markets, Business and Regulation* (Geneva: UNRISD).
Lim Keng-Yaik (2004) *Water Services Reform – The Way Forward.* Keynote address Water Services Reform Seminar, Kuala Lumpur.
Malaysian Water Association (MWA) (2004) *Malaysia Water Industry Guide* (Kuala Lumpur: MWA).
Malaysian Water Association (MWA) (2003) *Malaysia Water Industry Guide* (Kuala Lumpur: MWA).
Malaysian Water Association (MWA) (2002) *Malaysia Water Industry Guide* (Kuala Lumpur: MWA).
Malaysian Water Association (MWA) (2001) *Malaysia Water Industry Guide* (Kuala Lumpur: MWA).
Naidu, G. and Cassey Lee (1997) 'The Transition to Privatization: Malaysia', in Ashoka Mody (ed.), *Infrastructure Strategies in East Asia: The Untold Story* (Washington, DC: World Bank).
Rachagan, S. Sothi (2003) *Managing Water... For People: Privatisation of Water – Who Benefits?* Paper presented at Environmental Protection Society of Malaysia's Annual Public Forum, 5 June, Kuala Lumpur.
Raja Dato' Zaharaton Raja Zainal Abidin (2005) *Water Services Agenda in the Ninth Plan.* Presentation at the Water Malaysia 2005 Conference, Kuala Lumpur, 12–13 April.
United States Agency for International Development (USAID) and Organisation for Economic Co-operation and Development (OECD) (2005) *Regional Assessment Survey and Workshop on Full Cost Recovery for Water Utilities in South-east Asia: Sharing International Experience and Best Practices.* Web publication at http://www.oecd.org/dataoecd/59/58/34617894.pdf (accessed 29 October 2007).
World Health Organization (WHO) (2005) *Minimum Water Quantity Needed for Domestic Use in Emergencies.* Technical Note No. 9 (Geneva: WHO).

# 7
# Hungary

*Zsolt Boda, Gábor Scheiring, Emanuele Lobina and David Hall*

## Introduction

After more than a decade of experimentation with private sector participation (PSP)[1] in the water sector, we still have no clear picture about the privatization process in Hungary and its impact. This chapter will try to provide an analysis of the impact of PSP in the water sector in Hungary. The Hungarian water sector has undergone a major transition since the early 1990s, which has affected both its economic and its social performance. Before the 1990s, under the centrally planned economy, drinking water was provided by the state. As a result, state-managed companies had almost no incentive to increase efficiency. Their main goals were to obtain enough subsidies from the government and to try to meet the goals set out in the economic plans.

During the socialist era household water and sanitation services were provided free of charge.[2] This ended only after the 1990 regime change, when user tariffs were introduced gradually. Although the tariff of water and sanitation have been steadily increasing in real terms over the past 15 years, these prices are kept low by local governments. The reason is that people were used to free water during the socialist era and making them pay high prices would be politically sensitive.

The local government act (1990) transferred the responsibility for water provision to local governments, declaring water provision to be mandatory. In 1991–1992 the 33 water companies were replaced by five regional companies. However, many local companies remained under the control of local governments. However, municipalities had the right to refuse the transfer and in some cases this is what happened. Thus, the changes resulted in a mixed ownership structure (about 20 per cent of the water companies are still state-owned) and a highly fragmented structure, with altogether 369 companies supplying drinking water and/or sewerage service by the end of 2001. Around half of the water companies run water services in only one town or village. The process of decentralization was also strengthened by the rise in operational costs and water prices. Those utilities that could provide water from local water sources were decoupled from the regional companies (Somlyódy *et al.* 2002). When the privatization of water services at the local level started in 1994 through concessions or management contracts, things became even more complex.

For the Central and Eastern Europe region, Hungary has been a pioneer in the privatization of public services (the entire energy sector and many of the water distribution services). Today about 40 per cent of the water is distributed by private companies/joint ventures, and about 20 per cent of the water companies are privatized. Some companies are Hungarian, but the well-known multinational companies have also been very active in Hungary: Veolia, SUEZ, RWE, E-on, and Berlinwaters, among others. The fact that different types of ownership are present in Hungary makes it suitable for a comparative analysis.

The intention of this chapter is to investigate the impact of PSP in the water supply industry on access and affordability of the poorest households, and how social policies are designed to help the poor. The study is based on a dataset provided by the Hungarian Waterworks Association.[3] This database contains data on 120 water and sewage companies from 1995 to 2004. In terms of the number of Hungarian water companies our database represents less than one-third of the total number of waterworks of a total of 369 water and sewage companies (in 2005). However, the database contains data on the members of the Hungarian Waterworks Association, which are essentially the largest water companies. Therefore the companies covered by the database actually provide more than 90 per cent of the water produced in Hungary, serving about 9.5 million people (of a total Hungarian population of around 10.2 million people). A great number of the Hungarian waterworks are extremely small village networks, and many of them are not members of the Association.

The structure of the chapter is as follows. First, we provide a general description of the Hungarian water sector, including data about access to and affordability of water. Secondly, we provide a presentation of the Hungarian social policies concerning water. Thirdly, we present an outline about the trends of water privatization in Hungary. Here we include the results of data analysis on private sector involvement and water prices. In the final section we draw some policy conclusions.

## Characteristics of the Hungarian water sector

### The meaning of access and affordability

*Access*

Access to water in Hungary is not a major problem in comparison with other developing countries, such as those in Africa or South Asia. According to the World Health Organization (WHO), access to water is defined as having a source of safe drinking water within 200 metres of one's home. In Hungary, piped water is available to almost all (99.7 per cent) of the settlements. In places where it is not feasible to provide piped networks, water is transported in tanks. Free public fountains are provided in towns and villages. As mentioned earlier, water provision is a local government obligation.

The fact that piped water is available in almost every settlement suggests that if people are not connected to the pipe network, it is for financial, rather than physical constraints. As Table 7.1 illustrates, although the national average figure shows that 96 per cent of the

*Table 7.1* Proportion of dwellings supplied with piped water by income groups (per cent) and the change between 1992 and 2003 (percentage)

| *Year* | *Income groups* | | | | | | | | | | |
|---|---|---|---|---|---|---|---|---|---|---|---|
| | *1* | *2* | *3* | *4* | *5* | *6* | *7* | *8* | *9* | *10* | *Average* |
| 1992 | 75.5 | 82.3 | 86.1 | 88.0 | 89.7 | 90.7 | 93.2 | 93.6 | 96.8 | 97.6 | 89.3 |
| 1993 | 73.4 | 82.8 | 85.9 | 88.2 | 88.7 | 89.7 | 92.9 | 95.5 | 96.6 | 98.3 | 90.2 |
| 1994 | 79.0 | 85.3 | 86.6 | 88.9 | 91.0 | 89.9 | 92.2 | 94.4 | 96.6 | 98.3 | 91.0 |
| 1995 | 75.8 | 84.9 | 86.8 | 87.0 | 89.8 | 93.0 | 93.3 | 93.9 | 97.3 | 97.9 | 91.0 |
| 1996 | 76.4 | 86.5 | 90.3 | 91.5 | 90.6 | 91.7 | 93.7 | 95.6 | 96.8 | 98.1 | 92.1 |
| 1997 | 73.3 | 86.1 | 90.5 | 90.1 | 90.7 | 91.4 | 92.5 | 95.9 | 97.7 | 98.7 | 91.8 |
| 1998 | 79.1 | 87.5 | 90.3 | 89.8 | 91.9 | 93.9 | 94.1 | 94.7 | 96.7 | 98.6 | 92.6 |
| 1999 | 77.6 | 85.9 | 89.2 | 90.7 | 92.6 | 93.7 | 94.1 | 96.6 | 97.3 | 98.9 | 92.8 |
| | *1st decile* | *1st quintile* | *2nd quintile* | *3rd quintile* | *4th quintile* | *5th quintile* | *10th decile* | | | | *Average* |
| 2000 | 80.7 | 85.7 | 92.0 | 93.9 | 97.2 | 99.0 | 99.4 | | | | 94.4 |
| 2001 | 77.8 | 84.2 | 93.8 | 95.9 | 98.0 | 99.4 | 99.4 | | | | 95.1 |
| | *1* | *2* | *3* | *4* | *5* | *6* | *7* | *8* | *9* | *10* | *Average* |
| 2002 | 79.1 | 90.8 | 92.5 | 94.5 | 95.5 | 96.8 | 97.0 | 98.5 | 98.5 | 99.3 | 95.2 |
| 2003 | 80.7 | 91.0 | 92.7 | 95.8 | 95.2 | 96.7 | 97.3 | 98.6 | 98.5 | 99.4 | 95.5 |

*Source*: Hungarian Central Statistical Office.

population is connected to piped water in their homes, it is very uneven in terms of income group. In 2003, only 81 per cent of the poorest families had piped water in their homes. This situation was a slightly improvement on the figure in 1992, when it stood at 76 per cent. There is almost universal access to piped water connection for the richest income groups in their residences.

Why do the poorest groups have no access to piped water in their homes? We could eventually redefine the question of access to piped water as an affordability question. In other words, although there is a piped network running in their settlement, the poor may be unable to pay for the necessary connections. It is not the physical and spatial marginalization of social groups (or regions) that creates inequalities in terms of access in the first place. It is more to do with the limited financial capacities of people to pay for the costs of connection. In other words, connection charges hamper access and not necessarily the consumption bills.

The hypothesis that the question of access is indeed a question of affordability is also reinforced by the data. Although the data on access show a slow, gradual increase for each income group over time, this rate of growth rose slightly after 2000. And 2000 was the first year after 1995 when overall household expenditures grew in real terms. This is also the year when water consumption started to increase, following seven years of decline. This suggests that connections may be determined by the relative income positions of households. If people have higher financial status, then they are willing to spend this on water connection and related infrastructure (bathroom, or non-essential uses).

As one would expect, inequalities also exist in regional terms and by type of settlements. Table 7.2 shows that rural areas lag considerably

*Table 7.2* Rate of residence supplied with piped water by settlement type (percentage)

| | *1992* | *1995* | *1998* | *2000* |
|---|---|---|---|---|
| Rate of residence connected to public water supply | 89 | 91 | 92 | 94 |
| Budapest | 98 | 98 | | 99 |
| Other towns | 90 | 92 | 94* | 93 |
| Rural areas | 73 | 82 | 87 | 87 |

*Source*: Hungarian Central Statistical Office.
*Note*: *With Budapest.

behind urban areas. Tables 7.1 and 7.2 show that most poor people in Hungary live in rural areas. In Hungary, the distribution of household income shows a strong correlation with the population size of the settlements.

*Affordability*

We use household expenditure data provided by the Central Statistical Office to assess the amount a household spends on water. As illustrated in Table 7.3, the amount spent on water grew between 1992 and 1995 for all income groups. During this period there was an economic recession in Hungary, with GDP dropping by about 15 per cent. Revenues were shrinking even more rapidly. Household expenditures for the first income group dropped in nominal terms by 13 per cent from 1992 to 1993. However, after 1995 we can distinguish three trends in spending on water.

The first five income groups saw their water spending stabilizing around 1.4–1.5 per cent of household expenditure between 1995

*Table 7.3* Affordability of water: water bills (without sewerage charges) according to income groups for Hungary (percentage of yearly household expenditure)

| *Year* | *Income groups* | | | | | | | | | |
|---|---|---|---|---|---|---|---|---|---|---|
| | *1* | *2* | *3* | *4* | *5* | *6* | *7* | *8* | *9* | *10* |
| 1992 | 1.1 | 1.2 | 1.1 | 1.1 | 1.1 | 1.0 | 0.9 | 0.9 | 0.9 | 0.8 |
| 1993 | 1.2 | 1.2 | 1.3 | 1.2 | 1.3 | 1.2 | 1.3 | 1.2 | 1.0 | 0.8 |
| 1994 | 1.2 | 1.3 | 1.3 | 1.2 | 1.2 | 1.3 | 1.2 | 1.1 | 1.0 | 0.8 |
| 1995 | 1.5 | 1.5 | 1.4 | 1.4 | 1.4 | 1.4 | 1.4 | 1.3 | 1.1 | 0.9 |
| 1996 | 1.4 | 1.5 | 1.5 | 1.4 | 1.4 | 1.3 | 1.4 | 1.2 | 1.2 | 0.9 |
| 1997 | 1.4 | 1.6 | 1.5 | 1.4 | 1.4 | 1.4 | 1.4 | 1.4 | 1.2 | 0.9 |
| 1998 | 1.4 | 1.4 | 1.3 | 1.4 | 1.4 | 1.3 | 1.2 | 1.3 | 1.1 | 0.9 |
| 1999 | 1.5 | 1.5 | 1.4 | 1.5 | 1.4 | 1.5 | 1.3 | 1.2 | 1.2 | 0.9 |

| | *1st decile* | *1st quintile* | *2nd quintile* | *3rd quintile* | *4th quintile* | *5th quintile* | *10th decile* |
|---|---|---|---|---|---|---|---|
| 2000 | 1.5 | 1.5 | 1.5 | 1.5 | 1.3 | 1.0 | 0.9 |
| 2001 | 1.4 | 1.4 | 1.4 | 1.3 | 1.2 | 0.9 | 0.8 |
| 2002 | 1.5 | 1.5 | 1.4 | 1.3 | 1.2 | 0.9 | 0.8 |

| | *1* | *2* | *3* | *4* | *5* | *6* | *7* | *8* | *9* | *10* |
|---|---|---|---|---|---|---|---|---|---|---|
| 2003 | 1.5 | 1.5 | 1.5 | 1.4 | 1.4 | 1.3 | 1.3 | 1.2 | 1.1 | 0.8 |

*Source*: Hungarian Central Statistical Office.

and 2003. This means a 36 per cent increase in water expenditure as a percentage of overall household expenditure for income groups one and three, and an increase of about 26 per cent for income groups two, four and five over the whole period. Income groups six to nine experienced a slow decrease of water spending in their household expenditures from 1995 to 2003. Water spending from household expenditures peaked around 1996–97 and after it has been decreasing slowly. For the whole period this means an increase in spending of around 30 per cent (groups six and eight), 44 per cent (group seven) and 22 per cent (group nine). The members of the richest income group have been spending almost the same on water throughout the whole period. In 2003 they devoted 0.8 per cent of their expenditures on water – the same percentage as in 1992.

We can say that these figures are not high enough to cause a burden on households. It is difficult to decide what is the benchmark. For example, Fitch and Price (2002) propose a threshold of 3 per cent of income spent on water services (water and sanitation together) as a definition of water poverty. This threshold has been widely used since. Internationally, it is accepted that water bills should not be more than 3–5 per cent of total income.

Table 7.4 refers to expenditure data instead of income. The combined water and sewerage expenditures do not reach 3 per cent, even in the case of the poorest income groups. This implies that water affordability does not seem to be a problem in Hungary. As shown in Figure 7.1, however, water consumption data may indicate that people were feeling the burden of increasing water prices. As water prices increased sharply in real terms during the 1990s, water consumption decreased, standing at 87 per cent of the 1995 consumption level at the end of the 1990s. This is a considerable fall in water consumption.

The picture is just a little bit different for the poorest income group (Figure 7.2). Water consumption dropped for the poorest between 1995 and 1999. This drop was even more pronounced than for the whole population (to 80 per cent of the 1995 level – compared to 87 per cent). However, with stabilizing water prices and rising household expenditures water consumption began to increase again, and by 2003 it had reached the same level as for the whole population (94 per cent of the 1995 level), despite the fact that income growth has been more modest than for the whole population.

Water consumption shows significant variations over time. This is perhaps a surprising finding since water is considered to be a basic necessity and therefore has a low price elasticity. One explanation would be that

*Table 7.4* Affordability of water: water bills and sewerage charges according to income groups for Hungary (percentage of yearly household expenditure)

| *Year* | *Income Groups* | | | | | | | | | |
|---|---|---|---|---|---|---|---|---|---|---|
| | *1* | *2* | *3* | *4* | *5* | *6* | *7* | *8* | *9* | *10* |
| 1995 | 1.98 | 1.94 | 1.87 | 1.84 | 1.79 | 1.96 | 1.81 | 1.77 | 1.56 | 1.30 |
| 1996 | 1.87 | 2.03 | 2.05 | 1.83 | 1.96 | 1.96 | 1.97 | 1.74 | 1.68 | 1.36 |
| 1997 | 1.81 | 2.15 | 2.05 | 1.88 | 1.93 | 1.94 | 1.92 | 1.99 | 1.79 | 1.40 |
| 1998 | 2.05 | 1.90 | 1.87 | 1.87 | 1.89 | 1.84 | 1.83 | 1.96 | 1.71 | 1.43 |
| 1999 | 2.10 | 2.20 | 1.96 | 2.16 | 2.01 | 2.14 | 2.04 | 1.90 | 1.94 | 1.44 |
| | *1st decile* | *1st quintile* | *2nd quintile* | *3rd quintile* | *4th quintile* | *5th quintile* | *10th decile* | | | |
| 2000 | 2.29 | 2.30 | 2.39 | 2.37 | 2.22 | 1.80 | 1.64 | | | |
| 2001 | 2.22 | 2.15 | 2.20 | 2.23 | 2.04 | 1.60 | 1.45 | | | |
| 2002 | 2.01 | 1.95 | 2.29 | 2.24 | 2.13 | 2.17 | 1.53 | | | |
| | *1* | *2* | *3* | *4* | *5* | *6* | *7* | *8* | *9* | *10* |
| 2003 | 2.47 | 2.63 | 2.62 | 2.53 | 2.45 | 2.38 | 2.42 | 2.21 | 2.07 | 1.72 |

*Source*: Hungarian Central Statistical Office.

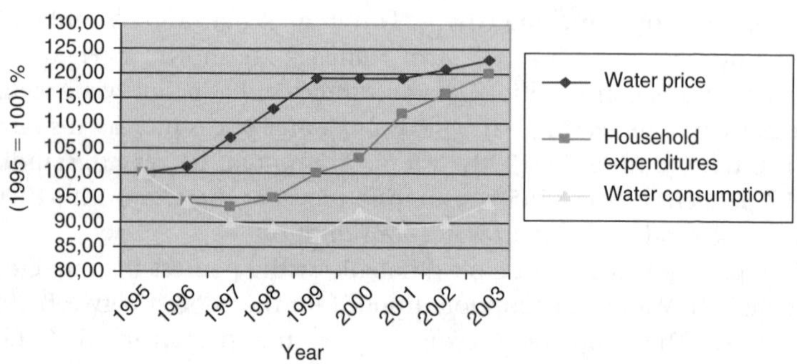


*Figure 7.1* Average household expenditures, average water price increase and household water consumption (percentage change in real terms, 1995 = 100)

rich people tried to reduce their consumption on non-essential items such as swimming pools or gardens whereas there is very little scope for the poor to decrease water consumption. As can be seen from Figure 7.2, water consumption has changed considerably, following the variations of water price and, to some extent, income.

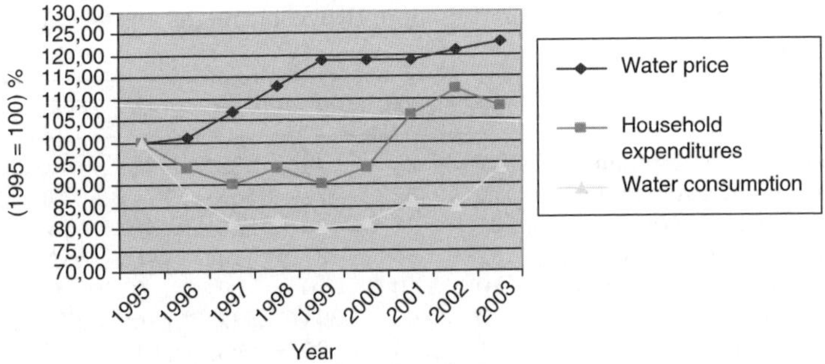


*Figure 7.2* Household expenditures of the 1st income decile, average water price increase and household water consumption (percentage change in real terms, 1995 = 100)

Did PSP in the Hungarian water industry impact on the increases in water prices observed over the past decade? Has private sector involvement contributed to rising water bills in Hungary? Even if water poverty does not seem to exist, people may be considered as water-poor, since water prices vary by a factor of three from one locality to another. We do not have local water expenditure data, but considering at water prices and their relation to PSP in water can provide some illumination as to whether or not water privatization has any effect (either positive or negative) on water affordability.

The reason is that water affordability, as measured in terms of water expenditures per total income (or expenditures), is a composite indicator, which depends upon water price, water consumption, and income. Income itself may be affected by social policies. Therefore using water expenditures per total income as an measure of affordability may obscure the effects of privatization on price. Increasing prices caused by privatization may be counterbalanced by falling consumption, increasing income or social policy measures.

### Social policies

#### *National-level social policies*

In order to comply with the European Union Water Framework Directive, the Hungarian water tariff compensation scheme has to be transformed no later than 2015. Among other things, this directive ensures that the prices charged to the consumers reflect the true price of abstraction, distribution and treatment – that is, the cost recovery principle. As mentioned earlier, in Hungary the price does not reflect the true cost

*Table 7.5* Water prices and compensation, HUF/cubic metre, 1993–99 (EUR1 = HUF250)

| | *1993* | *1994* | *1995* | *1996* | *1997* | *1998* | *1999* |
|---|---|---|---|---|---|---|---|
| Producer price minimum | 19 | 25 | 44 | 32 | 34 | 49 | 30 |
| Producer price maximum | 79 | 362 | 1,472 | 1,565 | 1,874 | 2,033 | 2,176 |
| Household price minimum | 21 | 27 | 50 | 36 | 38 | 55 | 34 |
| Household price maximum | 52 | 66 | 87 | 114 | 146 | 182 | 207 |
| Compensation minimum | 0 | 0 | 0 | 0 | 0 | 0 | 0 |
| Compensation maximum | 32 | 302 | 1,394 | 1,537 | 1,696 | 1,871 | 1,991 |
| Compensation ratio (with maximum prices) (%) | 41 | 83 | 95 | 98 | 91 | 92 | 92 |

*Source*: Hajós (2000: 43), and own calculations.

and is based on a subsidy scheme. The amount of subsidy is decided yearly within the national budget. This sum is distributed among those water companies, of which the costs of water production (and therefore the water prices) exceed a given threshold. Companies receiving the compensation can lower their water prices to the threshold level. The threshold changes yearly, being the function of the sum to be distributed. Since this sum has decreased constantly in real terms, the threshold of subsidy has increased constantly over the past ten years. The subsidy is able to reduce the price of water in those few localities where (for either geographical or technical reasons) the costs of water provision are very high. There is a tenfold difference between the water utilities with the lowest and the highest costs of water production (see below).

There is certainly a justification for state intervention in tariffs. Our study shows the importance of state and local government intervention in keeping the prices at an acceptable level (taking into account that water was free in the socialist era). Although the affordability data show that water tariffs are not a problem, we should bear in mind that the costs of water provision vary to a considerable extent.

*Weight and significance of the national compensation scheme*

Without state intervention, water prices in some regions would be very high. Table 7.5 shows the amount of water compensation between 1993 and 1999 per cubic metre of water. We can see that water prices are widely dispersed, ranging from HUF30 to HUF2176 per cubic metre in 1999 (EUR1 = HUF250). In the case of the highest producer prices central government subsidies cover the majority of the price, reaching above 90 per cent from 1995. The amount of compensation decreased after 1995

*Table 7.6* Household water-services compensation (billion HUF; EUR1 = HUF250)

| | 1992 | 1993 | 1994 | 1995 | 1996 | 1997 | 1998 | 1999 | 2000 | 2001 | 2002 | 2003 | 2004 | 2005 |
|---|---|---|---|---|---|---|---|---|---|---|---|---|---|---|
| By year | 1.5 | 1.5 | 1.5 | 2.0 | 2.5 | 3.0 | 3.4 | 3.8 | 4.1 | 4.5 | 4.9 | 5.6 | 5.9 | 5.5 |
| At 2002 base value | 6.5 | 5.3 | 4.5 | 4.6 | 4.7 | 4.8 | 4.7 | 4.8 | 4.7 | 4.7 | 4.9 | | | |

*Source*: Koskovics and Rákosi (2002) and budget acts.

and 1996, as a result of the steep rise in the absolute value of compensation transferred to local governments (increase in production costs and inflation). This shows that the central budget subsidies could not keep abreast with the rise of producer prices.

By looking at the absolute figures for central government household water compensation (Table 7.6), we can see that it had been increasing constantly from 1995 onwards (HUF1.5 to HUF2.0 billion) until recently, with only a HUF0.4 billion drop in 2005 at nominal value. Calculated at 2002 base value we can see that the subsidy has fallen significantly in the first years, and oscillated around HUF4.8 billion during the following years. With a tight budget in 2005, the government had to cut spending. Water subsidy was reduced, offsetting the real increase of the first years of the 2000s. The amount spent on water compensation represents only a marginal part of the government budget (0.0422 per cent). The total value of household water consumption calculated at average minimum price for the year 2003 was HUF63.625 billion[4] (EUR1 = HUF250). Accordingly, the state subsidy in 2003 corresponds to 8.8 per cent of the total household water consumption. This does not seem to be a huge amount. However, we should not forget that this subsidy is somehow intended for those operators where the production costs are excessively high. Together with local authorities' right to set the prices, this 'small' amount of central subsidy plays an important role in securing the basic rights and welfare of citizens.

In 2002, 12 out of 80 water companies in our database (15 per cent of the companies) received central budget subsidies, among them three privatized operators (one multinational company and two small, local operators).

We could argue that keeping household water prices very low by excluding some cost elements from the calculation is considered a hidden social policy. For example, Ungvári and Mohai (2004) argue that prices are usually set very low, which excludes investment and depreciation costs. Prices are not even able to cover the operational costs. In most cases, utilities are not responsible for investments, since it is the municipality's responsibility with subsidies from central government and some EU funding (Koskovics and Rákosi 2002). Upon agreement (as in the case of Budapest) a so-called 'improvement ratio' may be added to the price to cover part of the investment costs, but this is very rare. By keeping prices low, the fairness of this policy tool is questionable, as it diverts flows towards the well-off[5].

In 2002 the threshold to which the central budget supported household water services was HUF240/cubic metre, and in the case of combined water and wastewater services it was HUF434/cubic metre. With the increase in operational costs and the amount requested from the central budget a ceiling had to be introduced – this stood at 95.4 per cent in 2002. This means that local governments received a maximum of 95.4 per cent of the difference in costs of the threshold value. As Koskovics and Rákosi (2002: 53) point out, the threshold value had been increasing faster than inflation, that is the real value of the highest household water tariffs also increased significantly, with approximately 20 per cent from 1997 to 1999.

### *Guidelines of the compensation*

As mentioned, the overall amount available for household water compensation is set annually in the national budget. In 1993, this was decided at an interministerial (interdepartmental) level. The central subsidy has to flow through the local government and cannot be transferred directly to the operator. The guidelines for considering individual applications are not defined in the budget acts: they are left to the ministry responsible for water issues. The ministry (or the interdepartmental committee) either issues a communication or, as has been the recent practice, a ministerial decree.

This practice has been criticized by the State Audit Office. Local governments have to report yearly about the subsidies. If they do not do so, the whole subsidy has to be transferred to the government. Initially, due to the frequent changes in the organizational structure of the water sector, the interdepartmental committee could not define standard universal principles; rather, it allocated the disposable sum based on individual deliberations. As the report of the State Audit Office (1996) points out, several local governments misused central budget subsidies by manipulating water prices and using the funds for other purposes.

For example, the guidelines of the application procedure for the 2005 compensation were set in a ministerial decree that stated the following among others: Those local governments may receive central budget drinking water price compensation that fulfills the following criteria:

- in the case of regions with sewerage services 60 per cent of the network is connected to the sewerage system;
- specific costs of drinking water service exceed HUF175/cubic metre in the case of water bought from another water utility;
- specific costs of drinking water service exceed HUF319/cubic metre in the case of regions without sewerage;
- specific costs of combined drinking water and sewerage services exceed HUF601/cubic metre in the case of regions with sewerage system.

The interdepartmental committee decides on the extent of individual compensations based on the following principles:

- depreciation does not exceed HUF200/cubic metre;
- the year-on-year rise in salaries does not exceed 6.5 per cent;
- the year-on-year rise in material-type costs does not exceed 2 per cent;
- the year-on-year rise in overall specific costs does not exceed 8 per cent;
- if the price-setting agency sets a different price for non-residential water consumption, this price must not be lower than the residential water price;
- in case of water bought from another water utility, water loss does not exceed 20 per cent.

*Monitoring and abuses*

The main tool to monitor and evaluate the use and efficiency of the water price subsidies is to compare actual water tariffs and producer prices. In terms of the impact of this national-level policy we can assume that it tries to ease the water services bills of households. This scheme could be criticized since it benefits the richer population more than the poor, since the upper and middle classes consume more water.

*Local-level social policies*

With no reliable data, we can provide only a general description of local-level social policies. We argue that the central government subsidy in pricing is quite significant, compared to the limited scope for social policies at the local level.

Local-level social support for water payments is provided in the general household maintenance supports: expenses on heating, house rental, fuel, electricity, gas, water, wastewater and waste collection. These charges are calculated together as household maintenance expenses. If these charges exceed a given amount, support can be given by reducing the bills. The local government transfers the money to the utility. The social support is usually operated by the social and health committee of local governments. An interesting example is that of Budapest where an additional Foundation was set up which receives funding from the water utility and provides assistance to the most vulnerable groups through an application-compensation scheme.

The local governments have a high degree of freedom to make decisions about social support schemes. The support they allocate varies from one municipality to another, and also from year to year, according to the financial situation of the individual local governments.

Based on our interviews with local government representatives, we conclude that this form of social support is much less important than the national-level tariff compensation, and especially the hidden support based on artificially low water prices. The main reason for this is that local governments have insufficient funds to support local social policies. Nevertheless, the scheme is important, because it impacts upon the poorest people.

To conclude, we have shown that the central government compensates for around 8–9 per cent of spending on water, by keeping water prices 5–90 per cent lower than full-cost recovery (depending on the locality). We also demonstrated that there is some assistance provided at the local level.

## Debates on privatization – under scrutiny

Here we pay some brief attention to the political debates surrounding water privatization within the Hungarian context (this may also be relevant to the situation in other transition economies). Privatization, including water privatization in Hungary, is introduced within the context of 'general' privatization and the transition to a market economy, which implies the selling off of state property. Generally, there is no specific sectoral debate regarding water utility privatization *per se*.

Privatization took place in an era of general political and economic transformation, and privatization itself was one important element in this transformation. The importance attached to privatization is understandable given the specificity of the centrally planned economies where almost all productive assets were in the possession – or under the tight control – of the state.

Privatization in the transition economies is unique in many respects, not 'just' because of the political importance assigned to it. The quantity of assets that changed ownership is very large and has touched upon almost every sector of the economy. The speed of the process, especially in those countries leading the reforms, such as Hungary, has also been unprecedented. The privatization process is also unique because it has happened in a dynamically changing environment. In Western Europe, for example, privatization is somehow defined by the existing legal, political, cultural and economic structures. But in the transition economies, the general regulatory or political framework has not yet been clearly defined.

Among the arguments leading to privatization were to increase the efficiency of public utilities, to increase government revenue, and to increase investment. These arguments are well researched and there is no need to go into detail here (Prasad in this volume). However, there are some specific points to be made within the context of Hungary. In order to increase efficiency, employment in the public sector was reduced dramatically. For example, the activity rate among people between the ages of 15 and 75 – that is, the rate of those adults who are working – is some 10 per cent lower in Hungary, than the EU average. In the water sector, Debrecen Waterworks halved its workforce within ten years. Regarding increasing government budget, it is argued that the Budapest Waterworks was (partially) privatized to secure revenue since it was already restructured, and there was no substantial need to investments.

Regarding the argument of seeking additional investment we show that the Szeged Waterworks (as a private company), for example, has not been more efficient in securing additional funds compared to local governments (who can seek cheaper loans to finance investments without serious price increases). In the case of Budapest Sewage Works, the most important investments were financed either by central government or by the city's budget. Another example comes from the city of Pécs with its partially privatized waterworks (1997 SUEZ). The local authorities are having difficulties since prices are increasing while no investments have been forthcoming. In addition, since the waterworks is partly privatized, the city is having difficulties securing EU funds for water infrastructure development.

We have shown that water privatization took place within the general wave of privatization and that no specific debate on water took place. However, a referendum in 2004 managed to block the privatization of health care services. There is a growing feeling in Hungary that government should operate basic services.

## PSP in the Hungarian water sector

### General trends of private sector involvement

As already mentioned, following the change in the political regime the ownership structure of the water system changed considerably. Currently, the ownership structure is not just fragmented, but it is also blurred: in some regions the state ownership remained, while the majority of the waterworks are owned and managed by the local municipalities. A further complication in management was created by introducing the privatization of water at the *local* level. The city of Szeged was the first to start negotiating a concession in 1994 and several other cities and regions followed. Now it is estimated that around 30 per cent of the water is distributed by private companies/joint ventures (Owen 2006).

We do not have a clear picture of the privatization process of the water sector for several reasons – the research behind the present study is the first systematic attempt to construct just such a general picture. One reason is that there is no Office of Water which would monitor the privatization process. The water authority deals only with technical, environmental and quality issues related to water management – the economic-financial aspects are not monitored. Local governments have a high degree of autonomy to make decisions without having either the expertise or the relevant information.[6] Another reason for not having a clear picture about the state of privatization in the Hungarian water sector is that even those companies which were not privatized were formally transformed into public corporations or limited liability companies, and the local government became the owner.

Looking at the brief Hungarian history of PSP we can see some major commonalities, but also some differences between the different privatization cases. Most importantly, full privatization, that is, the complete acquisition of state, local government assets by private companies, is illegal. Hungarian local governments may choose from the following options: outsourcing, long-term concessions and management contracts or setting up a joint company. All of these forms occur in Hungary with a special preference towards joint ventures and management contracts.

Since local governments cannot sell all of the assets (as in the case of Szeged, Budapest, Pécs and several other cities), local authorities have opted mostly for partial privatization – in other words, only a minority (less than 50 per cent) stake of the company is transferred to the private sector. This gives the municipality control, potentially giving them power to protect the public. However, this is often offset by the privatization agreement, which gives management rights to its private partners, thus limiting the authority of the municipality. The minority owners – typically a multinational company or a consortium of companies – are granted the management rights for a long-term concession contract for 15 or (as in the case of Budapest) 25 years.

The privatization contracts – or at least some parts of them – are kept secret. We have made attempts to obtain enough information on the content of these contracts. In most of the contracts, there is no obligation for investment – the owners only have to maintain the infrastructure (Juras and Schenk 2005). For example, the city of Pécs expressed its discontent (over the fact that no additional investments were required, but water prices were increasing) by threatening to withdraw from the contract.[7] This is even more alarming since water prices do not reflect the cost-recovery principle.

### Company size

We identified 12 privatized companies in our company database, which make up between 13 and 20 per cent of the sample. This is below the estimated rate of privatized waterworks, which is around 30 per cent (Ungvári and Mohai 2004). Of these 12 privatized companies, we differentiated the multinationals (six companies) out of which five operate in cities (Budapest, Pécs, Szeged, Kaposvár, Hódmezövásárhely) and one is a regional company. The rest of the privatized companies consist of a small number of Hungarian firms which manage the waterworks for villages or small towns.

Measured in terms of the number of employees there is no significant difference, on average, between the sizes of community-owned and private companies. In terms of the average number of employees, the multinationals are larger companies, while the other privatized ones are small firms. The difference is even more accentuated if we consider the value of company assets. The value of the assets of multinationals is four or five times bigger than the average, while the other private companies are much below the average.

However, this picture can be misleading. When considering company assets one key problem is that capital account balances of water companies are extremely unreliable (Ungvári and Mohai 2004: 29). The average length of the water pipeline per person served would be a more appropriate measure. Multinational companies have the lowest figures, because they operate in cities, while many other publicly owned and operated large companies are regional water utilities. Another feature of the privately operated water companies is that they have grown faster than the community-owned firms. This is illustrated by the rate of increase of the average length of water pipeline operated by a company. We find that the pipeline systems of multinationals have grown by 15 per cent. This increase could have occurred as a result of new constructions or through a process of mergers and acquisitions. Evidence from Hungary suggests that in this instance the latter may have played a more important role.

**Efficiency/productivity**

One general argument for privatization is that private operators might increase the efficiency of a company. In order to consider this hypothesis we looked at some efficiency indicators. We limited our attention to some general aspects of company productivity. For example, turnover per employee increased for the community-owned waterworks and also for the multinationals. The magnitude is the same (around 30 per cent), but the trend seems to be steadier for the multinationals. On the other hand, no efficiency improvement can be noted for the small private waterworks. An increase in productivity can be noticed for all types of water companies during the past ten years, as measured by the length of water pipeline operated per employee. For community-owned companies the average length of pipeline per employee has grown by 40 per cent, compared to 88 per cent for multinationals, and about 30 per cent for other privately operated companies.

We assumed that larger companies might have more opportunities for increasing productivity (laying off people). Our data reveal (Table 7.7) that the 20 largest water companies shed fewer employees than the average of the community-owned firms. Multinationals have been leading the way in reducing their workforce.

We find that the multinational companies pay wages that are, on average, 14–25 per cent higher than community-owned companies. The lowest average wages are paid by the small private waterworks. Again, we assumed that larger companies may pay higher wages, so we compared the average wage paid by the multinationals to the wages of the 20 largest companies. Indeed, although the advantage of the multinationals has been somewhat reduced, it still remains.

However since we lack data about the profitability, amount of investment and cost of operation we cannot obtain a complete picture of

*Table 7.7* Change in the number of employees, percentage (1995 = 100)

| *Year* | *Community-owned companies* | *The 20 largest companies* | *Multinationals* | *Other private* |
|---|---|---|---|---|
| 1995 | 100 | 100 | 100 | 100 |
| 1996 | 92 | 92 | 88 | 106 |
| 1997 | 80 | 90 | 81 | 115 |
| 1998 | 75 | 89 | 78 | 107 |
| 1999 | 74 | 90 | 76 | 110 |
| 2000 | 75 | 87 | 68 | 121 |
| 2001 | 72 | 86 | 65 | 100 |
| 2002 | 70 | 84 | 62 | 97 |
| 2003 | 72 | 83 | 62 | 93 |
| 2004 | 74 | 82 | 61 | 87 |

the efficiency of different companies. We can only confirm that multinational companies shed labour to improve efficiency and productivity.

## The effect of private sector involvement on water price

With an increase in efficiency observed in most types of company, we would like to investigate who benefits from such improvements. Does it lead to a decrease in prices, increase in coverage or do the companies take them as profits?

These questions would be meaningful only in a full-cost recovery setting, which is not the case in Hungary. As discussed above, water prices are below the level needed to cover investment and depreciation costs, and they, only barely hardly cover operation costs. As mentioned earlier, the main reason is that local municipalities do not allow their prices to rise faster, for political reasons. Therefore, if in the past ten years water prices have grown more quickly than inflation (as indeed they have), this should be seen as normal from a business point of view. If there are differences between the prices of privatized and non-privatized companies, this might signal at least a difference in relative bargaining power of the firms.

However, in our case price analysis has some problems and shortcomings. First, some of the cases in the database are conglomerates of several small, local companies. Being conglomerates, they are still not very large companies, because they bring together small, village water utilities. But they still set different prices for the different settlements. In other words, about 25 companies do not have not one but two water prices in the

*Table 7.8* Average household water prices, minimum values (HUF, nominal values, EUR1 = HUF250)

| *Year* | *Community-owned* | | *Private operators* | | *Total* | |
|---|---|---|---|---|---|---|
| | *Price* | *N* | *Price* | *N* | *Price* | *N* |
| 1995 | 57.23 | 52 | 51.63 | 8 | 56.49 | 60 |
| 1996 | 71.49 | 56 | 60.96 | 10 | 69.89 | 66 |
| 1997 | 86.52 | 63 | 83.35 | 11 | 86.05 | 74 |
| 1998 | 101.13 | 70 | 103.22 | 12 | 101.43 | 82 |
| 1999 | 116.14 | 71 | 121.42 | 12 | 116.90 | 83 |
| 2000 | 126.74 | 68 | 141.02 | 11 | 128.73 | 79 |
| 2001 | 140.18 | 70 | 146.54 | 12 | 141.11 | 82 |
| 2002 | 148.83 | 71 | 155.28 | 12 | 149.76 | 83 |
| 2003 | 160.37 | 70 | 164.68 | 12 | 161.00 | 82 |
| 2004 | 172.91 | 67 | 177.02 | 12 | 173.54 | 79 |

database for each year: a minimum and a maximum price they set for their consumers. Since water prices are in general lower in towns (because of the lower marginal cost of supplying water) minimum price would reflect the reality.

Table 7.8 shows that from 1998, the prices of private operators are 2–11 per cent higher than the prices charged by community-owned companies. We conducted some statistical analysis to see if ownership was instrumental in having different price. From our findings, we can say that water privatization has not led to price increase in Hungary. For instance, for multinationals water prices in 2004 vary from HUF124–HUF277 among the six companies (Table 7.9). We also observe that small private companies have higher prices than the multinationals. The prices of the multinationals correspond almost exactly to the prices of the community-owned waterworks. The other, small privatized companies have prices that are, on average, some 10 per cent higher.

Other factors (apart from ownership per se) might also have an impact on price differences. These might include technology used by the individual companies, the geographical characteristics, the availability of water and so on. But it might also be that other, external factors explain the price variations – for example, political decisions made by the given municipality.

However, we need to be cautious since geography (cost of production) and type of ownership may be linked. In this case, the prices may be higher in private firms, on a relative, rather than an absolute

*Table 7.9* Average household water prices, minimum values (HUF, nominal values, EUR1 = HUF250)

| *Year* | *Community-owned companies* | | *Multinationals* | | *Other private* | | *Total* | |
|---|---|---|---|---|---|---|---|---|
| | *HUF* | *N* | *HUF* | *N* | *HUF* | *N* | *HUF* | *N* |
| 1995 | 57.23 | 52 | 50.97 | 6 | 53.60 | 2 | 56.49 | 60 |
| 1996 | 71.49 | 56 | 59.95 | 6 | 62.47 | 4 | 69.89 | 66 |
| 1997 | 86.52 | 63 | 81.55 | 6 | 85.52 | 5 | 86.05 | 74 |
| 1998 | 101.13 | 70 | 97.15 | 6 | 109.28 | 6 | 101.43 | 82 |
| 1999 | 116.14 | 71 | 113.82 | 6 | 129.01 | 6 | 116.90 | 83 |
| 2000 | 126.74 | 68 | 126.50 | 6 | 158.44 | 5 | 128.73 | 79 |
| 2001 | 140.18 | 70 | 138.87 | 6 | 154.21 | 6 | 141.11 | 82 |
| 2002 | 148.83 | 71 | 149.95 | 6 | 160.60 | 6 | 149.76 | 83 |
| 2003 | 160.37 | 70 | 158.68 | 6 | 170.67 | 6 | 161.00 | 82 |
| 2004 | 172.91 | 67 | 168.40 | 6 | 185.64 | 6 | 173.54 | 79 |

scale. Since the costs of water production are different in different places (experts say that there is a tenfold difference between the costs of the most and the least expensive water production sites in Hungary), the private operators could have chosen those settlements where the production costs tend to be low in absolute terms. In those places even a low price might hide an increased profit, given that the costs are so low. Indeed, there are signs of 'cherry-picking', especially from multinational investors who carefully focus on larger cities with high population densities. One would expect that water tariffs should be lower in bigger cities. This might suggest that some overpricing is indeed happening in towns and cities.

Another plausible explanation might be that private investors have been seeking to increase efficiency and have tried to raise their profits by reducing costs, instead of increasing prices. As we saw earlier, multinationals were in the frontline in reducing their workforce. A third, and also very plausible explanation would suggest that the institutional setting of the privatization context determines the behaviour of the companies. Our case studies suggest that there are guaranteed fixed management fees for private companies. Or, as in the case of Budapest, the management fee is not linked to the profits, but rather to the improvements in efficiency. If so, the private investors do not necessarily have to increase the prices in order to realize gains. This leads us to our previous explanation of why private companies may choose to increase efficiency rather than increase prices.

## Conclusion

In this chapter we demonstrated that there is a lack of state capacity to control and monitor PSP in the water sector in Hungary. PSP often takes place at the local (municipal) level, and there is no central authority (Office of Water) that controls or monitors the process. The National Water Authority deals only with environmental, water management and technical issues. However, local governments do not necessarily have the capabilities to regulate the private operators. We argued that PSP in water started in Hungary without the proper institutional and legal framework and that this led to several local conflicts.

We also demonstrated that Hungary has some strong social policies in place. We argued that water prices in Hungary are heavily subsidized, including cross-subsidization (household water prices are lower than industrial prices), water prices are kept low by local governments (for political reasons), which is regarded as a hidden subsidy. Water tariffs are not able to cover the operation costs. We also highlighted the role of central subsidies in keeping prices below a threshold, where the central government covers a non-negligible part of the water costs from the state budget.

Such social policies in keeping the prices low lead us to argue that water affordability does not appear to be a problem in Hungary. However, water prices have been increasing steadily in Hungary since the regime change of the early 1990s. Despite this rapid increase, the poorest income group spends no more than 1.5 per cent of their household expenditure on water (or 2.63 per cent if we take water and sewerage services). Similarly, by international standards access to water is not a problem in Hungary. Piped water is available in practically every settlement, and public fountains are provided free of charge to everyone living within 200 metres. However, an important fraction of the population, accounting for almost 20 per cent of the poorest households, does not have piped water in their homes. This access problem is, in fact, an affordability problem: people do not have the financial capacities for connecting to the main pipes.

The rate of observed price increases is slightly higher in the private companies than in the community-owned companies. However, privatized companies do not seem to have higher water tariffs. We formulated three explanations for this (none of these should be regarded as exclusive): the specificities of the social policies, which provide other incentives for the private operators (fixed management fees or fees linked to cuts in costs, and so on); the efficiency improvements made by the private operators (which allow them to realize gains without necessary increasing prices); and the 'cherry-picking' of private investors (choosing those regions where efficiency gains could be easily realized and prices are not high).

In conclusion, it is clear that private water companies (especially multinational corporations) have been successful in increasing efficiency (productivity). However, this has not led to falling prices. Private companies have not contributed to investments in the infrastructure.

## Notes

1. When we refer to 'privatized water companies' we mean a partially privatized company owning long-term management rights.
2. This was a general policy during the socialist era: the prices of public services were kept artificially low (or they were non-existent). This was a social transfer (welfare measure) which partly compensated people for the low level of salaries.
3. The database was provided by the Hungarian Waterworks Association (Magyar Vízközmü Szövetség). We would like to thank the Association, and in particular Dr. Mária Papp, the president of the Association, for the help given to our project.
4. Total water consumption by households (excluding non-household consumption) was 395,187,800 cubic metres in 2003. The average water price in 2003 is HUF161/cubic metre (calculated as the average of the minimum prices, the average maximum was HUF176 – however, the majority of the providers falls into the first category).
5. We could also observe the same type of hidden social policy in the case of energy, especially household gas prices, that were kept artificially low by the previous government to ease household burdens. The issue became highly politicized during the elections in 2002, and is still a central topic. Certainly, this is a legacy of the old socialist system, in which the prices of public services were kept artificially low.
6. For instance, the transfer of ownership from the state to local governments was undertaken without a proper evaluation of the value of the assets, or after making a careful inventory of state ownership. Local governments do not even know the value and the physical status of the assets they possess.
7. Pécs offers an interesting example, because some years ago the city took back the previously privatized waste collection company for similar reasons: it turned out that prices increased and infrastructure development became more difficult to finance, since the private operator did not invest, but the city had difficulties in accessing EU funds for a formally private company.

## References

Barghouti, S. (1999) 'Growing Challenges to Water Resources Management', *Sustainable Development International* 1 (Launch Edition), 43–52.

Boda, Zs. (2005) 'No Limits? Privatization in Central and Eastern Europe', in Ernst Ulrich von Weizsäcker, Oran Young and Matthias Finger (eds), *Limits to Privatization: How to Avoid Too Much of a Good Thing* (London: Earthscan).

Boda, Zs., G. Scheiring, D. Hall and E. Lobina (2006) *Social Policies and Private Sector Participation in Water Supply: The Case of Hungary*. Programme on Markets, Business and Regulation (Geneva: UNRISD).

Brooks, D.B. (2002) *In Focus: Water, Local Level Management* (Ottawa: International Development Research Centre).

Brubaker, Elisabeth (2001) *The Promise of Privatization* (Toronto: Energy Probe Research Foundation). http://www.environmentprobe.org/enviroprobe/pubs/Ev548.htm, accessed on 23 September 2005.

Cosgrove, W.J. and F.R. Rijsberman (2000) *World Water Vision: Making Water Everybody's Business* (London: Earthscan).

Debreceni Vizmü (1999) *Extract from the Debrecen Waterworks Inc. Account for the Year 1998* (Debrecen).

Fitch, M. and H. Price (2002) *Water Poverty in England and Wales* (Leicester: Centre for Utility Consumer Law and Chartered Institute of Environmental Health).

Gergely, P. (1999) *The Szeged Case*. Report (August), based on articles published in Hungarian periodicals, including Népszabadság and Napi Világgazdaság. PSIRU database.

Gleick, Peter H. (2003) 'Global Freshwater Resources: Soft-path Solutions for the 21st Century', *Science*, 302, 1524–8.

Gleick, Peter H. (2000) 'The Changing Water Paradigm: a Look at Twenty-first Century Water Resources Development', *Water International*, 25(1), 127–38.

Hall, D. (1998) 'Restructuring and Privatization in the Public Utilities – Europe', in L. De Luca (ed.), *Labour and Social Dimensions of Privatization and Restrucuring (Public Utilities: Water, Gas and Electricity)* (Geneva: published for the International Labour Office).

Hall, D. and E. Lobina (2004) 'Private and Public Interests in Water and Energy', *Natural Resources Forum*, 28, 268–77.

Hall, D. and E. Lobina (1999) *Water and Privatisation in Central and Eastern Europe, 1999*. Public Services International Research Unit, University of Greenwich. www.psiru.org/reports/9909b-W-CEE.doc, accessed on 10 October 2005.

Hungarian Central Statistical Office (2004) *Public Utilities 2003* (Budapest: Hungarian Central Statistical Office).

Juras, Alexander and Todd Schenk (2005) 'Budapest Sewage Works: Partial Privatization of a Central European Utility', in Ernst Ulrich von Weizsäcker, Oran Young and Matthias Finger (eds), *Limits to Privatization: How to Avoid Too Much of a Good Thing* (London: Earthscan).

Kalotay, Kálmán and Gábor Hunya (2000) 'Privatization and FDI in Central and Eastern Europe', *Transnational Corporations*, 9(1), April, 39–66.

Koskovics, Éva and Judit Rákosi (2002) *Az önkormányzati környezetvédelmi közszolgáltatásokat érintö európai uniós szabályozások megvalósításának feltételei*. A Budapesti Közgazdaságtudományi és Államigazgatási Egyetem Környezettudományi Intézetének tanulmányai (Budapest, October).

KVVM (2005) *Európai összefogás a vizek jó állapotáért: A Víz Keretirányelv végrehajtásának helyzete Magyarországon és a Duna-vízgyüjtökerületben*. October (Budapest: Környezetvédelmi és Vízügyi Minisztérium).

Lobina, E. (2005a) 'Problems with Private Water Concessions: a Review of Experiences and Analysis of Dynamics', *International Journal of Water Resources Development*, 21(1), 55–87.

Lobina, E. (2005b) *D11: WaterTime Case Study – Arezzo, Italy*. WaterTime Deliverable D11, 4 March 2005. http://www.watertime.net/docs/WP2/D11_Arezzo.doc.

Lobina, E. (2001) *Water Privatisation and Restructuring in Central and Eastern Europe, 2001. PSIRU Reports*, November. http://www.psiru.org/reports/2001-11-W-CEE.doc.

Mohajeri, Shahrooz, Bettina Knoothe, David-Nicolas Lamothe and Jean-Antoine Faby (eds) (2003) *Aqualibrium: European Water Management between Regulation and Competition* (Brussels: European Commission, Directorate General for Research).

National Research Council (2002) *Privatization of Water Services in the United States* (Washington: National Academy Press).

Ostrom, Elinor (1990) *Governing the Commons: The Evolution of Institutions for Collective Action* (Cambridge: Cambridge University Press).

Owen, D.L. (2006) *Pinsent Masons Water Yearbook, 2006–2007* (London: Masons Solicitors).

Péter, Judit (2004) *WaterTime National Context Report – Hungary*. A research project supported by the European Commission. www.watertime.org, accessed on 13 September 2005.

Péter, Judit (2005a) *WaterTime Case Study – Budapest, Hungary*. A research project supported by the European Commission. www.watertime.org, accessed on 13 September 2005.

Péter, Judit (2005b) *WaterTime Case Study – Szeged, Hungary*. A research project supported by the European Commission. www.watertime.org, accessed on 13 September 2005.

Rees, Judith A. (1998) *Regulation and Private Participation in the Water and Sanitation Sector* (Stockholm: Global Water Partnership, Swedish International Development Cooperation Agency).

Rose, Carol M. (2002) 'Common Property, Regulatory Property and Environmental Protection: Comparing Community-based Management to Tradable Environmental Allowances', in Elinor Ostrom *et al.* (eds), *The Drama of the Commons* (Washington, DC: National Academy Press).

Serafy, Salah L. (1991) 'The Environment as Capital', in Robert Costanza (ed.), *Ecological Economics: The Science and Management of Sustainability* (Columbia: Columbia University Press).

Somlyódy, László, Buzás Kálmán, Clement Adrienne and Licskó István (2002) 'Települési vízgazdálkodás', in László Somlyódy (ed.), *A hazai vízgazdálkodás stratégiai kérdései* (Budapest: Hungarian Academy of Sciences).

State Audit Office (1996) *Jelentés a helyi önkormányzatok közüzemi víz- és csatornaszolgáltatási feladatainak és az ehhez kapcsolódó lakossági díjtámogatási rendszer müködésének viszgálatáról* (Budapest: State Audit Office).

Szegedi Vizmü (2004) *Szegedi Vízmü Rt – Víz az élet forrása*. Leaflet.

Szegedi Vizmü (1996) No title. Leaflet, 4 July.

Trawick, Paul (2003) 'Against the Privatization of Water: an Indigenous Model for Improving Existing Laws and Successfully Governing the Commons', *World Development*, 31(6), 977–96.

Trawick, Paul (2001) 'Successfully Governing the Commons: Principles of Social Organization in an Andean Irrigation System', *Human Ecology*, 29(1), 1–26.

Ungvári, Gábor and Zsuzsanna Mohai (2004) *Assesment and Development of Municipal Water and Wastewater Tariffs and Effluent Charges in the Danube River Basin.* National Profile for Water and Wastewater Management in Hungary. UNDP/GEF Danube Regional Project.

# 8
# Burkina Faso

*Issaka Kouanda and Mouhamad Moudassir*

## Introduction

As discussed in the introductory chapter of this book, there has been a worldwide trend towards the privatization of state-owned companies in the water sector over the past two decades. Africa has been no exception to this phenomenon: under the aegis of the World Bank (WB) and the International Monetary Fund (IMF), many countries have privatized their water sectors. The primary justification for this reform was based on the idea that public ownership meant inefficiency and mismanagement and that the state could not inject the additional investments required. It was argued that with the *status quo* scenario with public management, the Millennium Development Goals (MDGs) of halving the number of people without access to potable water would not be achieved.

In order to solve water problems, commercialization and private sector participation (PSP) were both encouraged. The intention was to increase the efficiency of public companies, and to increase both investment and coverage across the population. Commercialization and privatization of the water sector has taken different forms in different countries. The situation is extremely complex. In the African context (especially in the countries of the Sahel), where the problem of access to safe water is characterized by geo-climatic conditions of scarcity of water resources and by socioeconomic conditions of high levels of poverty among the population.

This case study shows how commercialization and PSP deals with issues of access and affordability in Burkina Faso. To our knowledge there has been no such previous study of this topic. The chapter also investigates the role of social policies in addressing issues of access and affordability. This case study is representative of other African countries. Burkina Faso is a landlocked country that suffers from extreme climatic conditions and it is also one of the poorest countries in the world. For a long time its public water policy has been marked by a strong state presence in charge of water production in urban and rural areas, and by the intervention of private water vendors in urban water distribution.

The first wave of public reforms in the area of water policy took place in the 1990s – this resulted in an overhaul of the status of the water offices and, in some cases, by their elimination. To cope with rapid population growth in urban areas, especially Ouagadougou (the capital), the government tried to increase the water supply by building additional infrastructure with the help of external funds. One of the conditions for such assistance was to involve the private sector. This was executed through a service contract between a group of service providers led by the multinational Veolia and the National Office of Water and Sewerage Purification (ONEA).

This chapter consists of five sections: the next gives an overview of the water sector in Burkina Faso, tackling the question of the scarcity of water resources, the structure of water production and industry performance over the past 15 years. Next we describe the involvement of private actors, their successes and failures, and this is followed by a description of institutional and social policies and their outcomes. The fifth part presents the results of an empirical analysis of the issues of access and affordability – it concentrates on how the situation has changed since Veolia entered the market. Finally, we conclude and offer some policy recommendations.

## Water production and supply in Burkina Faso – an overview

### Organization of the Burkinabe water sector

The water sector in Burkina Faso is structured and organized in such a way as to manage a rare, but valuable good in a specific social and political context. The water policy concentrates on three major goals: the improvement of the quality of the supply for connected population; the expansion of coverage for the growing urban population; and increasing access to the rural population.

#### *Water – a fundamental scarce resource*

In order to understand current water policy in the country, it is important to study it through the context of a specific country. The scarcity of potable water in Burkina Faso is linked intrinsically to the climatic and hydrological characteristics of the country. It has insufficient rainfall. Burkina Faso has a Sudanese-Sahelian climate characterized by an alternation of dry and rainy seasons. Rainfalls in Burkina Faso are insufficient in regard to their cycles (concentrated on average over a four-month period) and prevailing high temperatures. This leads to a rapid subterranean infiltration and a rapid evaporation of rainwater. The rainfall situation seems to have worsened since the 1976 drought, as a decrease of 10–20 per cent of the rainfall has been observed since then.

This leads to a problem of scarcity of inbound water resources. The hydrographical network is composed of many streams and rivers, located mainly in the southern zone of the country, but these are not inbound sources. The hydrographical network is composed of three main basins, from where the main rivers of neighbouring countries take their source. A 2001 survey by the Ministry of Environment and Water concluded that, according to the fluctuation of the aquifers over the last 20 years, there is almost no renewable subterranean water in Burkina Faso. The scarcity of water is worsened by the difficulties of exploiting it. Due to the geological conditions, the subterranean extraction of water is extremely expensive in areas suffering from lack of rain. In the north east of the country, a very dry region, drilling ranges from 10 to 60 metres to get water (Groen *et al.* 1988). One possible solution offers construction of dams. This is not only expensive but climatic conditions hamper the expected results.

*Access to water in Burkina Faso*

In Ouagadougou, only 30 per cent of the city's population are connected to the public distribution network.[1] During the hottest three months of the year (April–June), when the water resources drop by one-third,[2] 60 per cent of the population experience frequent water cuts. As illustrated in Table 8.1, in general, access to potable water (as measured by the World

*Table 8.1* Access rates to safe water

| | *1994* | *1998* | *2003* |
|---|---|---|---|
| Access rate in urban centres | — | 82.9 | 85.8 |
| Access rate in rural areas | 31 | 44.7 | 53.9 |
| Nation average | 43.1 | 51.9 | 60.7 |
| ONEA's coverage rate in the existing centres | 54 | 67 | 78 |

*Sources*: INSD (1994, 1998, and 2003) for the access rate, and ONEA (1990 and 2004) for the coverage rate and volume consumed.

Health Organization's definition of having a source within 200 metres of one's residence) has improved over the last decade, but the coverage remains insufficient. 40 per cent of the total population still lack access to potable water. We also observe that water consumption has decreased slightly between 1994 and 1998. The problem is more acute in rural, areas where only 50 per cent have access to water supply. ONEA has been making considerable progress in increasing network coverage in its 36 principal centres.

*1 Urban centres.* ONEA is in charge of producing, distributing and purifying water in the main cities of Burkina Faso. In fact, its work is concentrated essentially in the capital (Ouagadougou), the second biggest town of the country (Bobo Dioulasso), and some smaller urban centres. The structure and organization of the office reflects the priority given to the larger cities. ONEA has 36 centres that are in charge of 36 urban communes of more than 10,000 inhabitants each and also has a regional directorate for Ouagadougou, one for Bobo Dioulasso and one for other centres. The allocation of resources reflects the priority given to the biggest cities (Table 8.2). For example, in terms of human resources allocated to the connection of potable water, 37 per cent of the office employees work for the Ouagadougou centre, which covers 56 per cent of the total population covered by ONEA.

From the industrial point of view, water production is fundamentally different in the two main directorates (Ouagadougou and Bobo) and in the auxiliary centres. For example, in Ouagadougou, the water is supplied

*Table 8.2* Resources and results of different centres of ONEA, 2004

| | *ONEA* | *Regional directorate for Quagadougou* | *Regional directorate for Bobo Dioulasso* | *Directorate for other centres* | *Ratio Ouagadougou/ ONEA (%)* |
|---|---|---|---|---|---|
| Number of employees working for water adduction in 2004 | 477 | 179 | 131 | 167 | 37 |
| Population supplied by private vendors | 760,390 | 454,350 | 195,760 | 85,840 | 59.6 |
| Population supplied by a hand pump | 1,349,285 | 724,873 | 310,124 | 314,288 | 53.7 |
| Total population supplied with water | 2,114,794 | 1,178,323 | 506,825 | 404,305 | 55.7 |

*Source*: ONEA (2004, 2005).

through private connections (38 per cent) and fountains (62 per cent) whereas in auxiliary centres, most of the water is supplied by fountains (77 per cent) and a small quantity by private connection (21 per cent).

*2 Rural areas.* It was following the 1974 drought that access to drinking water in rural areas became a particularly important issue and international cooperation (mainly NGOs) became active outside the main cities. Wells were drilled in collaboration with the state-owned ONPF (the National Office for Wells and Boreholes). But the latter encountered various difficulties and was dissolved by 1995, thus allowing private companies to operate in the countryside. There has been an increase in access to safe water from 31 per cent in 1994 to 54 per cent in 2003 (Table 8.1). Despite the MDG leitmotiv, the state budget remains too small to significantly improve access to water for the rural population and the external funds continue to be too unpredictable to initiate any structured policy reform. The unpredictability of funds might also discourage private companies from investing in the rural water sector. A report from the Danish development cooperation shows that in 2002, 211 companies were involved in the rural sector.[3] These actors have to compete for an unstable and irregular market, which is unattractive, as it generally offers insufficient financial resources and does not allow a continuous development. In addition, the procedure for granting market shares lacks rigour.[4] Together with weak control, this leads to the creation of a *jungle environment* in the water sector and also to a poor quality of service. As a result, the Ministry of Water classified 25 per cent of the drillings in rural areas as faulty.[5]

## Institutional complexity

As discussed earlier in this chapter, the organization of the water supply is extremely complex because of both the scarcity of the resource and also the diversity of the actors involved. The law on water management 002-2001/AN of 8 February 2001 confirms the state's key role in the formulation of a national water policy.[6] Laws 40–2 of August 1998 on the territorial organization mention that the management of the water resources is the responsibility of the local authorities, but does not specify the precise role that the decentralized authorities have to play in the water supply.

Historically, the water policy has always been attributed to a particular ministry that has been in charge of defining the trends to be followed, as well as their application.[7] The National Council of Water manages the water used for any purpose other than agriculture, but the Ministry of

Agriculture remains in charge of the integrated management of water resources throughout the country. However, this management depends on three other ministries: the Ministry of Agriculture, Hydrographical and Fishing Resources with a minimum of six directorates, including the General Directorate for Potable Water; the Ministry of Animal Resources; and the Ministry of Environment and Living Environment.

The multitude of different actors involved in this sector renders the organization opaque. The General Directorate of Potable Water controls ONEA, advises and coordinates the interventions of NGOs in rural areas and, with the assistance of external funds, builds up hydrographical infrastructures. Water supply in urban centres is even more complex, despite ONEA being the only competent authority. ONEA was functioning under the umbrella of EPIC (Public Enterprise of Industrial and Commercial Nature) and was thus dependent directly upon the Ministry of Water for its operations as well as its resources. As was stipulated in its status, when dealing with the water supply in the urban centres, ONEA was following the instructions set by the Ministry of Water. Prices were fixed by the Council of Ministers and state subsidies were given to ONEA to compensate for the losses, as prices did not include all production costs. In 1994, under the framework of the World Bank's reform process, ONEA received the status of a Corporate Statutory Body and therefore it now benefits from autonomy of management. However, the relations between ONEA and the state have remained nearly unchanged. ONEA is still under the control of the General Directorate for Potable Water. Its activities and modalities of work are decided with mutual consent by the two actors. As a result, the state still influences the pricing decisions: ONEA proposes a price based on the results of surveys and the final prices are debated and fixed at the Council of Ministers, by the different ministries concerned.[8] Prices are published by the Ministry of Trade and thus take effect nationwide.

## Progress and challenges

As mentioned above, over the past decade water supply and access to safe water has improved in Burkina Faso. Water production has doubled between 1990 and 2004 and the length of the potable water network tripled from (from 948 km to 3,143 km) over the same period. But these improvements have benefited principally the larger cities such as Ouagadougou and Bobo Dioulasso and, to a lesser extent, semi-urban centres or rural areas. As mentioned earlier, ONEA's efforts vary substantially between the main and secondary urban centres. However, due to the lack of data, it remains difficult to analyse the performance of the

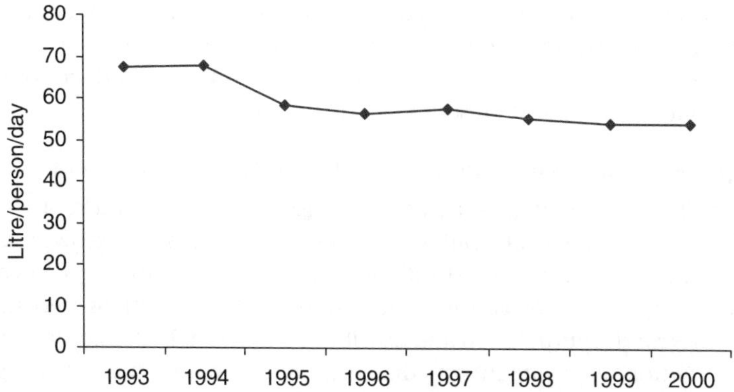


*Figure 8.1* Evolution of the water consumption per capita between 1993 and 2000
*Source*: ONEA (2004).

water network in the rural areas. Although coverage has improved, this does not imply that the water consumption per person has also increased. On the contrary, there was a decrease observed between 1993 and 2000 (Figure 8.1). The increase of the water supply was accompanied by a decrease in the water consumption per capita. This could be explained by an increasing population, increased consumption by non-domestic users, or price increase which discourages people to consume (see later on impact of price increase).

Lack of coverage also impacts upon the sanitary conditions of the population. It is estimated that one-third of households are not equipped with sanitary facilities and do not use water in their homes for their own hygiene. In rural areas, it is common to use watercourses (rivers, streams) for own consumption and hygiene. In addition, 65 per cent people relieve themselves in nature, which is a major health concern. One-third of the rural population fetch drinking water from watercourses, which are contaminated by human and animal faeces, resulting in outbreaks of water-borne diseases. It is reported by the World Health Organization that 19 per cent of deaths of children under five years of age are due to diarrhoeal diseases, as are 3 per cent of neonatal deaths.

## Intervention of private actors in the water sector

It is important to understand the involvement of different types of private actors in the water sector in Burkina Faso. The modes of intervention of private actors in the water sector have taken two forms: either that of a simple participation in the distribution of the water produced by ONEA, or that of a support to the organization of the water production and distribution, in terms of resources and methods.

## Typology of the actors and rationalism for their involvement

According to certain experts, the obstacles to the extension of a water network are largely attributable to poverty, population growth and unplanned urban growth (Collignon and Vezina 2000). This uncontrolled growth is not accompanied by the development of necessary facilities for the purification and distribution of water. In this context, the intervention of private intermediaries is crucial because they contribute to the extension of the water distribution network (for example, through fountains that they subcontract from ONEA, and door-to-door resellers, or water tankers).

It is instructive to consider urban policy in order to understand Ouagadougou's current water problems. It is argued that urban policy[9] affected the water demand negatively. Before 1983, almost 70 per cent of the city constructions were unauthorized. This led to a negative impact on the global demand of water. First, due to ONEA's limited capacity of production, the water distribution network remained unchanged, and, secondly, it attracted many people to the city. But this rapid increase of population has resulted in many inhabitants living in areas that were previously unreachable by basic services, including potable water.[10] Since then, the population has been growing and has thus created a space for private actors. Water, produced by ONEA, is sold to fountain managers, who resell it directly to the households (they come to the fountains or to resellers who deliver the water door to door). Nationwide, 53 per cent of the water produced by ONEA is distributed by private intermediaries (62 per cent in the city of Ouagadougou). Countrywide, it is difficult to estimate the exact number of resellers and the percentage that they represent in the water distribution since most of them are in the informal sector and therefore are not included in any evaluations or statistics. The role of the fountain managers and water resellers is to extend the distribution network, even to the more remote consumers.

In order to cope with the growing population, the country has embarked on efforts to increase the production capacity. The construction of the Ziga dam to increase the water supply to Ouagadougou is an example. With a storage capacity of 5,400 cubic metres, it will enable the creation of a second and third distribution network of respectively 210 and 1,200 kilometres. About 45,000 new private connections to the network and 400 fountains are planned to be opened in the capital. It is expected that, by the end of 2007, 800,000 people would have a direct supply, which is a significant increase on the 300,000 people connected in 1999. As a result, 95 per cent of the population will have access to potable water in 2004.[11] The pipeline works are now completed and Ouagadougou is supplied through the Ziga dam. At this stage, the extension of the second and third networks is yet to be completed. Only one pilot project, for 5,000 connections, was underway in 2006 and it is expected that this objective will be achieved.

In order to embark on this colossal project, Burkina Faso, under the aegis of the World Bank, had to borrow FCFA150 billion.[12] As a condition for such a loan, the donors requested that ONEA be privatized. Finally, it was agreed to have a service contract. This contract gives Veolia the right to apply principles and practises of management that generate sufficient profit margins to develop its activities and to pay back ONEA's debt.

## Juridical arrangements

In this section we will analyse, the relations between ONEA and the fountain managers and also the service contract between ONEA and Veolia.

### *Partnership between ONEA and the fountain managers*

Fountain managers sign a contract with ONEA that specifies the rights and obligations of each party to the agreement. The partnership between both entities could be seen as a delegation of public services because the activities of the fountain managers are strictly ruled by ONEA.[13] For ONEA, a manager is its client and not its employee. This client, however, has an important task – to improve the access to potable water. The manager[14] should be a non-salaried worker (private or public), fully available and living close to his/her working place. The manager also needs to respect ONEA's measures of hygiene and purification. ONEA's obligation towards the manager is to supply potable water. Both parties perform the maintenance of the infrastructure. In case of small reparations, the manager provides the spare parts and ONEA provides the manpower. For larger operations, such as water meter, pipelines, connections, only ONEA is responsible.

The price at which ONEA sells water to the fountain manager and the price charged by the fountain manager to the consumer are fixed by the Council of Ministers, since the role of a fountain manager is considered to be a public service. ONEA makes sure that the tariffs are respected and terminates contracts in cases of non-compliance. Contracts could also be terminated if the delay of payment is regular or if the manager has delegated his/her job to a third party. Other reasons for the termination are: violation of hygiene rules, lack of commercial viability and the change of residence of the fountain manager away from his/her working place. Door-to-door resellers have no obligations towards ONEA, as they are part of the informal sector.

*Service contract between Veolia and ONEA*

The legal aspect of the partnership between ONEA and the fountain managers reflects ONEA's position of strength over its partners, as ONEA has a monopoly over water production and distribution. On the other hand, the legal framework of the service contract signed by ONEA and Veolia governs a transfer of competences from the former to the latter.

The general and particular administrative clauses of the service contract are similar to any contract between a client (ONEA) and a service provider (Veolia). They stipulate that ONEA is the owner of the project and has delegated the execution of the project to Veolia. It will be paid with a loan from the International Development Association (IDA).[15] Each party has right to terminate the contract on the basis of a *force majeure* and if the other party fails to respect its obligations.

Veolia is responsible for the management of the contract, for commercial and human resources management and also for all financial reporting. In addition, Veolia gets a financial commission on the turnover realized by ONEA – a commission that depends upon measurable commercial and financial performances.[16]

As mentioned earlier, the donors' main concern was to improve ONEA's financial and management position so that the latter could pay its debts. In practice, Veolia has taken over ONEA's competences. Although the contract stipulates that ONEA is the decisive entity in charge of the production and distribution of potable water, it is Veolia that defines it. ONEA's organization chart reflects the power transferred to Veolia: its two chief officers have a power equal to that of one of their counterparts in ONEA. But fundamentally, the transfer of competences from ONEA to the group lies in the missions carried out by Veolia, which go beyond simple assistance to the management. Veolia operates quasi-totality of ONEA's activities from operational activities, human resources to management.

Veolia is obliged, in the short term, to strengthen ONEA's financial management as well as its capacity to finance investment and repay debts. In order to reinforce ONEA's investing capacity and solvency, Veolia has to put in place a tariff policy that allows, in the medium term, a comprehensive coverage of the costs. Therefore, Veolia has a major role in fixing the price.

## Stakes of the private sector

As mentioned earlier, different private actors are involved in both distribution and production. Each has different objectives. For those actors involved in the distribution chain, the main concern is the way in which water is bought and sold to the households. For actors such as Veolia, the stake will be the global supply policy.

### *Informal actors and prices*

ONEA can control the activities and prices applied by their intermediaries – that is, fountain managers – because their collaboration is legally defined and also because of their physical proximity to ONEA's offices. However, it is unable to control the price applied by the informal actors since they work independently of the state. Resellers fix their prices according to the distance between the fountain and the household that they supply and according to the commercial relationship with the consumers.[17] Table 8.3 provides prices applied by the resellers in a regular period (water sufficiently available).

It is clear that the further a person lives from the distribution point, the more expensive the water will be. It is generally recognized that the poorest people are those living in the suburbs or outskirts of the cities. It follows that the poorest face the highest prices. This inequality is worsened during the hottest period of the year (April to June), which witnesses a shortage of water, when the prices can triple or even quadruple. Even though this phenomenon has been familiar for some considerable time, the government has been unable to control it, as it has no way of to

*Table 8.3* Prices used by resellers in normal period (average prices, sample of 516 resellers in Ouagadougou in 2003, in FCFA per barrel)*

| *Type of clients* | *Price as a function of the distance between the hand pump and the place of delivery (Metres)* | | | |
|---|---|---|---|---|
| | *50–200* | *200–500* | *500–1000* | *1000–2000* |
| Regular clients | 215 | 260 | 335 | 470 |
| Occasional clients | 255 | 310* | 400* | 560** |

*Source*: ISL, HYDROCONSULT, SAHEL CONSULT 2003.
*Notes*: *US$1 = FCFA650.
**Author's own extrapolation based on the data found in the first column 255/215.

pressuring the resellers to maintain their prices at an acceptable level. But the impact of this phenomenon on the water supply is small, compared to the effects of Veolia's involvement.

*Veolia: efficiency versus social welfare*

Veolia's productivity objectives are not necessarily compatible with the government's social objectives. As has been mentioned already, Veolia is expected to improve ONEA's financial and accounting management. A better human and financial resources management would allow the extension of ONEA's distribution network (dam construction) and increase new connections at affordable prices to low-income households. It is still too early to evaluate whether the level of coverage has increased. As shown in Table 8.4, ONEA's productivity has indeed improved since the arrival of Veolia, such as administrative recovery rates has increased, debt collection delays has been reduced and staff productivity increased.

Similarly, there are noticeably positive results in terms of commercial performance. ONEA's improved performance is also noticeable on a financial level. For example, adequate results were achieved by over-matching the model by 3 per cent for the volume of water sold, and by 21 per cent for the finances at the end of the year. The role of Veolia in ONEA's achievement of better productivity is part of a global redefinition of the supply policy for potable water.

The 2004 contract plan gives ONEA five years to reach its objectives. It also fixed some stringent rules to be followed with respect to the market approach. For example, the plan stipulates that: *ONEA will not plan any*

*Table 8.4* Level of performance of the commercial department in 2004

| *Indicators* | *Initial data* | *2004 set objective* | *2004 actual performance* |
|---|---|---|---|
| Administration recovery rate at 4 months (%) | 65 | 70 | 27* |
| Private clients' recovery rate at 4 months (%) | 86 | 90 | 88 |
| Average term of payment of administrative debts (in days) | 255 | 210 | 137 |
| Average term of payment of private clients debt (in days) | 130 | 100 | 82 |
| Improvement of staff productivity (number of membership/agent) | 378 | N/A | 532 |

*Source*: ONEA (2005a: 25–8).

*investment for the centres and for any extensions of the already existing centres, if their financial profitability is not shown and if the population is less than 10,000 inhabitants.*[18] The demographic criterion of 10,000 inhabitants is necessary but not as important as the financial profitability for a development project to be launched in a rural commune. The contract clearly states that the government will not oblige ONEA to operate a project in a commune if it has been proven that it will not be profitable. It is a major turning point in ONEA's water supply policy. Previously, it supplied water according to national territorial development directives and on the basis of urban needs, and not on profitability or commercial objectives. Ouagadougou and Bobo will be given priority through the Ziga dam and the exploitation of the new reserves in Bobo. Consequently and progressively, ONEA will prioritize the most solvent customers. The dismantling of former subsidies and social measures are also part of this new approach.

## Regulation and social policies

In this section, we will analyse the social and institutional policies related to the improvement of the access to water for poor urban households by comparing the situations before and after the involvement of Veolia.

### Previous system of subsidies

The social policies aimed at the improvement of the access to safe water are based on tariff measures. Burkinabe tariff policy tried to integrate the notion of the water scarcity and the concern of providing potable water to the poorest. Before the present cost-recovery policy, ONEA received subsidies to finance its social policy. The World Bank observed that before 1998, the average price cost of water was FCFA400 (per cubic metre)[19] whereas its selling price was FCFA390, with the government paying the difference to ONEA.[20]

Since 1994, ONEA's progressive tariff system, based on the principle of cross-subsidies, was introduced to reach a long-term financial balance, with the biggest clients subsidizing the smallest.[21] This objective should have been reached by the price equalization principle, which indicates that ONEA sets a unique price for its centres nationwide, taking into account the differentials of all production costs, so that the profits realized in the main centres compensate the deficits of the secondary centres. This institutional agreement was irreversible (to ensure a continuous water supply).

The financial equilibrium was achieved by adjusting selling prices according to different categories of consumers. The system of progressive tariffs and cross-subsidies aimed to reach this adjustment by creating different groups of consumers classified according to their level of water consumption. A consumption scale goes from a social bracket (small consumers) to the category of big consumers. Small consumers pay a price that is much lower than the cost of production and the largest consumers pay a price higher than the marginal cost of production. By doing so, three objectives were sought: a financial balance by taking into account the cost of production, social fairness as big consumers pay for the smallest, and the respect of the environment as the prices vary according to the volume of water consumed and thus limits wastage of water. Past institutional measures allowed the subsidizing of consumers at the fountains and at autonomous water post. They benefited mainly the small consumers (belonging to the social bracket) and to a lesser extent the medium consumers. Veolia's intervention brought a progressive dismantling of such tariff policy.

**A progressive dismantling of social policies**

In this section, we will analyse how the policy of cross-subsidies has been reformed, and we will then analyse the consequences of the affordability of water for the poorest households.

*Price increase*

As a result of applying strict commercial objectives, the price of water started to increase. Table 8.5 illustrates the system of progressive tariffs. Lower prices are paid by those consumers defined as the social bracket and by consumers collecting water at the water fountains. Price increases remained constant between 1995 and 2000 for all categories of consumers, with a larger increase for the larger consumers. This increase had a negative impact on the level of consumption and therefore conflicted with ONEA's financial and commercial forecasts. The results of the 2001 tariffs survey show that, following the 1995 price increase, consumption per private connection, per person and per day, decreased by on average 17.3 per cent (nationwide), by around 17.5 per cent for Ouagadougou and Bobo and by 13.3 per cent in auxiliary centres. The 1997 and 1999 increases provoked a further reduction of the consumption by 4 per cent.[22] In reaction to these consumption reductions and in line with its new commercial strategy, ONEA decided to dismantle the cross-subsidies progressively. This was aimed at boosting the demand for water by larger consumers.

*Table 8.5* Evolution of ONEA's tariffs between 1995 and 2000 (CFA/cubic metre)

| | *January 1995* | | *December 1997* | | *January 1999* | | *February 2000* | *Variation (%) 2000/1995* | *Tax/tariff ratio in 2000* |
|---|---|---|---|---|---|---|---|---|---|
| | *Tariff* | *Increase rate (%)* | *Tariff* | *Increase rate (%)* | *Tariff* | *Increase rate (%)* | | | |
| Water sold to fountain managers | 174 | 2 | 178 | 2 | 182 | 2 | 186 | 6.8 | |
| Water sold to PEA | 87 | 2 | 89 | 2 | 91 | 2 | 93 | 6.8 | |
| 1–10 $m^3$ (social category) | 164 | 2 | 168 | 2 | 172 | 2 | 176 | 7.3 | 2.159 |
| 11–25 $m^3$ | 320 | 6 | 338 | 5 | 356 | 5 | 376 | 17 | 1.013 |
| 26–50 $m^3$ | 800 | 8 | 860 | 7 | 924 | 7 | 993 | 14 | 0.382 |
| >50 $m^3$ | 840 | 2 | 860 | 7 | 924 | 7 | 993 | 18 | 0.382 |
| Tax | 380 | | 380 | | 380 | | 380 | | |

*Source*: Ministère de l'industrie et du commerce, Ministère de l'eau 1995, 1997, 1999, 2000.

*Table 8.6* ONEA's new tariffs since 2003 (CFA/cubic metre): water sold to households by ONEA

| | |
|---|---|
| 0–6 $m^3$ (Social Category) | 188 |
| 6–30 $m^3$ | 393 |
| More than 30 $m^3$ | 1040 |
| Tax | 1000 |
| Decontamination | 21 |
| VAT > more than 50 $m^3$ (payment on decontamination and consumption) | 0.18 |

*Source*: Ministère de l'industrie et du commerce, Ministère de l'eau 2003.

*Increase of the water expenses for small consumers*

In order to increase the volume of water sold, ONEA stimulated the demand of the big consumers by revising the cost of water on all consumer categories. This meant an increase in the price paid by low-income households, and a reduction of the price paid by big consumers in the cross-subsidies system. The increase in volume sold was supposed to be achieved by two means: reduction of the size of the social bracket, and an increase in the connection tax.

*Reduction of the size of the social bracket.* This objective was clearly stated in the tariffs survey: 'the social bracket that received subsidies will be reduced to households consuming 6 $m^3$ instead of 10 $m^3$. This will generate a net reduction of the needs of cross-subsidies paid by the upper tariffs classes and so, a reduction of the selling price necessary to reach ONEA's financial objective. It would also stop the negative reaction to price increase from consumers of upper tariff class who have a high purchasing power.'[23]

As shown in Table 8.6, the new price structure not only reduced the quantity for social bracket (from ten to six cubic metres), but also resulted in a reduction of water consumption by households belonging the social bracket, or a significant increase of their water expenses if they use more than the maximum volume.

*A rise in the connection tax.* Another way to increase revenue for ONEA was a rise in the connection tax. This amounted to FCFA1000 in 2003,[24] which meant a threefold increase compared to the previous figure of CFA380. For the households belonging to the social group, with water expenditures of FCFA1,200 for six cubic metres of water, the FCFA1,000 connection tax represents 80 per cent of their total water bill – a 40 per cent increase in their water expenses.

Prior to 2003, a household in the social bracket was paying less than the consumers supplying themselves from the fountains.[25] In order to correct this inequality, the price paid by this social category has been levelled by ONEA to the price paid by all clients of the water fountains and autonomous water points. Once again, this price adjustment obeyed commercial logic and not the social protection principle.

### The new institutional extensions of the social policy

The analysis made above highlights the impact of the new water supply policy on the conditions of access to drinking water for the households from a connection to the network. However, the social dimension of the problem of access cannot be analysed with a simple reference to the connected households. It must also be approached in comparison to the needs of the other categories of households who are not connected and are facing great difficulties in their daily access to safe water. Has the PSP influenced the conditions of access to drinking water for these categories of households? If not, what are the existing options and how are they articulated?

## Evaluation and perspectives of the public–private partnership

The first assessment of the Veolia–ONEA partnership reveals the limitations of increasing water coverage (through the introduction of commercial objectives) and an increase in the price paid by poor households. For this category of households, the consequences of this are a reduction in their quality of access (reduction of the ceiling of subsidized consumption) or a deterioration of their affordability (due to higher prices of water).

Although the tariff reform reduced the level of subsidies for poor customers, it did not necessarily lead to their elimination. The new policies are more disadvantageous to the poorest households, but not to other groups of customers. By assuming a fixed cost of producing a cubic metre of water in Ouagadougou between 2001 and 2003 (that is, FCFA590/cubic metre), one will note, that, until 2003, four categories of consumers paid a lower price and were thus subsidized. These were the consumers supplying themselves at the fountains and households belonging to the first three categories of the old tariff system. The ceiling of the subsidized consumption was fixed at 25 cubic metres. After 2003, the number of categories of consumers paying water at a price lower than FCFA590 was limited to three, but the ceiling of subsidized consumption was raised to 30 cubic metres. This means that the gap widened at the top, logically inducing an increase in the number of subsidized households, even if the ceiling for subsidized consumption is reduced (falling from ten cubic metres to six cubic metres). This favours those middle-class consumers who are paying a price closer to the production cost, at the expense of the social category. However, the reform did not necessarily lead to a reduction of the scale of the subsidies. The subsidy policy was reoriented towards achieving financial sustainability to increase coverage by extending the infrastructure for the population located in the peripheral districts. There is thus a prospect for increasing water supply and, therefore, for improving access. This can eventually lead to improving affordability for the households that relied on door-to-door sellers at relatively higher prices. These changes could potentially be beneficial to the poorest households, which are concentrated in the peripheral districts.

However, the extent to which it will benefit the poorest households remains less optimistic. The water coverage concerns only the parcelled zones and therefore the poorest households will be less affected since they are concentrated mainly in the non-parcelled zones. Moreover, even if these zones were covered by the new projects, their population would not be able to afford the connection costs (it is estimated that the poorest would be willing to pay only 40 per cent of the connection cost, compared to 60 per cent of the population in the parcelled zones).[26] Conscious of this, ONEA envisaged the realization of 400 new fountains to support the access to water for the populations in these zones.[27]

It is becoming clear that although the ONEA–Veolia partnership has good intentions, it is unable to provide affordable services to the poorer sector of the population. One way to tackle this is through community-driven projects.

## The search for new institutional methods

With all of the difficulties in providing affordable access to water (informal settlements, high prices charged by informal resellers, and so on), community-based self-help provides an alternative. Such actions fall under the logic of a decentralized supply and are based on the principle of partnership between the various categories of actors (state, regions, NGOs, urban communities) in terms of the mobilization of resources and also in terms of the definition of the objectives to be reached. Such achievements are small scale and are conceived on the basis of simple technologies that allow urban communities to appropriate it.

One example of such initiatives started in 2002, on the basis of a loan of US$30 million[28] in Ouagadougou and Bobo Dioulasso. About 27 per cent of the population of these two cities were involved with the project. As a result, 107 fountains were built, giving access to drinking water to more than 400,000 people.[29] The price of the barrel of 220 litres of water was brought down to FCFA60 compared to FCFA200 (charged by the retailers). These actions are implemented through innovative methods and are meant to cover all levels of the drinking water supply (from the production to the direct distribution to the households).

We have argued that although Veolia's intervention led to the improvement of ONEA's efficiency, affordability of water for the poorest has deteriorated. In order to get a clear picture of our argument, we will use some empirical analysis and statistics.

## Results from the statistical analysis of access to drinking water and water affordability in Burkina Faso

### Data

For the purposes of our analysis we used two databases: household surveys from 1998 and 2003.

### Access to safe water

We previously defined that a household would have access to drinking water if it supplies itself through at least one of the three means – namely a tap, a fountain or a borehole. A household which does not use at least one of these three sources is viewed as having no access to drinking water. The share of households having access to water rose from 52 per cent in 1998 to 61 per cent in 2003. Although there was an improvement in the access to water, this does not indicate how the access is distributed by different income categories, and which of these classes have benefited from these improvements.

Figure 8.2 shows the share of access broken into quintiles. As expected, we see that high-income households have a higher rate of access to water than households of low-income classes in 1998 and 2003. However, the graph also indicates that *all* of the income classes have benefited from the increase in the rate of access to water. The percentage of the households with access to water rose from 43 per cent in 1998 to 54 per cent in 2003 for the first quintile (that is, by 11 percentage points, which is slightly above the national average).

Nevertheless, since the intervention in the water sector has taken place mostly in the urban rather than the rural areas, it is appropriate to analyse

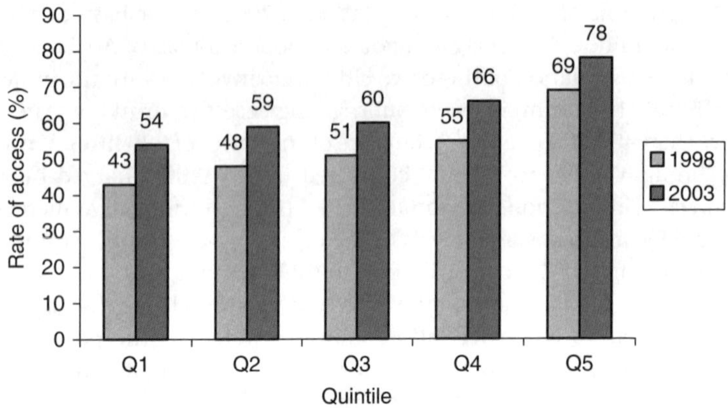


*Figure 8.2* Percentage of access (national) to safe water by income level, 1998–2003
*Source*: INSD (1998, 2003).

the access in both areas separately. If one isolates the performance of the urban centres from the national performance, we find that the rate of access in urban areas was 83 per cent in 1998 and 86 per cent in 2000. Although moderate, this evolution indicates clearly that there has been a real improvement in the access if we take into account the population growth. In order to observe the evolution of the rate of access for low-income households in the urban centres, we analyse the five income classes separately (Figure 8.3).

It appears that the rate of access increases progressively as a household moves upwards from a low-income class: the access rate for the low-income class was 76 per cent in 1998 while that for high-income families was 92 per cent. These rates changed, respectively, to 71 per cent and 95 per cent in 2003 – in other words, there was a fall for the lowest income quintile and a rise for the richest group. The level of access for the middle-income quintiles also rose. This leads us to believe that in urban areas, where the private sector is present, the poor have seen their levels of access fall, even though there has been a general improvement in the access rate. What could explain this fall in access to drinking water? Is it the increase in the price of water, the elimination of the state subsidy, or could it be the new pricing policy applied by Veolia that has adversely affected the poor? To answer these questions, we will use data on average spending allocated to water bill.

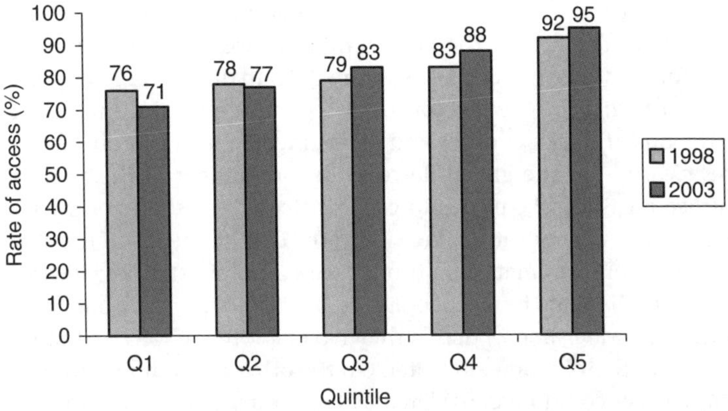


*Figure 8.3* Rate of access to safe water in urban centres by income level, 1998–2003
*Source*: INSD (1998, 2003).

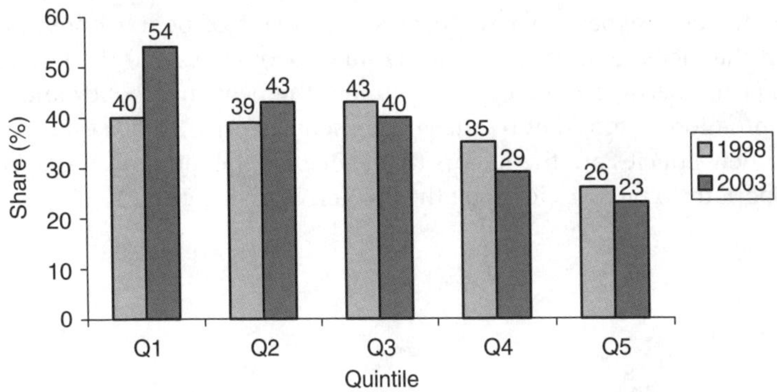


*Figure 8.4* Percentage of the water-poor by income class with a 3 per cent threshold in the urban centres
*Source*: INSD (1998, 2003).

## The water-poor

In this study we considered a household to be water-poor if it spends more than 3 per cent of its income on water.[30] Adopting a 3 per cent threshold for the urban centres in Burkina Faso, we find that the proportion of households that spend more than 3 per cent of their income on drinking water has decreased slightly – from 34.3 per cent in 1998 to 33.3 per cent in 2003. Figure 8.4 shows the break-down of the water-poor into income classes in urban centres.

As expected, the share of the water-poor decreases progressively as one moves from the first to the last quintile. However, if we compare the shares of the water-poor in 1998 and in 2003 in different income classes, we observe that it increased for the two poorest quintiles and decreased for the quintiles at the other end of the income distribution. This indicates clearly that the global decrease in the number of the water-poor in urban areas may be misleading. In particular, the shares of the water-poor in the lowest quintiles have increased despite the fall in the average rate. A possible explanation (although we cannot substantiate it with any data) could be that the households belonging to quintiles one and two are the true water-poor – that is they have no other choice but to spend so much of their income on water. On the other hand, households from quintiles 3–5 could be considered as false water-poor since consuming more than 3 per cent on water could be used on non-essentials (gardens, and so on). Given that they use a lot more water, their water spending might be artificially inflated. If they restricted their water consumption to the essential needs, that share of spending would be far smaller.

One could expect that the decrease in access of poorer households and the increase in the share of the water-poor are due to the fact that water has become more expensive under the new tariff policy and the elimination of subsidies by the government. In order to make sure that the new policies are the factors that influence spending on water, it is important to break it down by the income class (Figure 8.5).

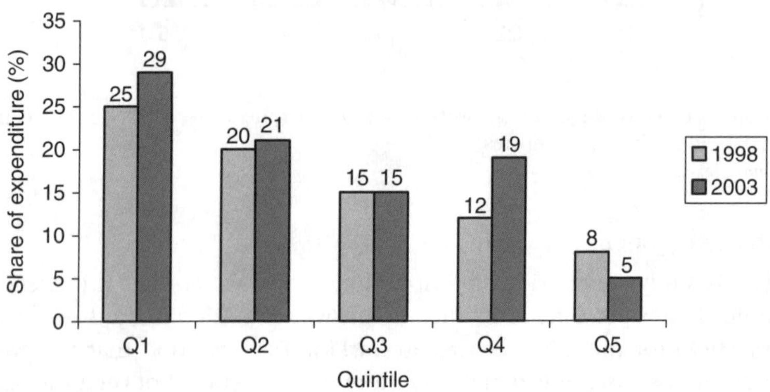


*Figure 8.5* Share of water expenditure by income class in urban centres in 1998 and 2003
*Source*: INSD (1998, 2003).

We observe that the share of spending on water decreases as we move towards the upper end of the income distribution. However, this share increases for households belonging to classes one and two and falls for households from groups four and five. The budget share that the households of the first income class allocates to water consumption reached 25 per cent of their total spending in 1998. This value was only 8 per cent for the richest income class. In 2003 that share rose for the former and fell for the latter group. The opposite movements in these two categories confirm that the new water policy has been regressive and that it has affected the poorest households negatively. As we have argued earlier, since the poorest are not generally connected to the network, they have to pay more from informal sellers.

### Distance to drinking water sources

In order to discuss the issue of access, it is imperative to consider the time spent on getting water. In other words, access is defined by the time a household spends to access a water source. Here we do not consider the means of supply, nor the quality of water consumed. Precisely, we presumed that a household does not have access to water if it spends more than 30 minutes to access a source.[31]

Based on our analysis, our results indicate that by commercializing ONEA, the time spent to accessing water has been reduced (as mentioned earlier this may be linked to the increase of pipe network).

## Conclusions and policy implications

The aim of the study was to evaluate the impact of commercializing water supply (through PSP–Veolia) in Burkina Faso and, specifically, its impact on the poorest households in regard to their access and affordability to safe water.

Over the last decade or so the supply and access to potable water has increased. This could be attributed partly to the commercial objective undertaken by ONEA with assistance from Veolia. The urban centres (Ouagadougou and Bobo Dioulasso) have benefited most from this increase in coverage. This was due mainly to the improvement of the infrastructure (Ouagadougou and the Ziga dam) and of ONEA's productivity over the last four years. The time spent to access water also seems to have improved, since the time dedicated to this task is now shorter. Nevertheless, these positive results are overshadowed by the observed reduction of water consumption per capita.

Our empirical results show that the affordability of water has been deteriorating for the poorest households as a result of ONEA's strict commercial objective. However, for the rich it has improved relatively. This result illustrates the new commercial orientation followed by ONEA aimed at delivering water to clients who can afford it. Obviously, this commercial objective has taken over the social objectives of the state. The new system of cross-subsidies implies a higher cost of water for the poorest families.

In the urban centres covered by ONEA, rich and middle-class families will see their level of water consumption increase whereas the poor households will be increasingly excluded. In Ouagadougou, as a result of the Ziga dam project, water availability will increase for the larger clients while the poorest households would be unable to pay extra money to obtain water and they will have to restrict their consumption.

In addition, in the present institutional context the limitation of ONEA's activities to commercially viable urban centres will provoke the marginalization of an important number of small communes in terms of access to water, and an increase of the demographic pressures on big cities and, specifically, on Ouagadougou. This may impact negatively on achieving the MDGs. To curtail such marginalization of small towns, the government of Burkina Faso would like to see private enterprises take over from ONEA. However, because of the problems of commercial viability, other private operators are unwilling to engage themselves in small towns or rural areas. If small towns continue to lack the minimal infrastructure and equipment to produce potable water, the population will migrate towards cities where water services are available. As a result, demographic growth will undermine the efforts that have so far been made in these centres. ONEA's reform to become a commercially viable institution has to be accompanied by appropriate social policies, such as increasing block tariffs, and cross-subsidies, subsidizing connection to the poorer households.

## Notes

1. The data were collected before the launch of a huge project aiming to improve access to potable water for the population of Burkina Faso. See World Bank (2001: 5).
2. The water resources drop from 15 million cubic metres in a normal year, to 10 million cubic metres in a dry year, as estimated in 1999. See World Bank (2001: 5).
3. DANIDA (2003).

4. The World Bank, for example, would like to see the contracts granted on the base of the production costs. The European Union, on the other hand, would like the technical skills and know-how to be taken into account.
5. Bingbourre (2005: 8).
6. Ministère de l'environnement et de l'eau (2001).
7. Up to 2001, Ministère de l'environnement et de l'eau (the Ministry of Water of Environment and Water) was in charge but in July 2002, it was taken over by the Ministère de l'agriculture, de l'hydraulique at des ressources halieutiques (the Ministry of Agriculture, Hydraulic and Fishing Resources).
8. Ministère de l'agriculture, de l'hydraulique et des ressources halieutiques (2004: 11).
9. Undertaken by Thomas Isidore Noël Sankara (1949–1987) from 1983 to 1987.
10. Collignon and Vezina (2000: 7).
11. World Bank (2001: 25).
12. US$1 = FCFA650 which is equivalent to around US$230 million.
13. The regulation specifies how the activity should be run: maintenance of the infrastructure, respect of the price and termination of contract, time and territory wise.
14. The manager is in charge of at most one well or water autonomous post.
15. ONEA (2001: 6).
16. ONEA (2001: Annex 1, p. 2).
17. ISL, HYDROCONSULT, SAHEL CONSULT (2003).
18. Ministère de l'agriculture, de l'hydraulique et des ressources halieutiques (2001: 5).
19. US$1 = FCFA650.
20. World Bank (2001: 5).
21. GOPA (1995).
22. GKW CONSULT GmbH (2001: Chapter 2, p. 17).
23. GKW CONSULT GmbH (2001: Chapter 3, p. 13).
24. US$1 = FCFA650.
25. According to the estimations of the tariffs survey, clients of the water fountains were paying FCFA5 for 20 litres, that is, FCFA250 per cubic metre, whereas household belonging to the social bracket were paying FCFA176 per cubic metre.
26. ISL, HYDROCONSULT, SAHEL CONSULT (2003: 19).
27. This phase of the project is apparently not in an operational phase.
28. From the World Bank, co-financed by the UNDP (United Nations Development Programme), the AFD (French Development Agency) and the ADB (African Development Bank), and co-financed by the communal authorities (20 per cent) and the urban communities (10 per cent).
29. World Bank (2003: 20).
30. Within the framework of poverty indicators measurement, the threshold has always been subject to debates and controversies. As far as the threshold of poverty is concerned, it has sometimes been defined as the half of the median. But for some decision makers, this rate does not reflect the true state of poverty. The same debates occur for the issue of water poverty. It is not easy to agree on a threshold as this can vary by country, by period, and by government policy. To avoid these traps, and for the purpose

of consistency with other studies we choose to maintain the 3 per cent rate.

31. Since time needed to access water depends on the distance, one could choose either time or distance travelled as the dependent variable.

## References


Amemiya, T. (1985) *Advanced Econometrics* (Cambridge MA: Harvard University Press).

Bayliss, K. (2002) 'Privatisation and Poverty: the Distribution Impact of Utility Privatisation', *Annals of Public and Cooperative Economics*, 73(4), 603–25.

Bayliss, K. (2003) 'Utility Privatisation in sub-Saharan Africa: a Case Study of Water', *Journal of Modern Studies*, 41(4), 507–31.

Bingboure, J.M. (2005) *Programme d'application du système de gestion des infrastructures hydrauliques d'alimentation en eau potable en milieu rural et semi-urbain.* Atelier sur la participation du secteur privé dans l'approvisionnement en eau (Ouagadougou), May.

Collignon, B. and M. Vezina (2000) *Independent Water and Sanitation Providers in African Cities. Full Report of a Ten-Country Study*, (Washington, DC: World Bank).

CREPA (1997) *Collaboration et renforcement des capacités institutionnelles pour la mise en œuvre de stratégies appropriées pour une gestion durable des ressources en eau en zones périurbaines. Cas du secteur 28 à Ouagadougou, Burkina Faso* (Ouagadougou).

DANIDA (2003) *Evaluation supplémentaire. Appui au secteur privé dans le domaine de l'eau et de l'assainissement au Burkina Faso* (Ouagadougou: Coopération danoise).

Estache, A. and R. Kouassi (2002) *How Different is the Efficiency of Public and Private Water Companies in Asia and Pacific Region?: What a Stochastic Cost Frontier Shows.* Policy Research Working Paper (Washington, DC: World Bank).

FAO (2005) *L'irrigation en Afrique en chiffres. Enquête AQUASTAT, Burkina Faso* (Rome: FAO).

Fitch, M. (2002) *Water Poverty in England and Wales.* Working paper (Leicester: Centre for Utility Consumer Law, University of Leicester).

GKW Consult GmbH, Mannheim (2001) *Etude tarifaire 2001–2005* (Ouagadougou: ONEA).

GOPA Conseils (1995) *Etude tarifaire*, tome 1 (Ouagadougou: ONEA).

Green, W.H. (1997) *Econometric Analysis*, 3rd edition (Englewood Cliffs, NJ: Prentice-Hall International).

INSD (1994) *Enquête prioritaire sur les conditions de vie des ménages* (Ouagadougou: Ministère de l'économie et des finances).

INSD (1998) *Enquête prioritaire 1998 sur les conditions de vie des ménages* (Ouagadougou: INSD, Ministère de l'économie et des finances).

INSD (2003) *Enquêtes prioritaires 2003* (Ouagadougou: Ministère de l'économie et des finances).

ISL, HYDROCONSULT, SAHEL CONSULT (2003) *Enquête marketing à Ouagadougou* (Ouagadougou, ONEA).

Johnstone, N. and L. Wood (2002) 'Introduction', in N. Johnstone and L. Wood (eds), *Private Firm and Public Water: Realising Social and Environment Objectives in Developing Countries* (Cheltenham: Edward Elgar).

Ministère de l'agriculture, de l'hydraulique et des ressources halieutiques (2001) *Contrat plan entre l'état Burkina Be et l'office national de l'eau et de l'assainissement* (Ouagadougou).

Ministère de l'environnement et de l'eau (2001) *Etat des ressources en eau et cadre de leur gestion* (Ouagadougou).

Ministère de l'environnement et de l'eau (1998) *Politique et stratégie en matière d'eau* (Ouagadougou).

Ministère de l'économie et des finances (1998) *Enquête prioritaire 1998 sur les conditions de vie des ménages* (Ouagadougou).

Ministère de l'industrie et du commerce, Ministère de l'eau (1995) *Tarifs de vente de l'eau* (Ouagadougou), January.

Ministère de l'industrie et du commerce, Ministère de l'eau (1997) *Tarifs de vente de l'eau* (Ouagadougou), December.

Ministère de l'industrie et du commerce, Ministère de l'eau (1999) *Tarifs de vente de l'eau* (Ouagadougou), January.

Ministère de l'industrie et du commerce, Ministère de l'eau (2000) *Tarifs de vente de l'eau* (Ouagadougou), February.

ONEA (1990) *Résultats d'exploitation* (Ouagadougou: ONEA).

ONEA (1994) *Résultats d'exploitation* (Ouagadougou: ONEA).

ONEA (2000) *Evolution de la tarification* (Bobo Dioulasso, Burkina Faso: ONEA).

ONEA (2001) *Contrat de services pour la gestion commerciale et le renforcement des opérations financières* (Ouagadougou: ONEA).

ONEA (2003) *Résultats d'exploitation* (Ouagadougou: ONEA).

ONEA (2004) *Résultats d'exploitation* (Ouagadougou: ONEA).

ONEA (2005a) *Audit du contrat de service. Rapport technique de l'auditeur* (Ouagadougou: ONEA).

ONEA (2005b) *Audit du modèle financier de l'ONEA* (Ouagadougou: ONEA).

Sawadogo, D. (2004) *Processus d'implication du privé: Cas de contrat de services à l'ONEA* (Ouagadougou).

Sawkins, J.H. and V. Dickie (2002) *Affordability of Water and Sewerage Services in Great Britain*. Report for ScotEcon.

Sidwaya, 13 April 2006, No. 5567 (Ouagadougou).

Thomas, A. (2000) *Econométrie des variables qualitatives* (Paris: Edition Dunod).

Water Aid (2004) *Problèmes avec la PSP dans le secteur de l'eau et assainissement dans les pays en transition et en voie de développement* (Public Services International Research Unit, University of Greenwich).

Wooldridge, J.M. (2001) *Econometric Analysis of Cross Section and Panel Data* (Cambridge, MA: MIT Press).

World Bank (2001) *Project Appraisal Document on a Proposed Credit to Burkina Faso for the Ouagadougou Water Supply Project*. Water and Urban 2 CD 15 (Washington DC: Africa Regional Office).

World Bank (2003) *Les communautés prennent en charge l'amélioration de leur environnement urbain en partenariat avec les acteurs institutionnels* (Burkina Faso: World Bank).

# Index